Object-Oriented Programming
With .Turbo Pascal®

Related Titles of Interest

Object-Oriented Programming With QuickPascal, Shammas
QuickPascal: A Self Teaching Guide, Weiskamp, Aguiar
Turbo Language Essentials: A Programmer's Reference, Weiskamp, Shammas, and Pronk
Turbo Algorithms: A Programmer's Reference, Weiskamp, Shammas, and Pronk
Turbo Libraries, Weiskamp, Shammas, and Pronk
Power Graphics Using Turbo C, Weiskamp, Heiny, and Shammas
Introducing C to Pascal Programmer's, Shammas
Advanced Turbo C Programmer's Guide, Mosich, Shammas, and Flamig
The Turbo C Survival Guide, Miller and Quilici
C Programming Language: An Applied Perspective, Miller and Quilici
Turbo C DOS Utilities, Alonso
Quick C DOS Utilities, Alonso
Turbo C and Quick C Functions: Building Blocks for Efficient Code, Barden
Power Graphics Using Turbo Pascal, Weiskamp, Heiny, and Shammas
Applying Turbo Pascal Library Units, Shammas
Programming with Macintosh Turbo Pascal, Swan
Turbo Pascal DOS Utilities, Alonso
Artificial Intelligence Programming with Turbo Prolog, Weiskamp and Hengl
Mastering HyperTalk, Weiskamp and Shammas

Object-Oriented Programming
With Turbo Pascal®

Namir Shammas

WILEY
John Wiley & Sons, Inc.

New York • Chichester • Brisbane • Toronto • Singapore

Publisher: Therese A. Zak
Editor: Katherine Schowalter
Managing Editor: Ruth Greif
Editing, Design and Production: Publication Services

HyperTalk is a registered trademark of Apple Computer
MS-DOS is a registered trademark of Microsoft Corporation
PC-DOS is a registered trademark of IBM
QuickPascal is a trademark of Microsoft Corporation
Turbo Pascal is a registered trademark of Borland International, Inc.

This publication is designed to provide accurate and authoritative information in regard to the subject matter covered. It is sold with the understanding that the publisher is not engaged in rendering legal, accounting, or other professional service. If legal advice or other expert assistance is required, the services of a competent professional person should be sought. FROM A DECLARATION OF PRINCIPLES JOINTLY ADOPTED BY A COMMITTEE OF THE AMERICAN BAR ASSOCIATION AND A COMMITTEE OF PUBLISHERS.

Library of Congress Cataloging-in-Publication Data

Shammas, Namir Clement, 1954-
    Object-oriented programming with Turbo Pascal / Namir Shammas
        p. cm.
    Incudes bibliographical references.
    ISBN   0-471-51702-X
    1. Object-oriented programming.   2. Pascal (Computer program
language)   3. Turbo Pascal (Computer program)   I. Title.
QA76.64.S472   1990
    005.26'2--dc20   89-29768
                                                          CIP

Printed in the United States of America
90 91 10 9 8 7 6 5 4 3 2 1

To my son Joseph,
the *little fella*.

Contents

Introduction   xi

Chapter 1   Object-Oriented Programming Basics   1

Overview   1
Basic Concepts of OOP   2
The Chicken and Egg Dilemma   6
Turbo Pascal OOP Features   7

Chapter 2   Advanced Object-Oriented Programming Issues   23

Naming Methods: The Good, the Bad, and the . . .   23
Enforcing Mandatory Initialization   26
Dynamic Objects and Methods   31
Dynamic vs. Static Objects   32
Dynamic Binding and Polymorphism   32
Exporting Classes   35
Assigning Objects   45
Arrays of Objects   46
Objects as Fields of Records   48
Compound Classes and Objects   48
Dynamic Objects   51
Accessing Subclasses   57

Chapter 3 Window Objects 59

The Screen Class   59
Screen Windows   61
Tiled Windows   62
Alternate Classes   72

Chapter 4 Screen Objects 75

Coding Screen Classes   76

Chapter 5 Screen, Cursor, and Text Objects 87

The Basics   87

Chapter 6 File Objects 101

The Basics   101
Generic File Classes   102
Text File Class   104
Binary File Class   105
Program File Class   106

Chapter 7 String Objects 127

It's Only Words   128
Items   129
Tokens   129
Your Title Is...   131
Connecting Different String Subclasses   145
Using Virtual Methods   148

Chapter 8 Array Objects 151

Array Objects   151
List Objects   153
Stack Objects   154
The Power of Inheritance   155

Chapter 9   Vector and Matrix Objects   169

The Basic Ingredients   169
Vector Class   169
Matrix Class   171
Spreadsheet Class   173
Statistics Matrix Class   175

Chapter 10   Polynomial Objects   203

The Basics   203
Suggested Extensions   214

Chapter 11   Linear Regression Objects   217

The Basics   217
Extended Precision   218
Linearized Regression   219
Regression Classes   219
Enhanced-Precision Class   221
Linearized Regression Class   222

Chapter 12   Electrical Circuit Objects   237

The Simplest Circuit   237
Series of Resistors   237
Parallel Resistors   238
Mixing Series and Parallel Resistors   239
Circuit Objects   240

Chapter 13   Calculator Objects   249

The Basic RPN Calculator   249
The Scientific RPN Calculator   251
The Financial Calculator Class   252

Chapter 14   Polymorphic Arrays   279

Other Polymorphic Arrays   296

Index   297

Introduction

Object-oriented programming (OOP) is a new discipline in software engineering. It offers a different way of planning, conceptualizing, designing, writing, updating, and maintaining software.

This book introduces you to the world of OOP using Borland's Turbo Pascal implementation (version 5.5) with a problem-solving approach. The main purpose of the book is to apply OOP to a variety of common problems. The focus is applied OOP, not its esoteric aspects.

The book is highly modular. You need to read Chapter 1 before proceeding to any other chapter if you are not familiar with OOP and the Turbo Pascal OOP syntax. Chapter 2 offers the advanced aspects of OOP using Turbo Pascal. You may wish to postpone reading it until after you look at the application chapters. You might also read it lightly before proceeding to the subsequent chapters. The application chapters, which make up the rest of the book, can be read in any order.

The application chapters offer examples in the following categories:

- Classes that model objects familiar to the computer user, such as the screen, windows, the cursor, and DOS files.
- Classes and objects that model data structures, such as arrays, strings, lists, stacks, vectors, and matrices.
- Classes and objects that model more abstract entities, such as mathematical polynomials and linear regression.
- Classes that model physical objects, such as calculators and electrical circuits.

I hope you find this book valuable in showing OOP at work.

Namir Clement Shammas

Object-Oriented Programming
With Turbo Pascal®

1 | Object-Oriented Programming Basics

Overview

High-level languages represent an intelligent interface between the programmer and the computer. Their evolution parallels software engineering techniques and methods. It is motivated by the desire to create robust and reusable software components that reduce software production cycles and time. This cutback in production time is even more important when a team of programmers are working on a software project.

The history of programming languages reflects the evolution from nonstructured (or semistructured) to structured to object-oriented languages. The Pascal language has played a major role in promoting structured programming and its accompanying programming disciplines. Indeed, Pascal and the other structured languages (such as C, Modula-2, and Ada) have appealed to the programmer as time-saving organized languages that foster better programming, with robust reusable code, ease of readability (which varies among languages), ease of update, and access to software libraries (which extend the language). As practicing Pascal programmers, we have all reaped the benefits of structured languages.

Structured languages are procedural languages wherein a program is divided into a set of procedures and functions. The sequence of routines describes how data is manipulated. Specifically, the programmer controls the interaction between the code and the data. The primary focus in procedural languages is the routine, while the second focus is the data being manipulated. In the seventies, the computer language scientists went back to the basics. They argued, "What if the data becomes the primary focus? After all, we live in a world of objects and not procedures." Look around you and you will see a variety of objects. Each one has its own set of features, characteristics, and functionalities. Some may be similar yet different, such as two chairs made of varying materials. These chairs share some common attributes and functionalities—yet they can be different. For example, an office chair is able to rotate and has wheels, while a regular chair does not.

Basic Concepts of OOP

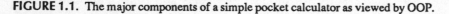

The highlight of object-oriented programming, as the name suggests, is objects. We are immersed in a universe of objects that vary in size, shape, functionality, and various other types of characteristics. To understand how OOP languages deal with objects, consider a four-function pocket calculator. Figure 1.1 shows a schematic of the major components of a calculator: the keyboard, the display, the CPU, and the internal registers. The same figure also divides the calculator components into two camps: the keyboard, which provides the calculator's functionality, and the other parts, which define the state of the calculator. The keyboard provides the functionality to run the calculator, thus affecting its state. The state of the machine includes whether it is on or off. In addition, while the calculator is on, the contents of the display and the internal registers are affected by what keys are pressed. Notice that

FIGURE 1.1. The major components of a simple pocket calculator as viewed by OOP.

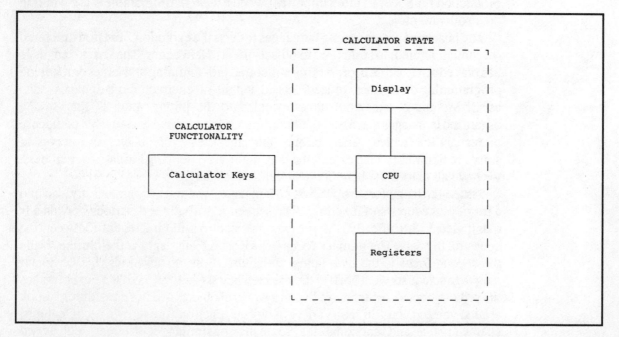

the number of keys is far less than the number of states that the calculator can possess(for one thing, there exists a huge number of possible digit combinations that can appear on the display).

Object-oriented languages treat an object as having a specific state that is attained and altered by the object's specific functionality. An object is an encapsulation of the object's data (maintaining its state) and the code that acts upon them. The calculator is a good example of an object with these two aspects, namely, the keyboard and the display. The functionality is represented uniquely by the set of keys. When you press a key of a calculator, you are sending an electric impulse to the CPU to cause it to perform a task that alters the state of the calculator. OOP views the process of pressing the key as sending a message to the CPU, which is the mind of the calculator. More about messages later.

In using a pocket calculator as an example of an object, I implicitly had my own calculator in mind. But calculators, like numerous other objects, have brands and model numbers. Each model is designed according to a fixed and well-defined set of specifications, and manufactured in mass using a collection of molds and templates. Thus, calculators, like all other objects, can be classified into categories. In object-oriented programming, classes are the software templates that are used to create objects. Classes parallel data types; however, they not only define the data fields used to determine the state of an object, but also specify the object's functionality. The concept of classes empowers you to categorize objects---after all, not all objects are created equal! Once you define a class you want to use, you can create instances of the class, called objects. For example, you can define a class of cars and then have a Buick LeSabre and a VW Quantum as instances of the class *car*.

Going back to our pocket calculator example, let's consider the role of the keys. Each key permits you to manipulate the calculator's state in a specific way. For

---

Definitions

A **class** describes the data fields of an object and the code that acts upon the data. Classes are similar to data types in Pascal.

An **object** is an instance or a member of a class, similar to a traditional variable in Pascal.

Note: The Borland manual for version 5.5 calls a *class* an *object* and calls an *object* an *instance of an object*. This nomenclature departs from all other OOP languages and implementations. I will be using the standard namings for classes and objects.

example, the plus key provides a method to add two numbers. Similarly, the other keys provide methods to perform other tasks. In object-oriented programming, a method is the code that is available for manipulating the state of an object. In other words, methods represent the ways an object can be manipulated, not the process of manipulation itself. The actual task of altering an object's state is called sending a message. In the calculator example, when a particular key is pressed to perform a required operation, the invoked key sends a message (using the OOP term) to the calculator object.

Sending messages brings a new syntax to Pascal. Let's look at a statement that assigns the square root of a variable to another variable. In a structured language you might write:

```
Y := SQRT(X);
```

which reads as follows:

Call function SQRT with X as its argument and assign the result to Y

Under OOP, the same can be written as:

```
Y := X.SQRT;
```

which reads as follows:

Tell X to apply its method SQRT and return the result to Y

Notice that in an OOP language the object X is addressed by passing a message to it. The message is to call *its* method SQRT. The word *its* is highlighted to stress the ownership of a method (that is, the association between a method and an object, as defined by the object's class).

Definitions

A **message** is a request sent to an object to call one of its methods. A message is *what* you do to an object.

A **method** is the procedure or function that is invoked to act on an object. A method specifies *how* a message is executed.

OOP fosters a more natural approach to manipulating data using objects that respond to messages. This approach cultivates a notion that objects in a program are similar to people working in an office---you send a memo or a message to a fellow worker (the object, in this case) requesting him to perform a specific task. Assuming the message is sent to the right person (this illustrates the importance of the message ownership concept), he or she will respond using their expertise and resources. The method by which the message is executed is up to the receiving object. The details of the response are transparent to the message sender.

Another feature of OOP is inheritance, a powerful feature that enables you to create subclasses. Each subclass inherits the characteristics of its parent class (also known as a superclass). A subclass adds new attributes to the inherited ones and may also override any inherited attributes. Turbo Pascal, which implements Object Pascal, supports only single (also known as linear) inheritance. This is a simple inheritance scheme wherein each subclass has only one parent class. Multiple or nonlinear inheritance (implemented in other OOP languages) permits a subclass to inherit attributes from two or more parent classes.

Figure 1.2 shows a sample class and its subclasses. Subclass C is a child of subclass B, a child of class A. Subclasses D and E are children of class A. Classes B, D, and E inherit the various attributes of class A. As I will show later, this means

FIGURE 1.2. Sample numeric class and its subclasses.

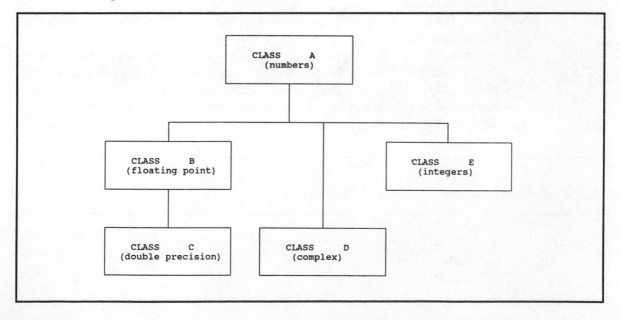

that attributes of A need not be restated when declaring subclasses B, C, and E---only the new and overridden attributes need to be declared. Similarly, subclass C inherits the attributes of subclass B and class A, and needs to declare only the new and overridden attributes.

Inheritance has a profound and significant impact on reducing coding. It enables you to avoid redundant coding and decrease software development time. Figure 1.3 shows the path of handling a message sent to an object of class C. If the message matches a method declared with class C, the matching method is invoked; otherwise, the message is passed to class B. If the message matches a method declared with class B, the matching method is invoked; otherwise, the message is passed to class A. This entire scenario is transparent to the programmer.

The Chicken and Egg Dilemma

Creating a class hierarchy involves defining the base class and the subclasses that represent refinements made on the base class. The selection of the base class and the subclasses may not always be easy. The rule of thumb to follow is the IsA relationship. For example, among the following classes: vehicles, cars, sports cars, buses, and trucks, it is easy to spot the base class *vehicle*. A car is a vehicle, as is a sports car, a bus, or a truck. Likewise, a sports car is a car; therefore, *sports car* is a subclass of *car*.

The IsA relationship is not always that clear. Consider the screen and windows. While some would select the screen as a base class and say "a window is a screen," others would state the reverse—"a screen is a window," their argument fueled by "virtual windows" (that is, the idea that the screen is merely a viewport into a virtual space). The selection of a base class in such a case may be resolved if the class hierarchy has at least three levels. When the grandchild class is in the process of being defined, it should become clear whether or not the base class was soundly selected.

FIGURE 1.3. Passing messages up the hierarchal class lineage.

```
                      Messages          Messages          Messages
Message ===>  for class C ====> for class B ====> for class A
to member
of class C
```

Programming Note

Designing a class hierarchy is an iterative process. The hierarchy that seems logical at first may prove to be awkward when coding the methods. Be prepared to redesign your class hierarchies—it is only part of the learning curve!

Turbo Pascal OOP Features

Turbo Pascal closely implements Object Pascal, an OOP extension of Pascal promoted by Apple Computer. The object-oriented language extensions are few, yet very powerful. The general syntax for declaring a class is shown here:

```
TYPE
    <class-name> = OBJECT | OBJECT(<parent class>)
        <list of data fields>
        <list of functions and procedures headings>
    END;
```

When a new class is defined, the keyword OBJECT is used. When a subclass is defined, the OBJECT keyword must enclose the name of the parent class in parentheses. The list of fields is implemented in the same manner as records, and just as with nested records, the fields of subclasses must be unique. The list of function and procedure headings is an implicit FORWARD declaration (the keyword FORWARD is not required).

I illustrate the basics of OOP in Listing 1.1. This program defines a class of objects that are character sets. Pascal supports the sets data type and implements the operations of set union, difference, and intersection. In addition, a programmer can create custom routines to manipulate sets as seen fit. Using structured programming techniques, all of the set manipulations are implemented in a fragmented way -- a few routines here, a few there. The program in Listing 1.1 presents a class of character sets that encapsulate a set-type field and the methods that act upon it. To avoid a long-winded example, I have kept the functionality to a minimum. Figure 1.4 illustrates the functionality of the character-set objects implemented in the program. This includes clearing the set membership, displaying the members, inserting new members, deleting existing members, and testing for set membership.

FIGURE 1.4. The functionality of a character-set object.

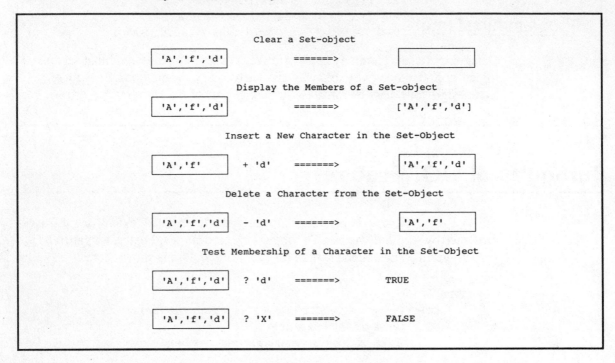

LISTING 1.1. Program ASETOBJ.PAS to illustrate the basics of OOP as applied to character-set object.

```
PROGRAM One_Set_Object;

{
 Program defines a general class of character sets.
}

Uses Crt;

TYPE CharSet = SET OF CHAR;

TYPE

TCharSet = OBJECT
        fSet : CharSet;
        fMembers : BYTE;
        PROCEDURE Clear;
        PROCEDURE WriteSet;
```

```pascal
            PROCEDURE InsertMember(AChar : CHAR);
            PROCEDURE DeleteMember(AChar : CHAR);
            FUNCTION CharInSet(AChar : CHAR) : BOOLEAN;
END;


PROCEDURE TCharSet.Clear;

BEGIN
    fSet := [];
    fMembers := 0;
END;

PROCEDURE TCharSet.WriteSet;

CONST QUOTE = '''';

VAR i : BYTE;

BEGIN
    WRITE('[');
    FOR i := 0 TO 255 DO
        IF CHR(i) IN fSet THEN
            WRITE(QUOTE, CHR(i), QUOTE, ',');
    WRITE(#8); { backspace }
    WRITELN(']');
END;

PROCEDURE TCharSet.InsertMember(AChar : CHAR);

BEGIN
    IF NOT (AChar IN fSet) THEN BEGIN
        fSet := fSet + [AChar];
        INC(fMembers)
    END;
END;

PROCEDURE TCharSet.DeleteMember(AChar : CHAR);

BEGIN
    IF AChar IN fSet THEN BEGIN
        fSet := fSet - [AChar];
        DEC(fMembers)
    END;
END;
```

```
FUNCTION TCharSet.CharInSet (AChar : CHAR) : BOOLEAN;

BEGIN
    CharInSet := AChar IN fSet
END;


PROCEDURE PressAnyKey;

VAR AKey : CHAR;

BEGIN
    WRITELN;
    WRITE('Press any key to continue ...');
    AKey := ReadKey;
    WRITELN;
    WRITELN;
END;


VAR ASCIISet : TCharSet;

BEGIN
    ClrScr;

    { test general character set }
    WRITELN('Testing general set object');
    ASCIISet.Clear;
    ASCIISet.InsertMember('A');
    ASCIISet.InsertMember('h');
    ASCIISet.InsertMember('0');
    ASCIISet.InsertMember('+');
    WRITELN('Set is ');
    ASCIISet.WriteSet; WRITELN;
    ASCIISet.DeleteMember('A');
    ASCIISet.DeleteMember('0');
    ASCIISet.DeleteMember('X');
    WRITELN('After deleting A, 0, and X, set is ');
    ASCIISet.WriteSet; WRITELN;
    WRITELN('Is char 0 in set ? ', ASCIISet.CharInSet('0'));
    WRITELN('Is char h in set ? ', ASCIISet.CharInSet('h'));
    PressAnyKey;
END.
```

The program defines the class TCharSet as follows:

```
TCharSet = OBJECT
        fSet : CharSet;
        fMembers : BYTE;
        PROCEDURE Clear;
        PROCEDURE WriteSet;
        PROCEDURE InsertMember(AChar : CHAR);
        PROCEDURE DeleteMember(AChar : CHAR);
        FUNCTION CharInSet(AChar : CHAR) : BOOLEAN;
END;
```

There are two data fields, namely, fSet and fMembers. The CharSet-typed fSet field keeps track of the characters that are members of the set object. The fMembers field retains the size of the membership. The class TCharSet defines five methods to alter the state of the objects that are instances of class TCharSet. The method Clear is used to initialize and reinitialize the object. The method WriteSet displays the members of the set using the ['<char>',<sequence of chars>] format. The InsertMember method inserts a nonexistent member and updates the membership size. The method DeleteMember removes an existing member and decreases the membership size. The CharInSet method queries the membership of a character, and returns TRUE if the character AChar is a member; otherwise it returns FALSE.

Looking at the code for the methods, notice the following:

1. Each method name is preceded by the class name and the dot access operator. This is a mandatory requirement to inform the compiler about the ownership of the methods. With a single class this rule does not seem to justify itself. Add another class or subclass, and the requirement becomes fully justified.
2. The data fields are directly accessed in the methods without requiring the qualifier *self*. The identifier *self* is a general reference to the target object. Using *self* is a very convenient way to make reference to one or more objects that are not yet created at runtime. The Turbo Pascal compiler uses an invisible WITH self DO statement that absolves you from using the *self* qualifier.
3. The program creates the object ASCIISet in the VAR declaration section, just like any other variable.
4. Messages are sent to the object ASCIISet using the <object>.<message> format. For example, the statement ASCIISet.Clear reads "send the Clear message to object ASCIISet." Object ASCIISet responds by executing method TCharSet.Clear and clearing the character set. Likewise, the statement ASCIISet.InsertMember('A'); reads "send the message

InsertMember('A') to object ASCIISet," to which object ASCIISet responds by executing method TCharSet.InsertMember and inserting character 'A' in the set.

The output for the preceding program is as follows:

```
Testing general set object
Set is
['+','0','A','h']
After deleting A, 0, and X, set is
['+','h']
Is char 0 in set ? FALSE
Is char h in set ? TRUE

Press any key to continue ...
```

The program in Listing 1.1 handled a single class and a single object. The power and versatility of OOP come from creating a hierarchy of classes. To illustrate this aspect of OOP, the example is expanded to include such a hierarchy. The class TCharSet, as defined by Listing 1.1, models character sets that include all the characters in ASCII table: control, punctuation, lower case, upper case, digits, and extended ASCII characters. In the next programs I will create the following subclasses of objects representing further refinement of the base class TCharSet:

1. A subclass of upper-case letters
2. A subclass of digits
3. A subclass of upper-case and lower-case letters

Figure 1.5 illustrates the hierarchy of the various character-set classes.

Let's look at how each subclass is created. Recall that the base class TCharSet is defined as follows:

```
TCharSet = OBJECT
    fSet : CharSet;
    fMembers : BYTE;
    PROCEDURE Clear;
    PROCEDURE WriteSet;
    PROCEDURE InsertMember(AChar : CHAR);
    PROCEDURE DeleteMember(AChar : CHAR);
    FUNCTION CharInSet(AChar : CHAR) : BOOLEAN;
END;
```

FIGURE 1.5. The hierarchy of the various character-set classes.

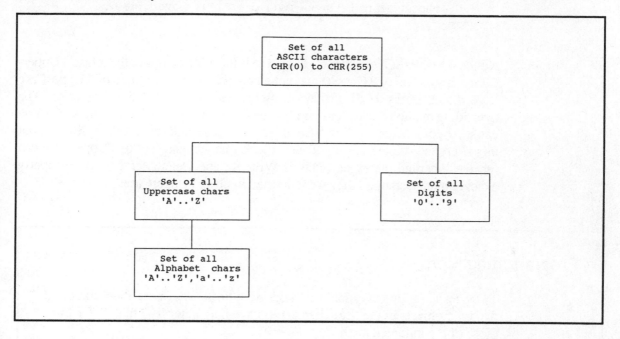

The first subclass of TCharSet is the set of upper-case letters; call it TUpperCase. How does this subclass differ from the TCharSet? First, consider the data fields. The fSet field serves an identical purpose in subclass TUpperCase of keeping track of the actual set membership. The data field fMembers can also be used in instances of TUpperCase to maintain the size of the set membership. Thus, the inherited data fields are useful to both TCharSet and TUpperCase classes. The TUpperCase subclass requires no additional data field to accommodate the associated functionality.

What about the methods inherited from class TCharSet? The methods TCharSet.Clear, TCharSet.WriteSet, TCharSet.DeleteMember, and TCharSet.CharInSet meet the functional requirements of the TUpperCase subclass. By contrast, the method TCharSet.InsertMember is inadequate for the class TUpperCase, and a new overriding version is needed to ensure that non–upper-case characters are screened out.

Based on this analysis, the definition of the TUpperCase class is as follows:

```
TUpperCase = OBJECT (TCharSet)
    PROCEDURE InsertMember (AChar : CHAR); { override }
END;
```

Notice that OBJECT(TCharSet) is used to inform the compiler that class TUpper-Case is a subclass of TCharSet and not a new base class. Instances of TUpperCase have direct access to all of the data fields and methods of the base class. The overriding method InsertMember is the new version of the inherited method. (You can still bypass the overriding methods and use those of the parent class. More about this after the listing is shown.) Thus, objects that are instances of TUpperCase can receive inherited messages, such as WriteSet and DeleteMember, and properly execute them as though they were defined in class TUpperCase.

Programming Note

Turbo Pascal allows overriding methods of static objects (more about static and dynamic objects in the next chapter) to have parameter lists that differ from those of the inherited methods.

The second subclass of TCharSet is the set of digits 0 to 9; call it TDigits. The inherited data fields, fSet and fMembers, serve this new subclass very satisfacto-rily. No new data fields need be added to subclass TDigits. All of the inherited methods, except TCharSet.InsertMember, work properly with the objects of class TDigits. A new version of method InsertMember is required to screen out nondigit characters. The declaration of subclass TDigits is as follows:

```
TDigits = OBJECT (TCharSet)
    PROCEDURE InsertMember (AChar : CHAR); { override }
END;
```

The power of inheritance is evident in this declaration, which includes a single new method—everything else is inherited from the parent class TCharSet!

The subclass TUpperCase may be used to declare another subclass that handles upper-case and lower-case characters; call it TAlphabet. Class TAlphabet differs from its parent class TUpperCase in the fact that members of the character set can be upper-case and lower-case letters. How does the difference in functionality impact the data fields of subclass TAlphabet? While the inherited fields are very adequate, I have added two more data fields, fUpCase and fLoCase, to keep track of the number of upper-case and lower-case letters, respectively.

As you might expect, a new version of the method InsertMember is required to work with subclass TAlphabet. In addition, a new version of method Clear is required to assign zeros to the new data fields, fUpCase and fLoCase. This assignment complements the inherited task of assigning a zero to data field fMembers and assigning an empty set to data field fSet.

Declaring new fields and overriding inherited methods as just described, the declaration of subclass TAlphabet is as follows:

```
TAlphabet = OBJECT (TUpperCase)
    fUpCase,
    fLoCase : BYTE;
    PROCEDURE Clear;
    PROCEDURE InsertMember(AChar : CHAR);  { override }
END;
```

LISTING 1.2. The SETSOBJ.PAS program, which demonstrates class hierarchy, inheritance, and overriding inherited methods.

```
PROGRAM Test_Set_Objects;

{
  Program defines four classes of character sets:
    1. General character set
    2. Upper-case letters
    3. Digits
    4. Alphabet characters

  The last three classes of characters are subclasses
  of their parent classes.  The program demonstrates when
  methods are inherited and when they are overriden.
}

Uses Crt;

TYPE CharSet = SET OF CHAR;
```

```
CONST ALPHABET : CharSet = ['A'..'Z','a'..'z'];
      UPPERCASE : CharSet = ['A'..'Z'];
      DIGITS : CharSet = ['0'..'9'];

TYPE

TCharSet = OBJECT
    fSet : CharSet;
    fMembers : BYTE;
    PROCEDURE Clear;
    PROCEDURE WriteSet;
    PROCEDURE InsertMember(AChar : CHAR);
    PROCEDURE DeleteMember(AChar : CHAR);
    FUNCTION CharInSet(AChar : CHAR) : BOOLEAN;
END;

TUpperCase = OBJECT(TCharSet)
    PROCEDURE InsertMember(AChar : CHAR); { override }
END;

TDigits = OBJECT(TCharSet)
    PROCEDURE InsertMember(AChar : CHAR); { override }
END;

TAlphabet = OBJECT(TUpperCase)
    fUpCase,
    fLoCase : BYTE;
    PROCEDURE Clear; { override }
    PROCEDURE InsertMember(AChar : CHAR); { override }
END;

PROCEDURE TCharSet.Clear;

BEGIN
    fSet := [];
    fMembers := 0;
END;

PROCEDURE TAlphabet.Clear;

BEGIN
    { send message using method of parent class }
    TUpperCase.Clear;
```

```pascal
        fUpCase := 0;
        fLoCase := 0;
    END;

PROCEDURE TCharSet.WriteSet;

CONST QUOTE = '''';

VAR i : BYTE;

BEGIN
    WRITE('[');
    FOR i := 0 TO 255 DO
        IF CHR(i) IN fSet THEN
            WRITE(QUOTE, CHR(i), QUOTE, ',');
    WRITE(#8); { backspace }
    WRITELN(']');
END;

PROCEDURE TCharSet.InsertMember(AChar : CHAR);

BEGIN
    IF NOT (AChar IN fSet) THEN BEGIN
        fSet := fSet + [AChar];
        INC(fMembers)
    END;
END;

PROCEDURE TAlphabet.InsertMember(AChar : CHAR);

BEGIN
    IF (NOT (AChar IN fSet)) AND
            (AChar IN ALPHABET) THEN BEGIN
        fSet := fSet + [AChar];
        INC(fMembers);
        IF AChar IN UPPERCASE THEN
            INC(fUpCase)
        ELSE
            INC(fLoCase);
    END;
END;

PROCEDURE TUpperCase.InsertMember(AChar : CHAR);
```

```
BEGIN
    IF (NOT (AChar IN fSet)) AND
            (AChar IN UPPERCASE) THEN BEGIN
        fSet := fSet + [AChar];
        INC(fMembers);
    END;
END;


PROCEDURE TDigits.InsertMember(AChar : CHAR);

BEGIN
    IF (NOT (AChar IN fSet)) AND
            (AChar IN DIGITS) THEN BEGIN
        fSet := fSet + [AChar];
        INC(fMembers);
    END;
END;



PROCEDURE TCharSet.DeleteMember(AChar : CHAR);

BEGIN
    IF AChar IN fSet THEN BEGIN
        fSet := fSet - [AChar];
        DEC(fMembers)
    END;
END;

FUNCTION TCharSet.CharInSet(AChar : CHAR) : BOOLEAN;

BEGIN
    CharInSet := AChar IN fSet
END;

PROCEDURE PressAnyKey;

VAR AKey : CHAR;

BEGIN
    WRITELN;
    WRITE('Press any key to continue ...');
    AKey := ReadKey;
    WRITELN;
    WRITELN;
END;
```

```
VAR ASCIISet    : TCharSet;
    Letters     : TAlphabet;
    UpChar      : TUpperCase;
    Digit       : TDigits;

BEGIN
    ClrScr;

    { test general character set }
    WRITELN('Testing general set object');
    ASCIISet.Clear;
    ASCIISet.InsertMember('A');
    ASCIISet.InsertMember('h');
    ASCIISet.InsertMember('0');
    ASCIISet.InsertMember('+');
    WRITELN('Set is ');
    ASCIISet.WriteSet; WRITELN;
    ASCIISet.DeleteMember('A');
    ASCIISet.DeleteMember('0');
    ASCIISet.DeleteMember('X');
    WRITELN('After deleting A, 0, and X, set is ');
    ASCIISet.WriteSet; WRITELN;
    WRITELN('Is char 0 in set ? ', ASCIISet.CharInSet('0'));
    WRITELN('Is char h in set ? ', ASCIISet.CharInSet('h'));
    PressAnyKey;

    { test alphabet character set }
    WRITELN('Testing alphabet set object');
    Letters.Clear;
    Letters.InsertMember('A');
    Letters.InsertMember('h');
    Letters.InsertMember('P');
    Letters.InsertMember('+');
    WRITELN('Set is ');
    Letters.WriteSet; WRITELN;
    WRITE('Set contains ', Letters.fUpCase, ' upper-case letters');
    WRITELN(' and ', Letters.fLoCase, ' lower-case letters');
    Letters.DeleteMember('A');
    Letters.DeleteMember('P');
    Letters.DeleteMember('X');
    WRITELN('After deleting A, P, and X, set is ');
    Letters.WriteSet; WRITELN;
    WRITELN('Is char A in set ? ', Letters.CharInSet('A'));
```

```
      WRITELN('Is char h in set ? ', Letters.CharInSet('h'));
      PressAnyKey;

      { test digit character set }
      WRITELN('Testing digit set object');
      Digit.Clear;
      Digit.InsertMember('0');
      Digit.InsertMember('5');
      Digit.InsertMember('9');
      Digit.InsertMember('+');
      WRITELN('Set is ');
      Digit.WriteSet; WRITELN;
      Digit.DeleteMember('0');
      Digit.DeleteMember('9');
      Digit.DeleteMember('X');
      WRITELN('After deleting 0, 9, and X, set is ');
      Digit.WriteSet; WRITELN;
      WRITELN('Is char 9 in set ? ', Digit.CharInSet('9'));
      WRITELN('Is char 5 in set ? ', Digit.CharInSet('5'));
      PressAnyKey;

      { test upper-case character set }
      WRITELN('Testing upper-case set object');
      UpChar.Clear;
      UpChar.InsertMember('A');
      UpChar.InsertMember('H');
      UpChar.InsertMember('Q');
      UpChar.InsertMember('+');
      WRITELN('Set is ');
      UpChar.WriteSet; WRITELN;
      UpChar.DeleteMember('A');
      UpChar.DeleteMember('Q');
      UpChar.DeleteMember('X');
      WRITELN('After deleting A, Q, and X, set is ');
      UpChar.WriteSet; WRITELN;
      WRITELN('Is char A in set ? ', UpChar.CharInSet('A'));
      WRITELN('Is char H in set ? ', UpChar.CharInSet('H'));
      PressAnyKey;
  END.
```

Notice the code for method TAlphabet.Clear:

```
PROCEDURE TAlphabet.Clear;

BEGIN
    { send message using method of parent class }
    TUpperCase.Clear;
    fUpCase := 0;
    fLoCase := 0;
END;
```

The first statement in that procedure is:

```
TUpperCase.Clear;
```

The method TAlphabet.Clear is able to invoke the inherited method it overrode in the first place by using the name of the parent class as the qualifier to the message Clear. This may look odd at first, but it makes sense when the overriding method simply adds one or more statements to the inherited code. In this case, the method TAlphabet.Clear must assign an empty set to the fSet data field and assign zero to fields fMembers, fUpCase, and fLoCase. The first two of these assignments need not be recoded—a call to the inherited method Clear does the job.

Programming Note

The mechanism of calling overridden inherited methods in Turbo Pascal allows you to specify the ancestor class. Be aware that this is true only within the declaration of methods---you cannot send an overridden inherited message to an object in Turbo Pascal.

Other object Pascal implementations, such as QuickPascal, use the IN-HERITED keyword to inherit overridden methods from parent classes only ("INHERITED Clear" would be used instead of TUpperCase.Clear). This is more limited than Turbo Pascal's mechanism. However, the tradeoff is that in such implementations you can issue similar types of messages to objects.

The output for the preceding program is as follows:

```
Testing general set object
Set is
['+','0','A','h']
```

```
After deleting A, 0, and X, set is
['+','h']

Is char 0 in set ? FALSE
Is char h in set ? TRUE

Press any key to continue ...

Testing alphabet set object
Set is
['A','P','h']

Set contains 2 upper-case letters and 1 lower-case letter
After deleting A, P, and X, set is
['h']

Is char A in set ? FALSE
Is char h in set ? TRUE

Press any key to continue ...

Testing digit set object
Set is
['0','5','9']

After deleting 0, 9, and X, set is
['5']

Is char 9 in set ? FALSE
Is char 5 in set ? TRUE

Press any key to continue ...

Testing upper-case set object
Set is
['A','H','Q']

After deleting A, Q, and X, set is
['H']

Is char A in set ? FALSE
Is char H in set ? TRUE
```

2

Advanced Object-Oriented Programming Issues

This chapter looks at the more advanced aspects of object-oriented programming with Turbo Pascal. You may wish to read this chapter later, after looking at the different application chapters that follow this one.

Naming Methods: The Good, the Bad, and the . . .

It won't take you long to discover the feature of overloading functions and procedures associated with classes. For disconnected classes that are involved in an application or a library unit, you can use the same names for methods (with identical or different parameter lists) as well as for data fields. As long as you explicitly qualify the data fields and methods with the names of the objects, there can be no mixup whatsoever. If you employ the WITH statement, then you need to be a bit more careful: do not include multiple objects that have any methods with the same name, even if the methods have different arguments. Attempting to do so yields a compiler error. Listing 2.1 contains a trivial program that demonstrates this point. It declares two unrelated classes, ClassA and ClassB, and their instances, objects A and B. These classes employ the same names for two methods: Init and GetA. The program has three similar sections. In the first section, all of the methods are explicitly qualified with the object names for maximum clarity and readability. In the second section, a WITH A DO statement is used. Methods of ClassB are still explicitly qualified with the B identifier and the dot operator. The third section is actually commented out since it produces a compiler error. Attempting to use a

WITH A,B DO statement makes the code confusing for both the compiler and the programmer.

LISTING 2.1. Program OVERLOAD.PAS, which illustrates overloading methods in unrelated classes.

```
Program Test_Overloading_Methods;

Uses Crt;

TYPE

ClassA = OBJECT
    A : INTEGER;
    PROCEDURE Init (I : INTEGER { input });
    FUNCTION GetA : INTEGER;
END;

ClassB = OBJECT
    A,
    B : INTEGER;
    PROCEDURE Init (I, J : INTEGER { input });
    FUNCTION GetA : INTEGER;
    FUNCTION GetB : INTEGER;
END;

PROCEDURE ClassA.Init (I : INTEGER { input });
BEGIN
    A := I
END;

FUNCTION ClassA.GetA : INTEGER;
BEGIN
    GetA := A
END;

PROCEDURE ClassB.Init (I, J : INTEGER { input });
BEGIN
    A := I;
    B := J
END;

FUNCTION ClassB.GetA : INTEGER;
BEGIN
    GetA := A
END;
```

```
FUNCTION ClassB.GetB : INTEGER;
BEGIN
    GetB := B
END;


VAR A : ClassA;
    B : ClassB;
    AKey : CHAR;


BEGIN
    ClrScr;
    { Explicit qualifiers are used to achieve
      maximum readability of code }
    A.Init(1);
    B.Init(10, 20);
    WRITELN('A.A = ', A.GetA);
    WRITELN('B.A = ', B.GetA);
    WRITELN('B.B = ', B.GetB);
    WRITELN;


    { The WITH statement is used with one object,
      but not the other }
    WITH A DO BEGIN
        Init(1);                   {The A. qualifier is not required}
        B.Init(10, 20);            {B. is still used as the qualifier}
        WRITELN('A.A = ', GetA);   {The A. qualifier is not required}
        WRITELN('B.A = ', B.GetA);
        WRITELN('B.B = ', B.GetB);
    END;
    WRITELN;


    { ------ WILL NOT COMPILE CORRECTLY ----- 
    WITH A, B DO BEGIN
        Init(1);
        Init(10, 20);
        WRITELN('A.A = ', GetA);
        WRITELN('B.A = ', GetA);
        WRITELN('B.B = ', GetB);
    }
    WRITELN;
    WRITE('Press any key to end the program ...');
    AKey := ReadKey;
END.
```

Enforcing Mandatory Initialization

Turbo Pascal and other implementations of Object Pascal do not support automatic initialization of objects, as does the rival language C++. In Turbo Pascal static objects are automatically created and removed, just like static variables. However, the process of initializing data fields is required in most applications. The question is: What happens if you accidentally forget to use the method (or group of methods) that initialize an object? The case of omitting a single initializing method is easy to spot and fix. The remedy is not so obvious when multiple methods contribute to initializing an object.

In the case of a single initializing method, you can employ a string-typed field that is assigned the string constant 'TRUE' (or any other string that distinguishes itself from garbage data) when the initializing method is called. All the other methods can check for the TRUE string in the initialization flag field. Usually the method is exited when the string is not TRUE. The program may even be halted altogether if matters are more critical. Sometimes a default initialization condition is employed. Listing 2.2 contains a program that creates a dynamic array. The class definition includes the data field DoneInit to report the initialization status. The method Init is used to allocate the size of the dynamic array, which is a required step. The method Fill fills the array with a value. This method examines the field DoneInit. If DoneInit is FALSE, the dynamic array is created using a default size (assuming that this action is acceptable to the application) and then the array is filled with numbers.

LISTING 2.2. Program MUSTINIT.PAS to test for mandatory initialization.

```
Program Test_Initialization;

{
Program illustrates how to test for mandatory
initialization and perform default initialization,
if applicable.
}

Uses Crt;
{$R-}

CONST DEFAULT_SIZE = 100;

TYPE
     OneRealArray = ARRAY [1..1] OF REAL;
     OneRealPtr = ^OneRealArray;
```

```
DynArray = OBJECT
    DoneInit : STRING;
    MaxSize : WORD;
    VecPtr : OneRealPtr;
    PROCEDURE Init (TheMaxSize : WORD { input });
    FUNCTION GetSize : WORD;
    PROCEDURE Fill (X : REAL { input });
    PROCEDURE Remove;
END;

PROCEDURE DynArray.Init (TheMaxSize : WORD { input });
BEGIN
    MaxSize := TheMaxSize;
    IF MaxSize < 1 THEN
        MaxSize := DEFAULT_SIZE;
    GetMem (VecPtr, MaxSize * SizeOf (REAL));
    DoneInit := 'TRUE'
END;

FUNCTION DynArray.GetSize : WORD;
BEGIN
    GetSize := MaxSize
END;

PROCEDURE DynArray.Fill (X : REAL { input });

VAR I : WORD;

BEGIN
    { implement default initialization }
    IF DoneInit <> 'TRUE' THEN
        Init (DEFAULT_SIZE);

    FOR I := 1 TO MaxSize DO
        VecPtr^[I] := X
END;

PROCEDURE DynArray.Remove;
BEGIN
    IF DoneInit = 'TRUE' THEN BEGIN
        FreeMem (VecPtr, MaxSize * SizeOf (REAL));
        DoneInit := 'FALSE'
    END;
END;
```

```
VAR A : DynArray;
    X : REAL;
    AKey : CHAR;

BEGIN
    ClrScr;

    { The initialization method is deliberately commented out }
    { A.Init(50) }
    X := 100.0;
    A.Fill(X); { initializes to default size }
    WRITELN('Filled dynamic array with ',X:4:0,'s');
    WRITELN('Dynamic array size is ', A.GetSize);
    A.Remove;
    WRITELN;
    WRITE('Press any key to end the program ...');
    AKey := ReadKey;
END.
```

In the case of multiple initializing methods, an array of Boolean flags (or a set of bits) is used to verify that every method is called to prepare the object. Listing 2.3 shows a program that calculates the future value of an investment based on the present value, the interest rate, and the number of investment periods. The class involved employs a separate initialization method for each of the three input parameters. An array of flags is used to ensure that (a) each initialization method has been called, and (b) proper values (positive values in this case) are assigned to the parameters. The method FV, which calculates the future value, examines the ANDed value of the flags. A logical TRUE result gives the green light for calculating the function value; otherwise, a −1 is returned as a numeric code for incomplete initialization.

LISTING 2.3. Program CHEKINIT.PAS demonstrates checking on initialization that employs multiple methods.

```
Program Test_Initialization;

{
Program illustrates how to check on initialization
that employs multiple methods
}

Uses Crt;
```

```
TYPE

ClassA = OBJECT
    PV,
    I,
    N : REAL;
    Flag : ARRAY [1..3] OF BOOLEAN;
    PROCEDURE InitPV(PVval : REAL { input });
    PROCEDURE InitI(Ival : REAL { input });
    PROCEDURE InitN(Nval : REAL { input });
    FUNCTION FV : REAL;
END;

PROCEDURE ClassA.InitPV(PVval : REAL { input });
BEGIN
    IF PVval > 0 THEN BEGIN
        PV := PVval;
        Flag[1] := TRUE
    END
    ELSE
        Flag[1] := FALSE;
END;

PROCEDURE ClassA.InitI(Ival : REAL { input });
BEGIN
    IF Ival > 0 THEN BEGIN
        I := Ival;
        Flag[2] := TRUE
    END
    ELSE
        Flag[2] := FALSE;
END;

PROCEDURE ClassA.InitN(Nval : REAL { input });
BEGIN
    IF Nval > 0 THEN BEGIN
        N := Nval;
        Flag[3] := TRUE
    END
    ELSE
        Flag[3] := FALSE;
END;

FUNCTION Power(Base, Exponent : REAL { input }) : REAL;
BEGIN
    IF Base > 0 THEN
```

```
            Power := Exp(Exponent * Ln(Base))
        ELSE
            Power := 0;
    END;

    FUNCTION ClassA.FV : REAL;

    VAR J : WORD;
        OK : BOOLEAN;

    BEGIN
        OK := Flag[1]; { initialize OK with first flag }
        J := 2;
        WHILE (J < 4) AND OK DO BEGIN
            OK := OK AND Flag[J];
            INC(J)
        END;
        IF OK THEN
            FV := PV * Power((1+I),N)
        ELSE
            FV := -1;
    END;


    VAR A : ClassA;
        PVval, Ival, Nval : REAL;
        AKey : CHAR;

    BEGIN
        ClrScr;
        WRITE('Enter present value : $');
        READLN(PVval); WRITELN;
        WRITE('Enter % interest rate : ');
        READLN(Ival); WRITELN;
        IF Ival > 1 THEN Ival := Ival / 100;
        WRITE('Enter number of periods : ');
        READLN(Nval); WRITELN;
        A.InitPV(PVval);
        A.InitI(Ival);
        A.InitN(Nval);
        WRITELN('Future value = $', A.FV:5:2);
        WRITELN;
        WRITE('Press any key to end the program ...');
        AKey := ReadKey;
    END.
```

Dynamic Objects and Methods

The objects shown so far are static. Turbo Pascal also implements dynamic objects. Static objects are compiled into machine code that runs faster than that of dynamic objects. On the other hand, dynamic objects offer more runtime flexibility and support polymorphism (this is discussed later in this chapter). In this section I present the syntax and rules for declaring and using dynamic objects.

Turbo Pascal draws some of its implementation of dynamic objects from C++ concepts and C++ keywords. The main vehicles for dynamic objects are virtual functions and procedures. The keyword VIRTUAL is placed in a separate statement following every declaration of a virtual method. Virtual methods must be accompanied by **constructors**, which are methods dedicated to initializing objects with virtual methods. The keyword CONSTRUCTOR is used instead of PROCEDURE when declaring a constructor. The suggested name for constructors is Init. Turbo Pascal also implements **destructors** which counter the effects of constructors. Their task is to perform any required "cleanup." The suggested name for destructors is Done.

The rules for declaring virtual methods are:

1. Once a method is declared virtual in a class, it must be declared virtual in all subclasses.
2. The first occurrence of a virtual method in a subclass may override nonvirtual methods in its ancestor classes.
3. Virtual methods *must have the same parameter list in every class in which it is used.*
4. Virtual methods can be inherited and need not be declared for every subclass.

The rules for using constructors are:

1. A constructor *must be called before* a virtual-message is sent to an object. Otherwise the system locks!
2. Multiple constructors are allowed to permit various ways of initializing an object.
3. Constructors can be inherited.

The rules for using destructors are:

1. A destructor should be called for proper cleanup. This is usually the recuperation of heap or EMS memory.
2. Multiple destructors are allowed to permit various ways of removing an object.

3.   Destructors can be inherited.
4.   Virtual destructors are allowed.

Dynamic vs. Static Objects

Turbo Pascal 5.5 offers you a choice between static and dynamic objects, each with its own advantages. Static objects enjoy a faster execution of methods, but use memory in the program's data/code segments. By contrast, dynamic objects use the heap, but execute a bit slower. If you are designing a large application, you may want to employ virtual methods to make use of the heap rather than the more limited data/ code segments.

Dynamic Binding and Polymorphism

Polymorphism is an OOP buzzword that means the ability of an object to respond to a command or message in a manner unique to it. The message itself is not monopolized by any single class. The champion of the polymorphism feature is the runtime late binding of methods. To understand polymorphism and late binding, consider the class hierarchy shown in Figure 2.1. The figure shows a class A with two methods A1 and A2, such that A1 calls on A2. An A1 message sent to an object of class A, call it ObjA, executes methods A.A1 and A.A2. The figure also shows class B as a subclass of A with method A2 overridden. If a message A1 is sent to an object of class B, call it ObjB, what is the sequence of methods executed? The answer is as follows:

1.   The runtime system takes the message ObjB.A1 and attempts to find a matching method among those of class B.

FIGURE 2.1. Late binding.

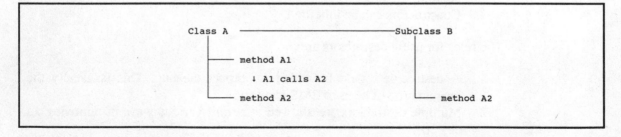

2.   The above action fails and the system resorts to examining the methods of the parent class A. The search is fruitful this time and the code for method A.A1 is used.

3.   Since method A.A1 calls on method A.A2, the runtime system must resolve the call. It first looks back at the methods of class B again (the class whose instance received the original message) and attempts to locate a method A2.

4.   The search is successful, and the system employs the code of B.A2 in resolving the call of ObjB.A1.

In the absence of late binding, the runtime system would have incorrectly (from the point of view of program logic) inserted the code of method A.A2 in resolving the call by method A.A1.

The sample program in Listing 2.4 illustrates how late binding works. Class A declares a constructor Init and the two methods Greetings and GetName. The former method calls on the latter to prompt you for a name. Class B, a child class of A, employs a virtual GetName method to prompt you with a different wording. Class B also utilizes the inherited constructor Init. The main part of the program sends the Greetings message to instances of both classes A and B. Because of late binding the messages sent display two different prompts.

LISTING 2.4. Program LATEBIND.PAS illustrates the effect of late binding.

```
Program Test_Late_Binding;

{
Program illustrates the effect of late binding.

Note: If the VIRTUAL; statements are commented out,
the objects become static and the absence of late
binding becomes evident by the identical prompts
emitted by the two Greetings messages.
}

Uses Crt;

TYPE

ClassA = OBJECT
    Name : STRING;
    CONSTRUCTOR Init;
```

```
        PROCEDURE Greetings;
        PROCEDURE GetName; VIRTUAL;
END;

ClassB = OBJECT (ClassA)
        PROCEDURE Getname; VIRTUAL;
END;

CONSTRUCTOR ClassA.Init;
BEGIN
     Name := ''; { initialize Name field to a null string }
END;

PROCEDURE ClassA.GetName;
BEGIN
     WRITE ('Your name please ? ');
     READLN (Name); WRITELN;
END;

PROCEDURE ClassA.Greetings;
BEGIN
     GetName;
     WRITELN ('Hello ', Name, ', how are you?');
     WRITELN;
END;

PROCEDURE ClassB.GetName;
BEGIN
     WRITE ('Enter your name -> ');
     READLN (Name); WRITELN;
END;

VAR A : ClassA;
    B : ClassB;
    AKey : CHAR;

BEGIN
     ClrScr;
     { initialize objects }
     A.Init;
     B.Init;
     { send Greetings message to objects A and B }
     A.Greetings;
     B.Greetings;
```

```
                    WRITELN;
                    WRITE('Press any key to end the program ...');
                    AKey := ReadKey;
              END.
```

Exporting Classes

Library units are excellent OOP development tools in Turbo Pascal. Listing 2.5 shows the SetsLib library unit, which is a library version of the sets program presented in Chapter 1. When you implement a class in a unit, the declaration of the class is placed in the interface part, while the detailed coding is put in the implementation segment.

Using library units enables you to use the divide-and-conquer strategy very effectively in software development. This manifests itself when you employ multiple levels of libraries. The low-level libraries export the classes that perform and manage underlying activities such as computations, sorting, and searching. The higher-level libraries export classes that deal with the user interface. The calculator object in Chapter 13 is an example of creating layers of classes using multilevel libraries.

LISTING 2.5. The source code for the SetsLib library unit.

```
      UNIT SetsLib;

   {========================================================


            Copyright (c) 1989, 1990  Namir Clement Shammas

      LIBRARY NAME: SetsLib


      VERSION:  1.0                              DATE 7/25/1989


      PURPOSE: Exports classes of character sets:
                   + General character set
                    + Alphabet
                      + Upper-case characters
                    + Digits


   ========================================================}
```

```
{*******************************************************************}
{***********************} INTERFACE {***************************}
{*******************************************************************}


Uses Crt;

TYPE CharSet = SET OF CHAR;

CONST ALPHABET : CharSet = ['A'..'Z','a'..'z'];
      UPPERCASE : CharSet = ['A'..'Z'];
      DIGITS : CharSet = ['0'..'9'];

TYPE

TCharSet = OBJECT
    fSet : CharSet;
    fMembers : BYTE;
    PROCEDURE Clear;
    PROCEDURE WriteSet;
    PROCEDURE InsertMember(AChar : CHAR);
    PROCEDURE DeleteMember(AChar : CHAR);
    FUNCTION CharInSet(AChar : CHAR) : BOOLEAN;
END;


TUpperCase = OBJECT(TCharSet)
    PROCEDURE InsertMember(AChar : CHAR); { override }
END;


TDigits = OBJECT(TCharSet)
    PROCEDURE InsertMember(AChar : CHAR); { override }
END;


TAlphabet = OBJECT(TUpperCase)
    fUpCase,
    fLoCase : BYTE;
    PROCEDURE Clear; { override }
    PROCEDURE InsertMember(AChar : CHAR); { override }
END;



{*******************************************************************}
{**********************} IMPLEMENTATION {***********************}
{*******************************************************************}
```

```
PROCEDURE TCharSet.Clear;

BEGIN
    fSet := [];
    fMembers := 0;
END;

PROCEDURE TAlphabet.Clear;

BEGIN
    { send message using method of parent class }
    TUpperCase.Clear;
    fUpCase := 0;
    fLoCase := 0;
END;

PROCEDURE TCharSet.WriteSet;

CONST QUOTE = '''';

VAR i : BYTE;

BEGIN
    WRITE('[');
    FOR i := 0 TO 255 DO
        IF CHR(i) IN fSet THEN
            WRITE(QUOTE, CHR(i), QUOTE, ',');
    WRITE(#8); { backspace }
    WRITELN(']');
END;

PROCEDURE TCharSet.InsertMember(AChar : CHAR);

BEGIN
    IF NOT (AChar IN fSet) THEN BEGIN
        fSet := fSet + [AChar];
        INC(fMembers)
    END;
END;

PROCEDURE TAlphabet.InsertMember(AChar : CHAR);

BEGIN
    IF (NOT (AChar IN fSet)) AND
            (AChar IN ALPHABET) THEN BEGIN
        fSet := fSet + [AChar];
```

```
            INC(fMembers);
            IF AChar IN UPPERCASE THEN
                INC(fUpCase)
            ELSE
                INC(fLoCase);
        END;
    END;


PROCEDURE TUpperCase.InsertMember(AChar : CHAR);

BEGIN
    IF (NOT (AChar IN fSet)) AND
            (AChar IN UPPERCASE) THEN BEGIN
        fSet := fSet + [AChar];
        INC(fMembers);
    END;
END;


PROCEDURE TDigits.InsertMember(AChar : CHAR);

BEGIN
    IF (NOT (AChar IN fSet)) AND
            (AChar IN DIGITS) THEN BEGIN
        fSet := fSet + [AChar];
        INC(fMembers);
    END;
END;


PROCEDURE TCharSet.DeleteMember(AChar : CHAR);

BEGIN
    IF AChar IN fSet THEN BEGIN
        fSet := fSet - [AChar];
        DEC(fMembers)
    END;
END;


FUNCTION TCharSet.CharInSet(AChar : CHAR) : BOOLEAN;

BEGIN
    CharInSet := AChar IN fSet
END;


END.
```

The following program (Listing 2.6) is a modified version of Listing 1.2 that uses the SetsLib library unit:

LISTING 2.6. Program TSSETLIB.PAS to test the set-classes exported by library unit SetsLib.

```
PROGRAM Test_Set_Objects;

{
    Program imports classes of sets exported by unit SetsLib
}

Uses Crt, SetsLib;

PROCEDURE PressAnyKey;

VAR AKey : CHAR;

BEGIN
    WRITELN;
    WRITE('Press any key to continue ...');
    AKey := ReadKey;
    WRITELN;
    WRITELN;
END;

VAR ASCIISet : TCharSet;
    Letters  : TAlphabet;
    UpChar   : TUpperCase;
    Digit    : TDigits;

BEGIN
    ClrScr;

    { test general character set }
    WRITELN('Testing general set object');
    ASCIISet.Clear;
    ASCIISet.InsertMember('A');
    ASCIISet.InsertMember('h');
    ASCIISet.InsertMember('0');
    ASCIISet.InsertMember('+');
    WRITELN('Set is ');
    ASCIISet.WriteSet; WRITELN;
    ASCIISet.DeleteMember('A');
```

```
ASCIISet.DeleteMember('0');
ASCIISet.DeleteMember('X');
WRITELN('After deleting A, 0, and X, set is ');
ASCIISet.WriteSet; WRITELN;
WRITELN('Is char 0 in set ? ', ASCIISet.CharInSet('0'));
WRITELN('Is char h in set ? ', ASCIISet.CharInSet('h'));
PressAnyKey;

{ test alphabet character set }
WRITELN('Testing alphabet set object');
Letters.Clear;
Letters.InsertMember('A');
Letters.InsertMember('h');
Letters.InsertMember('P');
Letters.InsertMember('+');
WRITELN('Set is ');
Letters.WriteSet; WRITELN;
WRITE('Set contains ', Letters.fUpCase, ' upper-case letters');
WRITELN(' and ', Letters.fLoCase, ' lower-case letters');
Letters.DeleteMember('A');
Letters.DeleteMember('P');
Letters.DeleteMember('X');
WRITELN('After deleting A, P, and X, set is ');
Letters.WriteSet; WRITELN;
WRITELN('Is char A in set ? ', Letters.CharInSet('A'));
WRITELN('Is char h in set ? ', Letters.CharInSet('h'));
PressAnyKey;

{ test digit character set }
WRITELN('Testing digit set object');
Digit.Clear;
Digit.InsertMember('0');
Digit.InsertMember('5');
Digit.InsertMember('9');
Digit.InsertMember('+');
WRITELN('Set is ');
Digit.WriteSet; WRITELN;
Digit.DeleteMember('0');
Digit.DeleteMember('9');
Digit.DeleteMember('X');
WRITELN('After deleting 0, 9, and X, set is ');
Digit.WriteSet; WRITELN;
WRITELN('Is char 9 in set ? ', Digit.CharInSet('9'));
WRITELN('Is char 5 in set ? ', Digit.CharInSet('5'));
```

```
        PressAnyKey;

        { test upper-case character set }
        WRITELN ('Testing upper-case set object');
        UpChar.Clear;
        UpChar.InsertMember ('A');
        UpChar.InsertMember ('H');
        UpChar.InsertMember ('Q');
        UpChar.InsertMember ('+');
        WRITELN ('Set is ');
        UpChar.WriteSet; WRITELN;
        UpChar.DeleteMember ('A');
        UpChar.DeleteMember ('Q');
        UpChar.DeleteMember ('X');
        WRITELN ('After deleting A, Q, and X, set is ');
        UpChar.WriteSet; WRITELN;
        WRITELN ('Is char A in set ? ', UpChar.CharInSet ('A'));
        WRITELN ('Is char H in set ? ', UpChar.CharInSet ('H'));
        PressAnyKey;
    END.
```

The output of this program is identical to that of Listing 1.2, shown at the end of Chapter 1.

Another benefit of using library units is data hiding. Turbo Pascal and the other implementations of OOP Pascal offer neither data hiding nor private methods—you can access every field and every method declared in a class! While you are discouraged from directly accessing data fields, the compiler will not stop you from doing so. I find this to be a weak aspect of OOP in the Pascal implementations, since data hiding is an important part of today's software engineering techniques.

To implement any kind of data hiding, your best bet is to do it in a library unit, and it is not easy! Here are suggestions for two possible routes:

1. Employ pointer-typed data fields in a class. Such fields are used as pointers to the hidden (or pseudohidden, if you like) data. The structures accessed by these pointers are defined inside the implementation section. This hides the details of the structures and makes access to their components very difficult for a client application.

2. Use a hidden-data manager to create and manipulate hidden data as each object of the same class is created. This means that each class with hidden data must have its own hidden-data manager. The data types of the hidden structures are declared within the implementation section. The initialization section of the library unit must initialize all the hidden-data managers.

Turbo Pascal does not support method hiding. The missing feature is useful when you declare methods in a class that are to be used only by other methods in the class. Invoking these methods from outside is an "unauthorized" act that disturbs the state of the object. How do you handle such cases? The answer is to implement pseudohidden methods—ones that respond properly only when called by other methods and exit when invoked directly. The steps involved in implementing pseudohidden methods are as follows:

1. Declare a Boolean filter variable that is local to the implementation section. This variable is hidden from all client applications and library units. Its purpose is to detect and filter out "unauthorized" messages.
2. The filter variable should be set to FALSE in the library initialization section.
3. A method that invokes the pseudohidden methods must set the filter variable to TRUE prior to sending the messages in question. When the caller is done, the filter variable must be set to FALSE again.

The foregoing steps are shown in the following example. Listing 2.7 contains a simple library unit HIDELIB.PAS which exports a class TClass. This class has two pseudohidden methods, Prompt and GetSquare, which are invoked by messages from the method Calculate. The Prompt method is used to prompt for the value of data field X. The GetSquare method calculates the value for data field Y by squaring the value of data field X. The method Calculate sends the messages Prompt and GetSquare to the instance of class TClass. The Boolean variable GoAhead, local to the implementation section, is used to prevent the messages Prompt and GetSquare from performing their tasks when sent from outside an instance of TClass. However, method Calculate manipulates GoAhead to enable methods Prompt and GetSquare to respond properly. The string-typed data field ErrorMessage and the method GetErrorMessage can be used to detect the status of the last message sent to an object.

LISTING 2.7. Library unit HIDELIB.PAS, which exports a class with pseudohidden methods.

```
UNIT HideLib;

{=====================================================================

          Copyright (c) 1989, 1990  Namir Clement Shammas

     LIBRARY NAME: HideLib

     VERSION:  1.0                              DATE 8/1/1989
```

```
                    PURPOSE: Gives an example of pseudohiding of methods using
                             library units.

        ───────────────────────────────────────────────────────────────}

    {*********************************************************************}
    {***********************} INTERFACE {***************************}
    {*********************************************************************}

    TYPE

    TClass = OBJECT
         X,
         Y : REAL;
         ErrorMessage : STRING;
         PROCEDURE Prompt; { Pseudohidden method }
         PROCEDURE GetSquare; { Pseudohidden method }
         PROCEDURE Calculate;
         FUNCTION GetErrorMessage : STRING;
    END;

    {*********************************************************************}
    {*********************} IMPLEMENTATION {***********************}
    {*********************************************************************}

    VAR GoAhead : BOOLEAN;

    PROCEDURE TClass.Prompt;
    BEGIN
         IF NOT GoAhead THEN BEGIN
             ErrorMessage := 'Attempt to call pseudohidden' +
                               ' method TClass.Prompt';
             Exit;
         END;
         WRITE ('Enter a number : ');
         READLN (X); WRITELN;
    END;

    PROCEDURE TClass.GetSquare;
    BEGIN
         IF NOT GoAhead THEN BEGIN
             ErrorMessage := 'Attempt to call pseudohidden' +
                               ' method TClass.GetSquare';
             Exit;
         END;
         Y := X * X;
    END;
```

```
PROCEDURE TClass.Calculate;
BEGIN
    GoAhead := TRUE;
    Prompt;
    GetSquare;
    WRITELN(X,'^2 = ',Y);
    WRITELN;
    ErrorMessage := '';
    GoAhead := FALSE;
END;

FUNCTION TClass.GetErrorMessage : STRING;
BEGIN
    GetErrorMessage := ErrorMessage
END;

BEGIN
    GoAhead := FALSE
END.
```

Listing 2.8 shows the program TESTHIDE.PAS, which demonstrates pseudohidden methods at work. The message TestObj.Calculate causes the program to prompt for a number, calculate its square, and display the results. The WRITELN statement that follows the TestObj.Calculate statement displays no wording for the error message, indicating that the message was successfully executed. By contrast, the messages Prompt and GetSquare, when sent to TestObj, perform no task and cause the display of error messages. Each error message describes the error and names the method that was improperly accessed.

LISTING 2.8. Program TESTHIDE.PAS to test pseudohidden methods.

```
Program TestHide;

{
 Program tests pseudohidden methods declared with class
 TClass, which is exported by unit HideLib.
}

Uses Crt, HideLib;

VAR TestObj : TClass;
    Akey : CHAR;

BEGIN
    ClrScr;
```

```
                    TestObj.Calculate;
                    WRITELN('Error message : ', TestObj.GetErrorMessage);
                    TestObj.Prompt;
                    WRITELN('Error message : ', TestObj.GetErrorMessage);
                    TestObj.GetSquare;
                    WRITELN('Error message : ', TestObj.GetErrorMessage);
                    WRITELN;
                    WRITE('Press any key to end the program ...');
                    Akey := ReadKey;
              END.
```

Assigning Objects

Turbo Pascal permits object assignment, similar to record assignment. In object assignment, the data fields of one object are copied into another. Pascal records of identical types are assigned to each other in a very straightforward fashion. The same applies to objects, *if they belong to the same class*. What about assigning objects that are in the same hierarchy of classes? Such assignment is allowed, but with the following limitation: an object of a subclass can be assigned to another of an ancestor class, but not the other way around. The reason for this rule is that since subclasses have more fields than their ancestor classes, an assignment of an ancestor-class object to a subclass object will leave the assignee with undefined data fields.

Warning!

Avoid assigning objects that have pointers. Instead, copy the nonpointer fields individually. Assignments among objects with pointer fields have the following side effects:

1. The process copies addresses of pointers, causing significant addresses to be lost. This means the loss of access to dynamic data on the heap.

2. This process makes one object an alias of another, something that should be avoided at all costs. Attempting to delete dynamic memory associated with an object and its alias will result in runtime error as the runtime system attempts to delete the same dynamic data twice!

Arrays of Objects

You can employ an array of objects as you can arrays of any other type. You can declare a type identifier for arrays of objects or declare them directly in the VAR section. In arrays, each object member is accessed using an index.

The program in Listing 2.9 declares the class Point to model screen coordinates. The type ObjArray is an array of Point-typed objects. One method associated with class Point defines the coordinates X and Y. The other method moves the cursor to set coordinates. The sample program performs the following tasks:

1. Declares the array.
2. Assigns random screen coordinates to each object.
3. Moves to the coordinates of each object and displays the string "Here!"
4. Moves to the coordinates of each object and slowly erases the text from the screen.

LISTING 2.9. Program ARROBJ.PAS illustrates an array of objects.

```
Program Test_Array_Of_Objects;

{
 Program uses an array of objects to display messages on
 the screen and then erases them.
}

Uses Crt;

CONST MAX_OBJ = 5;
      MESSAGE = 'Here!';
      LEN = Length (MESSAGE);
TYPE


Point = OBJECT
     X, Y : BYTE;
     PROCEDURE Define (XX, YY : BYTE { input });
     PROCEDURE MoveTo;
END;


ObjArray = ARRAY [1..MAX_OBJ] OF Point;
```

```
PROCEDURE Point.Define(XX, YY : BYTE { input });
BEGIN
    X := XX MOD 80;
    IF X = 0 THEN X := 1;
    Y := YY MOD 25;
    IF Y = 0 THEN Y := 1;
END;


PROCEDURE Point.MoveTo;
BEGIN
    GotoXY(X, Y);
END;


VAR A : ObjArray;
    I, J : BYTE;
    AKey : CHAR;


BEGIN
    ClrScr;

    FOR I := 1 TO MAX_OBJ DO
        A[I].Define(Random(80),Random(25));

    FOR I := 1 TO MAX_OBJ DO BEGIN
        A[I].MoveTo;
        WRITE(MESSAGE);
        Delay(1000)
    END;


    FOR I := 1 TO MAX_OBJ DO BEGIN
        A[I].MoveTo;
        FOR J := 1 TO LEN DO BEGIN
            WRITE(' ');
            Delay(100)
        END;
        Delay(1000)
    END;

    WRITELN;
    WRITE('Press any key to end the program ...');
    AKey := ReadKey;
END.
```

Objects as Fields of Records

Classes may be regarded as super-records that include fields that are procedures and functions. However, the superiority of classes over records should not prevent a program from having object-typed fields as part of a record. Such records are used when a group of like objects is managed using a data structure, such as a linked list, stack, queue, or tree. Since these structures are most frequently implemented as dynamic data, dynamic objects come into play. This is discussed in the final section of this chapter and the final example shows how records containing object fields are used to implement a dynamic stack of objects.

Compound Classes and Objects

The real world is full of objects that contain other smaller objects. For example, a car contains an engine. The engine is a separate object. Combining the engine and the car's body, electrical system, and other parts (or objects) results in the familiar functionality of an automobile. You can say that a car has an engine. Similar statements can be made about the other parts of the car. This points to the HasA relationship between an object and its component objects. These nested or contained objects may or may not be in the same hierarchy. You can even have similar object-components—a car has four similar wheels.

The next program (Listing 2.10) illustrates a compound class: the Display class representing the screen. A screen has a cursor and displayable text—objects that are related to the screen via a HasA relationship.

The classes Cursor and Strings are declared separately. The Cursor class is used to move the cursor on the screen. The method Define supplies the instances of class Cursor with a screen location, while the method MoveTo causes the cursor to move to the set screen location. The Strings class is involved in displaying a string at the current cursor location. The method GetString obtains the string to be displayed one or more times, while ShowString displays the string. The compound class Display declares fields of both classes Cursor and Strings. The method Init initializes the nested objects. The Boolean field DoneInit is used to avoid erroneous re-initialization.

The program displays the string "Here!" at five random screen locations. The messages for compound objects will have two dot operators in the absence of any WITH DO statement. The WITH A DO statement used in the program serves to shorten the messages.

LISTING 2.10. Program COMPOUND.PAS demonstrates compound classes and objects.

```
Program Show_Compound_Objects;

{ Program demonstrates how two unrelated classes, Cursor and
  Strings, form a compound or nested class, Display.
  The instance of the compound class taps into the data
  fields and methods of both objects to display strings
  in various screen locations.
}

Uses Crt;

TYPE

{ first simple class }
Cursor = OBJECT
    X,
    Y : BYTE;
    PROCEDURE Define(XLoc, YLoc : BYTE { input });
    PROCEDURE MoveTo;
END;

{ second simple class }
Strings = OBJECT
    AString : STRING;
    PROCEDURE GetString(S : STRING { input });
    PROCEDURE ShowString(UseCR : BOOLEAN { input });
END;

{ compound class }
Display = OBJECT
    fCursor : Cursor;
    fStrings : Strings;
    DoneInit : BOOLEAN;
    PROCEDURE Init;
END;

PROCEDURE Cursor.Define(XLoc, YLoc : BYTE { input });
BEGIN
    X := XLoc;
    IF NOT (X IN [1..80]) THEN X := 1;
    Y := YLoc;
```

```
        IF NOT (Y IN [1..25]) THEN Y := 1
END;


PROCEDURE Cursor.MoveTo;
BEGIN
    GotoXY(X, Y)
END;


PROCEDURE Strings.GetString(S : STRING { input });
BEGIN
    AString := S
END;


PROCEDURE Strings.ShowString(UseCR : BOOLEAN { input });
BEGIN
    WRITE(AString);
    IF UseCR THEN WRITELN;
END;


PROCEDURE Display.Init;
BEGIN
    IF DoneInit THEN Exit; { don't initialize more than once }
    fCursor.Define(1,1);
    fStrings.GetString('');
    DoneInit := TRUE
END;


VAR A : Display;
    I : BYTE;
    AKey : CHAR;


BEGIN
    A.Init; { initialize fields }
    ClrScr;
    WITH A DO BEGIN
        fStrings.GetString('Here!');
        Randomize;
        FOR I := 1 TO 5 DO BEGIN
            fCursor.Define(Random(80),Random(25));
            fCursor.MoveTo;
            fStrings.ShowString(FALSE);
            Delay(1000);
        END;
```

```
                        fCursor.Define(1,24);
                        fCursor.MoveTo;
                END;
                ClrEol;
                WRITELN;
                WRITE('Press any key to end the program ...');
                AKey := ReadKey;
        END.
```

Chapter 5, "Screen, Cursor, and Text Objects," gives a more complete example of using compound objects in screen output.

Dynamic Objects

Turbo Pascal 5.5 has extended the use of the predefined New and Dispose procedures. The New statement can now include the name of a constructor (along with the constructor's argument list) as a second parameter, as shown in the following general syntax:

```
NEW(<pointer>, <constructor>(<parameter list>));
```

which replaces the following set of statements:

```
NEW(<pointer>);
<pointer>^.<constructor(<parameter list>));
```

Similarly, the Dispose procedure can include the name of a destructor, as shown in the following general syntax:

```
DISPOSE(<pointer>, <destructor>(<parameter list>));
```

which replaces the following set of statements:

```
<pointer>^.<destructor(<parameter list>));
DISPOSE(<pointer>);
```

Listing 2.11 contains a simple program that illustrates a dynamic object. The program implements a stack using a dynamic array. Random values for the screen coordinates are pushed onto and popped off the stack. The size of the array is

determined at runtime. Once set, it remains fixed. Consequently, the stack, which
is based on the dynamic array, also has a fixed size. The program defines the Cursor
class as follows:

```
Cursor = OBJECT
    PointPtr : ArrayPtr;
    fSize, Index : WORD;
    CalledInit : BOOLEAN;
    CONSTRUCTOR Init(dSize : WORD); { allocate dynamic memory }
    FUNCTION PushXY(XLoc, YLoc : BYTE { input }) : BOOLEAN;
    FUNCTION PopXY : BOOLEAN;
    DESTRUCTOR Done;
END;
```

The PointPtr field is a dynamic pointer to an array of Point-typed records that
store the cursor's coordinates. The fSize field stores the size of the dynamic array
used to implement the stack. The Index field keeps track of the stack height. The
CalledInit field is used to flag whether the constructor Init has been called.

The program defines a constructor and destructor to allocate and deallocate the
dynamic data, respectively. The methods PushXY and PopXY are used to push and
pop the cursor coordinates. These methods return TRUE when successful, and
FALSE when not.

The program employs the following statements to create and remove the pointer
to the object and its dynamic array:

```
New(A, Init(TEST_SIZE)); { to create }
Dispose(A, Done); { to remove }
```

Notice that the carat symbol is used after the identifier A when sending the PushXY
and PopXY messages, since A is a formal Pascal pointer. The program displays the
string "Here!" on five random screen locations.

LISTING 2.11. Program DYNOBJ.PAS demonstrates simple dynamic objects.

```
Program Show_Simple_Dynamic_Objects;

{
Program defines a class Cursor and its pointer-type, Turtle.
The pointer to the class is used to create a dynamic instance.
Messages are sent using the pointer.
}
```

```
Uses Crt;
{$R-}

CONST TEST_SIZE = 5;

TYPE

{---------------- structures -------------------}

Point = RECORD
    X,
    Y : BYTE;
END;


OnePointArray = ARRAY [1..1] OF Point;
ArrayPtr = ^OnePointArray;


{-------------------- classes -------------------}


Cursor = OBJECT
    PointPtr : ArrayPtr;
    fSize, Index : WORD;
    CalledInit : BOOLEAN;
    CONSTRUCTOR Init (dSize : WORD); { allocate dynamic memory }
    FUNCTION PushXY (XLoc, YLoc : BYTE { input }) : BOOLEAN;
    FUNCTION PopXY : BOOLEAN;
    DESTRUCTOR Done;
END;


Turtle = ^Cursor;

CONSTRUCTOR Cursor.Init (dSize : WORD { input });
BEGIN
    GetMem (PointPtr, dSize);
    fSize := dSize;
    Index := 0;
    CalledInit := TRUE
END;

DESTRUCTOR Cursor.Done;
BEGIN
    FreeMem (PointPtr, fSize);
    fSize := 0;
```

```
        Index := 0;
        CalledInit := FALSE
END;


FUNCTION Cursor.PushXY(XLoc, YLoc : BYTE { input }) : BOOLEAN;


BEGIN
     IF (NOT CalledInit) OR (Index = fSize) THEN BEGIN
         PushXY := FALSE;
         EXIT
     END
     ELSE
         INC(Index);
     IF NOT (XLoc IN [1..80]) THEN XLoc := 1;
     IF NOT (YLoc IN [1..25]) THEN YLoc := 1;
     PointPtr^[Index].X := XLoc;
     PointPtr^[Index].Y := YLoc;
     PushXY := TRUE
END;


FUNCTION Cursor.PopXY : BOOLEAN;
BEGIN
     IF CalledInit AND (Index > 0) THEN BEGIN
         GotoXY(PointPtr^[Index].X, PointPtr^[Index].Y);
         DEC(Index);
         PopXY := TRUE
     END
     ELSE
         PopXY := FALSE;
END;


VAR A : Turtle;
    I : BYTE;
    AKey : CHAR;


BEGIN
     New(A, Init(TEST_SIZE));  { allocate space for pointer type
                                 and initialize cursor coordinate }


     ClrScr;
     Randomize;
     WHILE A^.PushXY(Random(80),Random(25)) DO
         { do nothing };
```

```
            WHILE A^.PopXY DO BEGIN
                WRITE('Here!');
                Delay(1000);
            END;
            Dispose(A, Done); { deallocate dynamic space and pointer space
        }
            GotoXY(1,24);
            ClrEol;
            WRITELN;
            WRITE('Press any key to end the program ...');
            AKey := ReadKey;
        END.
```

Dynamic objects come into play when dealing with a collection of similar objects that are managed within a data structure. Listing 2.12 contains a program that handles a stack of dynamic objects. The stack itself employs a linked list. Two New statements are used in creating a stack element: the first allocates space for the pointer element, and the second allocates the pointer to the object. Likewise, two Dispose statements are used to remove dynamic data in a reverse sequence.

The program creates five stacked instances of the class Cursor. Each object receives random screen locations and is then pushed onto the stack. After the stack is built, a WHILE loop is used to pop off the objects. As each object is popped off, it is sent the MoveTo message, causing the cursor to move to a screen location. At that location, the string "Here!" is emitted by a WRITE statement. Since a stack is a Last-In-First-Out structure, the screen locations are visited in reverse of the order in which they were created.

LISTING 2.12. Program DYNOBJ2.PAS illustrates a stack of dynamic objects.

```
Program Show_Dynamic_Stack_of_Objects;

{
  Program illustrates the use of a dynamic stack of objects.
  Objects are pushed onto the stack and popped off it.
}

Uses Crt;

TYPE

Cursor = OBJECT
    X,
    Y : BYTE;
```

```
        BeenUsed : BOOLEAN;
        PROCEDURE Define (XLoc, YLoc : BYTE { input });
        PROCEDURE MoveTo;
    END;


    Turtle = ^Cursor;

    StackPtr = ^StackObj;

    StackObj = RECORD
        T : Turtle;
        LastPtr : StackPtr
    END;


    PROCEDURE Cursor.Define (XLoc, YLoc : BYTE { input });
    BEGIN
        X := XLoc;
        IF NOT (X IN [1..80]) THEN X := 1;
        Y := YLoc;
        IF NOT (Y IN [1..25]) THEN Y := 1;
        BeenUsed := TRUE
    END;


    PROCEDURE Cursor.MoveTo;
    BEGIN
        GotoXY (X, Y)
    END;


    CONST TEST_SIZE = 5;

    VAR TopOfStack, Aptr : StackPtr;
        C : Cursor;
        I : BYTE;


    BEGIN
        ClrScr;
        TopOfStack := NIL;
        Randomize;
        FOR I := 1 TO TEST_SIZE DO BEGIN
            IF TopOfStack = NIL THEN BEGIN
                New (TopOfStack);
                TopOfStack^.LastPtr := NIL;
            END
```

```
        ELSE BEGIN
            New(Aptr);
            Aptr^.LastPtr := TopOfStack;
            TopOfStack := Aptr;
        END;
        New(TopOfStack^.T);
        TopOfStack^.T^.Define(Random(80),Random(25));
    END;

    WHILE TopOfStack <> NIL DO BEGIN
        TopOfStack^.T^.MoveTo;
        APtr := TopOfStack;
        TopOfStack := TopOfStack^.LastPtr;
        Dispose(APtr^.T);
        Dispose(APtr);
        WRITE('Here!');
        Delay(1000);
    END;

    GotoXY(1,24);
    ClrEol;

END.
```

Accessing Subclasses

Object-oriented programming is aimed at better modeling real-world objects. In many cases objects interact with other objects. These objects may or may not be part of the same hierarchy of classes. What happens if a class of objects needs to interact with its subclasses? While this seems to contradict the philosophy of OOP, there are applications, such as modeling chemical reactions, that produce such cases. Since the subclass is defined after the parent class, you cannot make an early reference to the subclass. This problem is solved using pointers. A pointer to the subclass can be declared early on without having the compiler flag any error. The pointer to the subclass can be supplied later as an argument to a method in the parent class.

3 | Window Objects

Text-based windows are among the most popular examples of classes, subclasses, and objects. Moreover, they are also some of the most relevant objects—we all look at screens and windows! Screens and windows are parts of the standard user (and programmer) interface. In this chapter, we look at how to create a screen class and its window subclasses. We will also discuss text-based video screens and windows and related classes.

The Screen Class

In a sense, the entire screen is the largest window you can view on your monitor. It has a specific number of rows and columns, which depends on the type of monitor and text mode. Other attributes are the foreground and background colors (if you have a color monitor). The displayed text for a video screen is stored in a special buffer. The starting address of the buffer is a parameter that can be optionally included as a class field. The buffer address is relevant in saving and restoring entire screens to memory.

Common screen operations include the following:

1. Clearing the screen.
2. Clearing to the end of the line.
3. Inserting a new line.
4. Deleting a line.
5. Displaying characters.
6. Emitting newline characters.
7. Moving the cursor.
8. Obtaining the cursor coordinates.

Other screen operations that are not so common but are worth including are:

1. Reselecting the screen. By default, the entire screen is the initial viewport. However, when you are handling windows and would like to access the entire screen again, you need to reselect it.
2. Saving and restoring the screen to a memory buffer.

These screen attributes and operations are defined by the following Pascal object:

```
ScrnObj = OBJECT
    Foreground,
    Background : BYTE;
    PROCEDURE SetColors ( ForeColor,              { input  }
                          BackColor : BYTE   { input });
    PROCEDURE Reselect;
    PROCEDURE ClearScr;
    PROCEDURE ClearEol;
    PROCEDURE InsertLine;
    PROCEDURE DeleteLine;
    PROCEDURE WriteText (S : STRING { input });
    PROCEDURE NewLine (NumLines : BYTE { input });
    PROCEDURE GotoXYC (X, Y: BYTE { input });
    FUNCTION WhereXC : BYTE;
    FUNCTION WhereYC : BYTE;
    PROCEDURE Save (    SegAdr          : WORD;          { input  }
                   VAR ScrArray   : ScreenBuffer { output });
    PROCEDURE Recall (  SegAdr          : WORD;          { input  }
                   VAR ScrArray   : ScreenBuffer { input  });
END;
```

The related constants and data types are listed below:

```
CONST MAX_SCREEN_ROW = 25;
      MAX_SCREEN_COL = 80;

TYPE ScreenBuffer = ARRAY [   1..MAX_SCREEN_COL,
                              1..MAX_SCREEN_ROW,
                              1..2] OF CHAR;
     ScreenPtr = ^ScreenBuffer;
```

Most of the routines associated with the ScrnObj class are exported by the standard Crt unit. Coding the class routines is, in most cases, a simple and straightforward call to the corresponding Crt routine.

Screen Windows

Turbo Pascal supports the Window statement, which empowers you to define a portion of the screen as a subscreen. The window, shown in Figure 3.1, is defined by the coordinates for the upper left and lower right corners. When a window is defined, it becomes the active viewport, with its own set of coordinates. In the window's coordinate system, the upper left corner of the window is coordinate (1, 1), while the lower right corner is $(X2 - X1 + 1, Y2 - Y1 + 1)$.

To define an untiled window (or viewport) object, you need a procedure that creates the window and defines its foreground and background colors. The coordinates that define the window must be included in the class declaration only if you select or reselect a window by using a handle ID. Otherwise, including these coordinates as class data fields is optional.

The majority of the other screen operations listed earlier can be simply inherited by the subclass of untiled windows. Therefore, no recoding of these routines is needed. However, there is one exception, namely, the Reselect procedure. To reselect a window you need to use the window limits instead of the video screen limits. Thus, the Reselect procedure should be overridden. The definition of the ScrnWindow class is shown following:

```
ScrnWindow = OBJECT (ScrnObj)
    FirstX, LastX,
    FirstY, LastY : BYTE;
    PROCEDURE CreateWindow(  X1,                      { input }
                             Y1,                      { input }
                             X2,                      { input }
                             Y2,                      { input }
                             ForeColor,               { input }
                             BackColor : BYTE         { input });
    PROCEDURE Reselect;
END;
```

FIGURE 3.1. Untiled window.

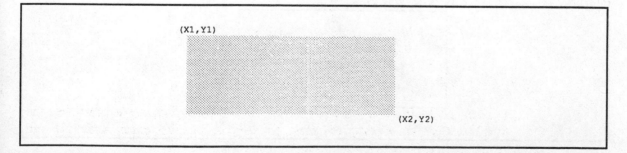

The reselect procedure employs the FirstX, FirstY, LastX, and LastY fields to reactivate the sought window region. The inherited fields Foreground and Background are used to reestablish the foreground and background colors associated with that window.

Tiled Windows

Tiled windows, are a special category of windows illustrated in Figure 3.2. They differ from untiled windows in two ways:

1. A tile is drawn at the four edges of the window, with an optional title placed at the top edge.
2. The available viewport of a tiled window is reduced by two rows and two columns, compared to an untiled window of the same size.

The differences between the classes of untiled and tiled windows warrant a single routine to be added. This routine must draw the tile, write any optional title, and adjust the size of the window available for text output.

The following is the definition of a tiled window class:

```
TiledWindow = OBJECT (ScrnWindow)
     PROCEDURE DefineTile(
                    Title           : STRING;    { input }
                    SingleTile      : BOOLEAN;   { input }
                    TileForeground,             { input }
                    TileBackground  : BYTE      { input });
     END;
```

FIGURE 3.2. Tiled window.

Notice that no new fields are added—the inherited fields are adequate. The DefineTile method enables you to choose single-line or double-line tiles, in addition to the tile's own foreground and background colors. This method should be called after invoking the inherited DefineWindow method.

The TiledWindow class inherits all of the methods from its ancestor classes. This includes the Reselect method, which the TiledWindow class inherits from its parent class ScrnWindow. There is no need to override Reselect, because the inherited coordinate fields describe the active window area inside the tiled window.

The foregoing classes are put together in the form of a library unit, shown in Listing 3.1.

LISTING 3.1. The source code for the ScrWndOb library unit.

```
Unit ScrWndOb;


{=====================================================================


                    Copyright (c) 1989, 1990   Namir Clement Shammas

        LIBRARY NAME: ScrWndOb

        VERSION 1.0 FOR TURBO PASCAL                  DATE 6/21/1989

        PURPOSE: Implements classes of screen, untiled windows,
                 and tiled windows.


=====================================================================}

{*********************************************************************}
{************************}INTERFACE{*********************************}
{*********************************************************************}

Uses Crt;

CONST MAX_SCREEN_ROW = 25;
      MAX_SCREEN_COL = 80;
      SCREEN_BUFFER_SIZE = 2 * MAX_SCREEN_ROW * MAX_SCREEN_COL;

TYPE

ScreenBuffer = ARRAY [ 1..MAX_SCREEN_COL,
                       1..MAX_SCREEN_ROW,
                       1..2] OF CHAR;
```

```
ScreenPtr = ^ScreenBuffer;

ScrnObj = OBJECT
    Foreground,
    Background : BYTE;
    PROCEDURE SetColors( ForeColor,              { input }
                         BackColor : BYTE    { input });
    PROCEDURE Reselect;
    PROCEDURE ClearScr;
    PROCEDURE ClearEol;
    PROCEDURE InsertLine;
    PROCEDURE DeleteLine;
    PROCEDURE WriteText(S : STRING { input });
    PROCEDURE NewLine(NumLines : BYTE { input });
    PROCEDURE GotoXYC(X, Y: BYTE { input });
    FUNCTION WhereXC : BYTE;
    FUNCTION WhereYC : BYTE;
    PROCEDURE Save(    SegAdr     : WORD;          { input }
                      VAR ScrArray: ScreenBuffer { output });
    PROCEDURE Recall(  SegAdr     : WORD;          { input }
                      VAR ScrArray: ScreenBuffer { input });
END;

ScrnWindow = OBJECT (ScrnObj)
    FirstX, LastX,
    FirstY, LastY : BYTE;

    PROCEDURE CreateWindow(  X1,                    { input }
                             Y1,                    { input }
                             X2,                    { input }
                             Y2,                    { input }
                             ForeColor,             { input }
                             BackColor : BYTE    { input });
    PROCEDURE Reselect;
END;


TiledWindow = OBJECT (ScrnWindow)
    PROCEDURE  DefineTile(
                 Title              : STRING;     { input }
                 SingleTile         : BOOLEAN;    { input }
                 TileForeground,                  { input }
                 TileBackground     : BYTE        { input });
END;
```

```
    {
Menu = OBJECT (TileWindow)
    MenuText : ARRAY [1..MAXMENU] OF STRING;
    HighChoice,
    SelectForeground,
    SelectBackground : BYTE;
    FUNCTION SelectMenu : BYTE;
END;
    }


{**********************************************************************}
{***********************}IMPLEMENTATION{***************************}
{**********************************************************************}


PROCEDURE ScrnObj.SetColors(  ForeColor,              { input }
                              BackColor : BYTE    { input });
{ Set the foreground and background colors.  This routine is
  used to initialize the screen colors. }
BEGIN
    Foreground := ForeColor;
    Background := BackColor;
END;


PROCEDURE ScrnObj.Reselect;
BEGIN
    Window(1,1,MAX_SCREEN_COL,MAX_SCREEN_ROW);
    TextColor(Foreground);
    TextBackground(Background);
END;


PROCEDURE ScrnObj.ClearScr;
{ clear the screen }
BEGIN
    TextColor(Foreground);
    TextBackground(Background);
    ClrScr;
END;


PROCEDURE ScrnObj.ClearEol;
{ clear to the end-of-line}
BEGIN
    ClrEol
END;
```

```
PROCEDURE ScrnObj.InsertLine;
{ insert a line }
BEGIN
    InsLine
END;

PROCEDURE ScrnObj.DeleteLine;
{ delete a line }
BEGIN
    DelLine
END;

PROCEDURE ScrnObj.WriteText(S : STRING { input });
{ write a string }
BEGIN
    WRITE(S)
END;

PROCEDURE ScrnObj.NewLine(NumLines : BYTE { input });
{ emit one or more newlines }
BEGIN
    WHILE NumLines > 0 DO BEGIN
        WRITELN;
        DEC(NumLines)
    END;
END;

PROCEDURE ScrnObj.GotoXYC(X, Y: BYTE { input });
{ move cursor }
BEGIN
    GotoXY(X,Y)
END;

FUNCTION ScrnObj.WhereXC : BYTE;
{ query X-coordinate of cursor }
BEGIN
    WhereXC := WhereX
END;

FUNCTION ScrnObj.WhereYC : BYTE;
{ query Y-coordinate of cursor }
BEGIN
    WhereYC := WhereY
END;
```

```
            PROCEDURE ScrnObj.Save(
                        SegAdr      : WORD;          { input  }
                  VAR   ScrArray    : ScreenBuffer { output });

VAR APtr : ScreenPtr;

BEGIN
    APtr := Ptr(SegAdr, 0);
    Move(APtr, ScrArray[1,1,1], SCREEN_BUFFER_SIZE);
END;


            PROCEDURE ScrnObj.Recall(
                        SegAdr      : WORD;          { input }
                  VAR   ScrArray    : ScreenBuffer { input });

VAR APtr : ScreenPtr;

BEGIN
    APtr := Ptr(SegAdr, 0);
    Move(ScrArray[1,1,1], APtr, SCREEN_BUFFER_SIZE);
END;


            PROCEDURE ScrnWindow.CreateWindow(
                        X1,                 { input  }
                        Y1,                 { input  }
                        X2,                 { input  }
                        Y2,                 { input  }
                        ForeColor,          { input  }
                        BackColor : BYTE { input  });
{ define window limits and foreground and background colors }
BEGIN
    FirstX := X1;
    LastX := X2;
    FirstY := Y1;
    LastY := Y2;
    Foreground := ForeColor;
    Background := BackColor;
    Window(X1,Y1,X2,Y2);
    TextColor(Foreground);
    TextBackground(Background);
END;


            PROCEDURE ScrnWindow.Reselect;
BEGIN
```

```
        Window(FirstX, FirstY, LastX, LastY);
        TextColor(Foreground);
        TextBackground(Background);
END;


PROCEDURE TiledWindow.DefineTile(
            Title         : STRING;   { input }
            SingleTile    : BOOLEAN;  { input }
            TileForeground,           { input }
            TileBackground: BYTE      { input });
{ draw tiled window }


VAR RUC, LUC, RLC, LLC, HOR, VER : CHAR;
    Row, Col,
    Wide, Long : BYTE;


BEGIN
    IF SingleTile THEN BEGIN
        RUC := #191;
        LUC := #218;
        RLC := #217;
        LLC := #192;
        HOR := #196;
        VER := #179;
    END
    ELSE BEGIN
        RUC := #187;
        LUC := #201;
        RLC := #188;
        LLC := #200;
        HOR := #205;
        VER := #186;
    END;
    { set tile colors }
    TextColor(TileForeground);
    TextBackground(TileBackground);
    { calculate width and length of window }
    Wide := LastX - FirstX + 1;
    Long := LastY - FirstY + 1;
    { draw bottom edge of window }
    GotoXY(1, Long);
    WRITE(LLC);
```

```
                    FOR Col := 2 TO Wide-1 DO
                        WRITE(HOR);
                    WRITE(RLC);
                    GotoXYC(1,1);
                    InsertLine;
                    { draw top edge of window }
                    WRITE(LUC);
                    FOR Col := 2 TO Wide-1 DO
                        WRITE(HOR);
                    WRITE(RUC);
                    IF Length(Title) > 0 THEN BEGIN
                        { put title }
                        GotoXY(3,1);
                        WRITE(' ',Title,' ');
                    END;
                    { draw left and right edges of window }
                    FOR Row := 2 TO Long-1 DO BEGIN
                        GotoXY(1,Row);
                        WRITE(VER);
                        GotoXY(Wide,Row);
                        WRITE(VER)
                    END;
                    { Adjust window limits to exclude tile area }
                    INC(FirstX);
                    INC(FirstY);
                    DEC(LastX);
                    DEC(LastY);
                    { employ window colors }
                    TextColor(Foreground);
                    TextBackground(Background);
                    { select window area }
                    Window(FirstX, FirstY, LastX, LastY);
                END;

            END.
```

Listing 3.2 shows a program that tests the various classes and methods exported by
unit ScrWndOb. The program performs the following simple tests:

1. Declares three objects to create single instances of each of the classes
   exported by the ScrWndOb library unit.
2. Tests the Screen object of class ScrnObj by assigning the screen colors and
   displaying messages on the first two lines.

3.   Creates an untiled window defined by the coordinates (1, 5) and (35, 10).
      The window colors are also specified and the window is cleared. Two lines
      of text are displayed.
4.   Creates a single-line tiled window defined by the coordinates (40, 14) and
      (75, 22). The window title is "Window 2." Four lines of text are displayed
      in the window. The last line is a "Wait please . . ." message.
5.   Reselects the untiled window and writes two more lines of text.
6.   Reselects the tiled window and erases the last message. Two new lines of text
      are written to that window.
7.   Reselects the entire screen by sending messages to the Screen object. The
      last set of Pascal statements saves the screen in a memory location, clears the
      screen, and recalls the previous image from memory after about 2 seconds.

LISTING 3.2.   Program that tests the various window classes and their methods.

```
Program Test_ScrWndOb_Unit;

{ Program to test the various classes exported by ScrWndOb unit }

Uses Crt, ScrWndOb;

CONST SCREEN_ADDR = $B800;

VAR Screen : ScrnObj;
    SWindow : ScrnWindow;
    TWindow : TiledWindow;
    MemScreen : ScreenBuffer;
    VideoMode : BYTE Absolute $0040:$0049;
    Flag : BOOLEAN;
    AKey : CHAR;

BEGIN

    IF VideoMode = 7 THEN BEGIN
        WRITELN;
        WRITELN ('You need a color monitor');
        WRITELN;
        HALT;
    END;

    { Test Screen object }
    Screen.SetColors (White, Blue);
```

```
Screen.ClearScr;
Screen.WriteText('Line 1 in Screen object');
Screen.NewLine(1);
Screen.WriteText('Line 2 in Screen object');
Screen.GotoXYC(1,24);

{ Test SWindow object }
SWindow.CreateWindow(1, 5, 35, 10, Red, White);
SWindow.ClearScr;
SWindow.WriteText('Line 1 in SWindow object');
SWindow.NewLine(1);
SWindow.WriteText('Line 2 in SWindow object');
SWindow.NewLine(2);

{ Test TWindow object }
TWindow.CreateWindow(40,14,75,22,Yellow,Green);
TWindow.DefineTile('Window 2', TRUE, White, Red);
TWindow.ClearScr;
TWindow.WriteText('1234567890123456789012345678901234567890123');
TWindow.NewLine(1);
TWindow.WriteText('Line 2 in TWindow object');
TWindow.NewLine(1);
TWindow.WriteText('Line 3 in TWindow object');
TWindow.NewLine(1);
TWindow.WriteText('Wait please ...');
TWindow.NewLine(2);
Delay(2000);

{ Reselect SWindow }
SWindow.Reselect;
SWindow.GotoXYC(1,3);
SWindow.WriteText('Line 3 in SWindow object');
SWindow.NewLine(1);
SWindow.WriteText('Line 4 in SWindow object');
SWindow.NewLine(2);
Delay(2000);

{ Reselect TWindow object }
TWindow.Reselect;
TWindow.GotoXYC(1,4);
TWindow.ClearEol;
TWindow.WriteText('Line 4 in TWindow object');
TWindow.NewLine(1);
```

```
TWindow.WriteText('Line 5 in TWindow object');
TWindow.NewLine(1);
Delay(2000);

Screen.Reselect;
Screen.Save(SCREEN_ADDR, MemScreen);
Screen.ClearScr;
Screen.WriteText('Wait please');
Delay(2000);
WRITE(^G);
Screen.Recall(SCREEN_ADDR, MemScreen);
Screen.GotoXYC(1,24);
Screen.WriteText('Press any key to end the program ...');
AKey := ReadKey;
Screen.GotoXYC(1,24);
Screen.ClearEol;
END.
```

Alternate Classes

In library unit ScrWndOb I defined and exported three related classes of windows. These classes serve as good illustrations for simple and frequently used classes and subclasses. The three classes can be merged into one class. Listing 3.3 shows the definition of the Window class, which encapsulates the three previous classes:

LISTING 3.3. Single class of Window objects.

```
CONST MAX_SCREEN_ROW = 25;
      MAX_SCREEN_COL = 80;

TYPE

ScreenBuffer = ARRAY [ 1..MAX_SCREEN_COL,
                       1..MAX_SCREEN_ROW,
                       1..2] OF CHAR;
ScreenPtr = ^ScreenBuffer;

Window = OBJECT
    {----------------------- data fields ----------------}
    Foreground,
```

```
                    Background : BYTE;
                    FirstX, LastX,
                    FirstY, LastY : BYTE;
                    {---------------------- methods -------------------}
                    PROCEDURE CreateWindow(    X1,                    { input }
                                               Y1,                    { input }
                                               X2,                    { input }
                                               Y2,                    { input }
                                               ForeColor,             { input }
                                               BackColor : BYTE   { input });
                    PROCEDURE DefineTile(
                            Title         : STRING;      { input }
                            SingleTile    : BOOLEAN;     { input }
                            TileForeground,              { input }
                            TileBackground : BYTE        { input });
                    PROCEDURE Reselect;
                    PROCEDURE ClearScr;
                    PROCEDURE ClearEol;
                    PROCEDURE InsertLine;
                    PROCEDURE DeleteLine;
                    PROCEDURE WriteText(S : STRING { input });
                    PROCEDURE NewLine(NumLines : BYTE { input });
                    PROCEDURE GotoXYC(X,Y: BYTE { input });
                    FUNCTION WhereXC : BYTE;
                    FUNCTION WhereYC : BYTE;
                    PROCEDURE Save   ( SegAdr     : WORD;          { input }
                                VAR ScrArray   : ScreenBuffer { output });
                    PROCEDURE Recall ( SegAdr     : WORD;          { input }
                                VAR ScrArray   : ScreenBuffer { input });
            END;
```

To access the entire screen simply use the coordinates (1, 1) and (80, 25) with the CreateWindow method. To use smaller viewports utilize other coordinates. The decision whether or not to employ a tile is tied to the choice of invoking method DefineTile. The Window class uses the same set of methods given in Listing 3.1. The Reselect method used is the overriding version defined for the ScrnWindow class.

4 | **Screen Objects**

In the last chapter I discussed classes and objects that are related to visible screens and windows. This chapter looks at classes of more abstract screens.

A video screen is a visible buffer of characters and their attributes. The video buffers contain a sequence of words (about 2000 words in an 80 by 25 display). The first byte of each word is the ASCII code of the character, while the second byte is the display attribute. The display attribute is calculated using the following:

```
Display attribute = foreground + 16 * background + 128 * blinking
```

To construct an abstract screen we start by defining the following data structure:

```
ScreenXXX = ARRAY [1..MAX_ROW,1..MAX_COL,1..2] OF CHAR;
```

The above three-dimensional matrix, represented in Figure 4.1, is an array of rows, with each row being an array of columns, with each column being a two-element array of characters (or bytes).

The next step is to recognize that the screen needs a memory area to store its contents. This can be one of three locations:

1. The user memory. In this case, the screen is not visible and its space needs to be allocated. Typically, dynamic allocation is used and the screen is accessed through a pointer. An application can possess several of such screens simultaneously.
2. The visible video buffer area. This is the unique visible screen. It is located at a fixed memory area (determined by the type of video adapter).
3. Other color video pages. These are memory areas available for holding invisible screens. The starting address of any page N is given by:

FIGURE 4.1. The three-dimensional array representing the matrices of text and attributes.

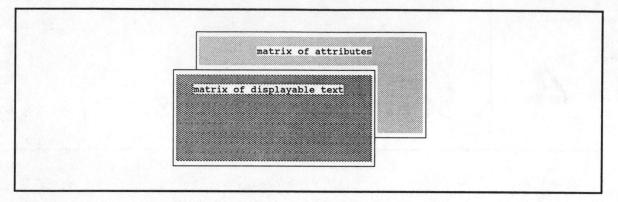

```
<Segment Address of Video>:<N * $1000>
```

In color video adapters in text mode, page 0 is used to display the visible screen. Thus, the visible CGA screen is located at $B800:$0000, page 1 is at $B800:$1000, page 2 is at $B800:$2000, and so on. The class of invisible CGA screens is something of a hybrid between the memory-based screen and the visible screen. While screens in the high video pages are not visible, their memory space is already available.

Table 4.1 summarizes the three types of screen.

Coding Screen Classes

To define a general class of screens we need to employ two fields to manage the following information:

1.   A pointer to a memory area that stores the characters and their attributes
2.   The segment address for the screen buffer area

TABLE 4.1. The three types of screen.

Screen Type	Is Visible	Uses Preallocated Memory
Visible screen	Yes	Yes
High video pages	No	Yes
Memory-based	No	No

The methods involved with screens are:

1. Initializating the screen. This sets up the data fields and dynamically allocates memory for the screen buffer, if needed.
2. Deallocating of dynamic memory, if used.
3. Clearing the screen by filling the buffer area with spaces.
4. Writing strings to a screen using a specified display attribute.
5. Displaying the contents of the memory-based screen.
6. Saving and recalling the screen to and from a file.

The following declaration of the ScreenObj class encapsulates all of the foregoing data attributes and methods:

```
ScreenObj = OBJECT
    ScrPtr : ScreenPointer;
    SegAdr : WORD;
    PROCEDURE Init(VideoSegAdr : WORD { input });
    { allocate the dynamic buffer using field ScrPtr }
    PROCEDURE Done;
    { deallocate dynamic buffer in memory }
    PROCEDURE ClearScr;
    { fill memory area with spaces }
    PROCEDURE WriteTo( X,                  { input }
                       Y      : BYTE;   { input }
                       S      : STRING; { input }
                       Attr   : BYTE    { input });
    { write string S starting at (X,Y) and using display
      attribute Attr }
    PROCEDURE Display(VideoBufAdr : WORD { input });
    { copy memory-based screen to video page of VideBufAdr }
    FUNCTION WriteScreen(Filename : STRING { input }) : BOOLEAN;
    { save screen to a file, return TRUE if successful }
    FUNCTION ReadScreen(Filename : STRING { input }) : BOOLEAN;
    { read a screen from a file, return TRUE if successful }
END;
```

where the ScreenBuffer and ScreenPointer types are declared as follows:

```
ScreenBuffer = ARRAY [1..MAX_ROW,1..MAX_COL,1..2] OF CHAR;
ScreenPointer = ^ScreenBuffer;
```

The screen is saved on file such that the characters are written first, then their attributes. This enables you to easily edit the image with a text editor.

The methods of class ScreenObj work with the memory-based as well as the video screens. Refinements to methods defined for ScreenObj can appear in a video screen subclass of ScreenObj. For example, the ClearScr method can be overridden to employ procedure ClrScr exported by unit Crt. The Display method can also be overridden with a do-nothing method, since the video screen is always visible. Other methods can be added to move and query the cursor. The VideoObj class is defined as follows:

```
VideoObj = OBJECT (ScreenObj)
    PROCEDURE ClearScr;
    { use ClrScr to clear screen }
    PROCEDURE Display (VideoBufAdr : WORD { input });
    { do-nothing override, argument is ignored }
    PROCEDURE GotoXYC (X,Y : BYTE { input });
    FUNCTION WhereXC : BYTE;
    FUNCTION WhereYC : BYTE;
END;
```

This declaration introduces no new data fields, since the inherited ones are adequate.

LISTING 4.1. Source code for the ScrnObj library unit.

```
Unit ScrnObj;


{================================================

        Copyright (c) 1989, 1990   Namir Clement Shammas


    LIBRARY NAME: ScrnObj


    VERSION 1.0 FOR TURBO PASCAL                    DATE 6/21/1989


    PURPOSE: Defines classes of memory-based and video-based
             screens.


==================================================}
```

```
{*******************************************************************}
{************************} INTERFACE {**************************}
{*******************************************************************}


Uses Crt;


CONST MAX_COL = 80;
      MAX_ROW = 25;
      COLOR_SCREEN_SEG_ADR = $B800;       {color monitor }
      MONO_SCREEN_SEG_ADR = $B000;        {monochrome monitor }

TYPE ScreenBuffer = ARRAY [1..MAX_ROW,1..MAX_COL,1..2] OF CHAR;
     ScreenPointer = ^ScreenBuffer;


ScreenObj = OBJECT
    ScrPtr : ScreenPointer;
    SegAdr : WORD;
    PROCEDURE Init (VideoSegAdr : WORD { input });
    { allocate the dynamic buffer using field ScrPtr }
    PROCEDURE Done;
    { deallocate dynamic buffer in memory }
    PROCEDURE ClearScr;
    { fill memory area with spaces }
    PROCEDURE WriteTo ( X,                       { input }
                        Y      : BYTE;           { input }
                        S      : STRING;         { input }
                        Attr   : BYTE            { input });
    { write string S starting at (X,Y) and using display
      attribute Attr }
    PROCEDURE Display (VideoBufAdr : WORD { input });
    { copy memory-based screen to video page of VideoBufAdr }
    FUNCTION WriteScreen (Filename : STRING { input }) : BOOLEAN;
    { save screen to a file, return TRUE if successful }
    FUNCTION ReadScreen (Filename : STRING { input }) : BOOLEAN;
    { read a screen from a file, return TRUE if successful }
END;


VideoObj = OBJECT (ScreenObj)
    PROCEDURE ClearScr;
    { use ClrScr to clear screen }
    PROCEDURE Display (VideoBufAdr : WORD { input });
    { do-nothing override, argument is ignored }
    PROCEDURE GotoXYC (X,Y : BYTE { input });
```

```
      FUNCTION WhereXC : BYTE;
      FUNCTION WhereYC : BYTE;
END;


{******************************************************************}
{*********************} IMPLEMENTATION {***********************}
{******************************************************************}


VAR VideoMode : BYTE Absolute $0040:$0049;

PROCEDURE ScreenObj.Init(VideoSegAdr : WORD { input });
BEGIN
    SegAdr := VideoSegAdr;
    IF VideoSegAdr = 0 THEN
      New(ScrPtr)
    ELSE BEGIN
      IF VideoMode = 7 THEN
        ScrPtr := Ptr(MONO_SCREEN_SEG_ADR, 0)
      ELSE
        ScrPtr := Ptr(COLOR_SCREEN_SEG_ADR, 0)
    END;

END;


PROCEDURE ScreenObj.Done;
BEGIN
    IF SegAdr = 0 THEN
      Dispose(ScrPtr);
END;


PROCEDURE ScreenObj.ClearScr;

VAR Row, Col : BYTE;

BEGIN
    FOR Row := 1 TO MAX_ROW DO
      FOR Col := 1 TO MAX_COL DO BEGIN
          ScrPtr^[Row, Col, 1] := ' ';
          ScrPtr^[Row, Col, 2] := CHR(White);
      END;
END;

PROCEDURE ScreenObj.WriteTo(    X,                  { input }
                                Y      : BYTE;    { input }
```

```
                                          S      : STRING;    { input }
                                          Attr   : BYTE       { input });
            VAR Row, Col, Count : BYTE;
                StrLen : BYTE Absolute S;

            BEGIN
                Count := 1;
                Col := X;
                Row := Y;
                WHILE Count <= StrLen DO BEGIN
                   ScrPtr^[Row, Col, 1] := S[Count];
                   ScrPtr^[Row, Col, 2] := CHR(Attr);
                   INC(Count);
                   INC(Col);
                   IF Col >= MAX_COL THEN BEGIN
                       Col := 1;
                       INC(Row);
                     END;
                END;
            END;


            FUNCTION ScreenObj.WriteScreen(Filename : STRING { input })
                              : BOOLEAN;


            VAR OK : BOOLEAN;
                FileVar : TEXT;
                Col, Row : BYTE;

            BEGIN
                Assign(FileVar, Filename);
                {$I-} Rewrite(FileVar); {$I+}
                OK := IOResult = 0;
                IF NOT OK THEN BEGIN
                   WriteScreen := FALSE;
                   EXIT
                END;

                { first write screen characters together }
                FOR Row := 1 TO MAX_ROW DO
                FOR Col := 1 TO MAX_COL DO
                   WRITE(FileVar, ScrPtr^[Row,Col,1]);

                { second, write the attributes }
                FOR Row := 1 TO MAX_ROW DO
```

```
            FOR Col := 1 TO MAX_COL DO
                WRITE(FileVar, ScrPtr^[Row,Col,2]);

        Close(FileVar);
        WriteScreen := TRUE
    END;


FUNCTION ScreenObj.ReadScreen(Filename : STRING { input })
                                       : BOOLEAN;


VAR OK : BOOLEAN;
    FileVar : TEXT;
    Row, Col : BYTE;


BEGIN
    Assign(FileVar, Filename);
    {$I-} Reset(FileVar); {$I+}
    OK := IOResult = 0;
    IF NOT OK THEN BEGIN
      ReadScreen := FALSE;
      EXIT
    END;

    { first, read screen characters together }
    FOR Row := 1 TO MAX_ROW DO
      FOR Col := 1 TO MAX_COL DO
          READ(FileVar, ScrPtr^[Row,Col,1]);

    { second, read the attributes }
    FOR Row := 1 TO MAX_ROW DO
      FOR Col := 1 TO MAX_COL DO
          READ(FileVar, ScrPtr^[Row,Col,2]);

    Close(FileVar);
    ReadScreen := TRUE
    END;

PROCEDURE ScreenObj.Display(VideoBufAdr : WORD { input });

VAR BufPtr : Pointer;

BEGIN
    IF VideoMode = 7 THEN
        BufPtr := Ptr(MONO_SCREEN_SEG_ADR,$0)
```

```
      ELSE
         BufPtr := Ptr(COLOR_SCREEN_SEG_ADR,$0);
      Move(ScrPtr^, BufPtr^, SizeOf(ScrPtr^));
END;

PROCEDURE VideoObj.ClearScr;
BEGIN
   ClrScr;
END;

PROCEDURE VideoObj.Display(VideoBufAdr : WORD { input });
BEGIN
   { do nothing, since text is already visible }
END;

PROCEDURE VideoObj.GotoXYC(X,Y : BYTE { input });
BEGIN
   GotoXY(X,Y)
END;

FUNCTION VideoObj.WhereXC : BYTE;
BEGIN
   WhereXC := WhereX
END;

FUNCTION VideoObj.WhereYC : BYTE;
BEGIN
   WhereYC := WhereY
END;


END.
```

Listing 4.2 shows a test program for the ScreenObj and VideoObj classes. The program performs the following tasks:

1. Declares single instances of the tested classes.
2. Sets the display attribute for white characters on a blue background.
3. Tests the instance of ScreenObj.
    3.1. Initializes and clears the MScreen object.
    3.2. Writes strings to lines 1, 10, 20, and 24 of the memory-based screen. The string on line 24 is a "wait please" message.
    3.3. Displays the screen.

4.   Tests the instance of the VideoObj class:
    4.1.   Initializes and clears the VScreen object.
    4.2.   Writes strings to lines 1, 10, 20, and 24 of the screen. The string on
        line 24 is a "wait please" message.
    4.3   Stores the screen in file SCREEN.DAT.
    4.4   Clears the screen and waits for 2 seconds.
    4.5   Recalls the stored screen.

LISTING 4.2. Program TSSCR2.PAS to test ScrnObj library unit.

```
Program Test_ScrnObj_Unit;

{ Program to test screen objects }

Uses Crt, ScrnObj;

CONST FILENAME = 'SCREEN.DAT';

VAR MScreen : ScreenObj;
    VScreen, VS : VideoObj;
    DispAttr : BYTE;
    AKey : CHAR;

BEGIN
    DispAttr := Ord(White) + 16 * Ord(Blue);

    { test MScreen object }
    MScreen.Init(0);
    MScreen.ClearScr;
    MScreen.WriteTo(1,1,'Line # 1', DispAttr);
    MScreen.WriteTo(10,10,'Line # 10', DispAttr);
    MScreen.WriteTo(20,20,'Line # 20', DispAttr);
    MScreen.WriteTo(1,24,'Wait please ...', DispAttr);
    MScreen.Display(SCREEN_SEG_ADR);
    Delay(2000);
    MScreen.Done;

    { test VScreen object }
    VScreen.Init(SCREEN_SEG_ADR);
    VScreen.ClearScr;
    VScreen.WriteTo(1,1,'Line # 1', DispAttr);
```

```
            VScreen.WriteTo(10,10,'Line # 10', DispAttr);
            VScreen.WriteTo(20,20,'Line # 20', DispAttr);
            VScreen.WriteTo(1,24,'Wait please ...', DispAttr);
            IF NOT VScreen.WriteScreen(FILENAME) THEN
                 HALT;
            Delay(2000);
            VScreen.ClearScr;
            Delay(2000);
            IF NOT VScreen.ReadScreen(FILENAME) THEN
                 HALT;
            Delay(1000);

            GotoXY(1,24);
        END.
```

The screen image is as follows:

Line # 1

            Line # 10

                    Line # 20

Wait please ...

5 | Screen, Cursor, and Text Objects

This chapter looks at compound objects: ones that are made up of nested objects. Compound objects implement the HasA relationship between an object and its component-objects. Compound objects model real-world objects that incorporate, rather than inherit, smaller objects.

In this chapter we will view the video screen, the cursor, and the displayable text as three distinct objects. A compound object will be defined to encompass the smaller ones.

The Basics

In the previous chapters, the various classes of screens and windows contained, as integral parts, fields and methods to manage the cursor and the displayable text. It is not difficult to view the cursor and the displayable text as separate objects, as shown in Figure 5.1. The cursor is an object with the following characteristics:

1. Visibility. The cursor can be turned on or off.
2. Shape. Using BIOS services, the shape of the cursor can be altered.
3. Location. The cursor has screen coordinates.

The manipulation of the cursor includes moving it to new screen coordinates and querying the current coordinates. Listing 5.1 defines the class Cursor as follows:

```
Cursor = OBJECT
   Visible : BOOLEAN;
   PROCEDURE GotoXYC(X,Y: BYTE { input });
```

FIGURE 5.1. Screen, cursor, and text objects.

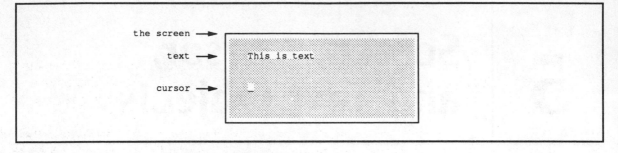

```
FUNCTION WhereXC : BYTE;
FUNCTION WhereYC : BYTE;
PROCEDURE CursorOff;
PROCEDURE CursorOn;
FUNCTION IsVisible : BOOLEAN;
PROCEDURE SetCursorShape( Start,                { input }
                          Finish : BYTE    { input });
```

The Visible field keeps track of the visibility status of the cursor. The values of that field are assigned by methods CursorOff and CursorOn. The first three methods of the Cursor class are shells that invoke the routines exported by the Crt library unit. The remaining methods include their own detailed coding and use the Register type exported by the DOS library unit.

The displayable text is an object that includes the characters emitted by an output statement (such as WRITELN) or echoed by an input statement. The displayable text is stored in a video buffer area. The video mode, the segment address of the video buffer, and a pointer to the buffer constitute the data attributes of the text object. These data fields are important in saving and restoring the screen, reading directly from the screen, and other direct video operations. Other methods associated with the text objects include screen I/O. I have defined the following class of VideoText in Listing 5.1.

```
VideoText = OBJECT
  SegAdr : WORD;
  VideoBufferPtr : ScreenPointer;
  VideoMode : BYTE;
  PROCEDURE Init;
  FUNCTION GetKey(Echo : BOOLEAN { input }) : CHAR;
  PROCEDURE WriteText(S : STRING { input });
  PROCEDURE NewLine(NumLines : BYTE { input });
```

```
        PROCEDURE Save (MemPtr : ScreenPointer { input });
        PROCEDURE Recall (MemPtr : ScreenPointer { input });
    END;
```

The method Init queries the video mode by examining the content of the memory location $0040:0049 and storing its value in field VideoMode. The SegAdr is assigned a value based on VideoMode. The VideoBufferPtr is made to point to the address SegAdr:0000.

The methods implemented perform keyboard character input (with and without echo), string output, newline emission, and video buffer swapping with RAM memory.

Concerning the screen itself I have defined the following class:

```
    Video = OBJECT
        Foreground,
        Background : BYTE;
        PROCEDURE SetColors ( ForeColor,              { input }
                              BackColor   : BYTE { input });
        PROCEDURE ClearScr;
        PROCEDURE ClearEolNum (LineNum     : BYTE { input });
        PROCEDURE ClearEol;
        PROCEDURE InsertLineNum (LineNum   : BYTE { input });
        PROCEDURE InsertLine;
        PROCEDURE DeleteLineNum (LineNum   : BYTE { input });
        PROCEDURE DeleteLine;
    END;
```

The Video class incorporates the foreground and background colors as data attributes. The methods associated with class Video offer nontext functionality, such as clearing the screen, inserting lines, and deleting lines.

These three classes are involved in creating the compound class Screen, declared as follows:

```
    Screen = OBJECT
        fVideo   : Video;
        fCursor  : Cursor;
        fText    : VideoText;
        PROCEDURE Init ( ForeColor,           { input }
                         BackColor : BYTE { input });
    END;
```

This declaration is represented by the following diagram:

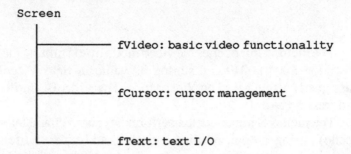

```
Screen

            |─────────────── fVideo: basic video functionality

            |─────────────── fCursor: cursor management

            |─────────────── fText: text I/O
```

By nesting objects, I have created the class Screen, which enjoys the attributes and functionality of the three objects. Objects of class Screen act as dispatchers, directing messages to the proper object-typed fields. For example, if TheScreen is an object of class Screen, messages are sent to TheScreen.fCursor object to manipulate the cursor. Similarly, messages are sent to TheScreen.fText to perform character I/O. The Screen class is a compound class integrating three objects that are closely related. The Init method performs a coordinated initialization for its three sub-objects.

LISTING 5.1. Source code for the library unit ScrnObj2.

```
Unit ScrnObj2;

{═══════════════════════════════════════════════════════════


          Copyright (c) 1989, 1990  Namir Clement Shammas


    LIBRARY NAME: ScrnObj2


    VERSION 1.0 FOR TURBO PASCAL                DATE 6/21/1989


    PURPOSE: Implements classes of screen, cursor, and video text.


    ═══════════════════════════════════════════════════════════}


{***************************************************************}
{***********************} INTERFACE {***************************}
{***************************************************************}
```

```
CONST MAX_COL = 80;
      MAX_ROW = 25;


TYPE ScreenBuffer = ARRAY [1..MAX_ROW,1..MAX_COL,1..2] OF CHAR;
     ScreenPointer = ^ScreenBuffer;


Video = OBJECT
    Foreground,
    Background : Byte;
    PROCEDURE SetColors( ForeColor,            { input }
                         BackColor : BYTE { input });
    PROCEDURE ClearSer
    PROCEDURE ClearEol Num (LineNum : BYTE { input })
    PROCEDURE ClearEol;
    PROCEDURE InsertLineNum(LineNum : BYTE { input });
    PROCEDURE InsertLine;
    PROCEDURE DeleteLineNum(LineNum : BYTE { input });
    PROCEDURE DeleteLine;
END;


Cursor = OBJECT
    Visible : BOOLEAN;
    PROCEDURE GotoXYC(X,Y: BYTE { input });
    FUNCTION WhereXC : BYTE;
    FUNCTION WhereYC : BYTE;
    PROCEDURE CursorOff;
    PROCEDURE CursorOn;
    FUNCTION IsVisible : BOOLEAN;
    PROCEDURE SetCursorShape( Start,            { input }
                              Finish : BYTE  { input });
END;


VideoText = OBJECT
    SegAdr : WORD;
    VideoBufferPtr : ScreenPointer;
    VideoMode : BYTE;
    PROCEDURE Init;
    FUNCTION GetKey(Echo : BOOLEAN { input }) : CHAR;
    PROCEDURE WriteText(S : STRING { input });
    PROCEDURE NewLine(NumLines : BYTE { input });
    PROCEDURE Save(MemPtr : ScreenPointer { input });
    PROCEDURE Recall(MemPtr : ScreenPointer { input });
END;
```

```
Screen = OBJECT
   fVideo  : Video;
   fCursor : Cursor;
   fText   : VideoText;
   PROCEDURE Init ( ForeColor,          { input }
                    BackColor : BYTE { input });
END;
```

```
{*********************************************************************}
{**********************}IMPLEMENTATION {******************************}
{*********************************************************************}
```

```
Uses Crt, Dos;
```

```
PROCEDURE Video.SetColors ( ForeColor,            { input }
                            BackColor : BYTE    { input });
{ Set the foreground and background colors.  This routine is
  used to initialize the screen colors }
BEGIN
    Foreground := ForeColor;
    Background := BackColor;
END;
```

```
PROCEDURE Video.ClearScr;
{ clear the screen }
BEGIN
    TextColor (Foreground);
    TextBackground (Background);
    ClrScr;
END;
```

```
PROCEDURE Video.ClearEolNum (LineNum : BYTE { input });
{ clear a specific line }
VAR PosY, PosX : BYTE;

BEGIN
    PosY := WhereY;
    PosX := WhereX;
    GotoXY (1, LineNum);
    ClrEol;
    GotoXY (PosX, PosY)
END;
```

```
PROCEDURE Video.ClearEol;
{ clear to the end-of-line}
BEGIN
    ClrEol;
END;

PROCEDURE Video.InsertLineNum(LineNum : BYTE { input });
{ insert a line at a specific screen row }
VAR PosY, PosX : BYTE;

BEGIN
    PosY := WhereY;
    PosX := WhereX;
    GotoXY(1, LineNum);
    InsLine;
    GotoXY(PosX, PosY)
END;

PROCEDURE Video.InsertLine;
{ insert a line }
BEGIN
    InsLine;
END;

PROCEDURE Video.DeleteLineNum(LineNum : BYTE { input });
{ delete a specific screen row }
VAR PosY, PosX : BYTE;

BEGIN
    PosY := WhereY;
    PosX := WhereX;
    GotoXY(1, LineNum);
    DelLine;
    GotoXY(PosX, PosY)
END;

PROCEDURE Video.DeleteLine;
{ delete a line }
BEGIN
    DelLine
END;

PROCEDURE Cursor.GotoXYC(X, Y: BYTE { input });
{ move cursor }
```

```
BEGIN
    GotoXY(X,Y)
END;


FUNCTION Cursor.WhereXC : BYTE;
{ query X-coordinate of cursor }
BEGIN
    WhereXC := WhereX
END;


FUNCTION Cursor.WhereYC : BYTE;
{ query Y-coordinate of cursor }
BEGIN
    WhereYC := WhereY
END;


PROCEDURE Cursor.CursorOff;
{ turn the cursor off }
VAR Regs : Registers;


BEGIN
    Regs.AX := $0100;
    Regs.CX := $2020;
    Intr($10, Regs);
    Visible := FALSE
END;


PROCEDURE Cursor.CursorOn;
{ turn cursor on }
VAR Regs : Registers;
    VideoMode : BYTE Absolute $0040:$0049;


BEGIN
    IF VideoMode = 7 THEN
        Regs.CX := $0C0D  { monochrome mode }
    ELSE
        Regs.CX := $0607; { color mode }
    Regs.AX := $0100;
    Intr($10, Regs);
    Visible := TRUE
END;
```

```
FUNCTION Cursor.IsVisible : BOOLEAN;
BEGIN
    IsVisible := Visible
END;


PROCEDURE Cursor.SetCursorShape(    Start,          { input }
                                    Finish : BYTE   { input });
{ set cursor shape }
VAR Regs : Registers;

BEGIN
    Regs.AX := $0100;
    Regs.CX := Start SHR 8 + Finish;
    Intr($10, Regs);
END;


FUNCTION VideoText.GetKey(Echo : BOOLEAN { input }) : CHAR;

VAR AKey : CHAR;

BEGIN
    AKey := ReadKey;
    IF Echo THEN
        WRITE(AKey);
    GetKey := AKey { return function value }
END;


PROCEDURE VideoText.WriteText(S : STRING { input });
{ write a string }
BEGIN
    WRITE(S)
END;


PROCEDURE VideoText.NewLine(NumLines : BYTE { input });
{ emit one or more new lines }
BEGIN
    WHILE NumLines > 0 DO BEGIN
        WRITELN;
        DEC(NumLines)
    END;
END;
```

```
PROCEDURE VideoText.Init;

VAR ModeVar : BYTE Absolute $0040:$0049;

BEGIN
    VideoMode := ModeVar;
    IF VideoMode = 7 THEN
        SegAdr := $B000
    ELSE
        SegAdr := $B800;
    VideoBufferPtr := Ptr(SegAdr, $0)
END;


PROCEDURE VideoText.Save(MemPtr : ScreenPointer { input });
BEGIN
    Move(VideoBufferPtr^, MemPtr^, 4000)
END;


PROCEDURE VideoText.Recall(MemPtr : ScreenPointer { input });
BEGIN
    Move(MemPtr^, VideoBufferPtr^, 4000)
END;


PROCEDURE Screen.Init(    ForeColor,          { input }
                          BackColor : BYTE { input });
BEGIN
    ()
    fVideo.SetColors(ForeColor, BackColor);
    fVideo.ClearScr;
    fCursor.CursorOn;
    fText.Init;
    ()
END;


END.
```

Listing 5.2 shows a test program for library unit ScrnObj2. The program performs the following:

1. Declares TheScreen object (and all of its sub-objects).
2. Displays a centered program heading, one character at a time. A Delay statement is used in slowly displaying the text. The cursor is turned off.

3. Displays toggled messages that indicate the visibility (or invisibility) of the cursor.
4. Prompts you to enter a string. A default input string is also displayed. Pressing [Enter] permits you to select the default string. When you type your input, the program reads the keystrokes one at a time. Provision is made for properly using the backspace key.
5. Displays the input string.

A WITH TheScreen DO statement is used to shorten the messages.

LISTING 5.2. Source code for the test program TESTSCR.PAS.

```
Program Test_ScrCursObj_Unit;

{
 Program that tests the compound object Screen exported by
 library unit ScrnObj2.
}

Uses Crt, ScrnObj2;

CONST DEF_STRING = 'Good morning everyone!';
      WAIT1 = 200;
      WAIT2 = 1000;
      WAIT3 = 2000;

VAR TheScreen : Screen;
    S : STRING;
    C : CHAR;
    PosX, I : BYTE;
    UseDefault : BOOLEAN;

BEGIN
    WITH TheScreen DO BEGIN
        Init(White, Blue);
        S := 'TESTING COMPOUND OBJECTS';
        fCursor.GotoXYC(40 - Length(S) div 2, 2);
        fCursor.CursorOff;
        FOR I := 1 TO Length(S) DO BEGIN
            fText.WriteText(S[I]);
            Delay(WAIT1);
        END;
```

```
fCursor.CursorOn;
FOR I := 1 TO 5 DO BEGIN
    fCursor.GotoXYC(1,4);
    fVideo.ClearEol;
    IF fCursor.IsVisible THEN BEGIN
        fText.WriteText('Now you see the cursor ');
        Delay(WAIT2);
        fCursor.CursorOff
    END
    ELSE BEGIN
        fText.WriteText('Now you don''t!');
        Delay(WAIT2);
        fCursor.CursorOn
    END;
END;
fCursor.CursorOn;
fCursor.GotoXYC(1,4);
fVideo.ClearEol;
fCursor.SetCursorShape(1,12);
fCursor.GotoXYC(1, 5);
fText.WriteText('Enter a string -> ');
PosX := fCursor.WhereXC;
Text.WriteText(DEF_STRING);
fCursor.GotoXYC(PosX, fCursor.WhereYC);
UseDefault := TRUE;
C := fText.GetKey(TRUE);
S := '';
WHILE C <> #13 DO BEGIN
    IF UseDefault THEN BEGIN
        UseDefault := FALSE;
        fVideo.ClearEol; { clear default input }
    END;
    IF C = #8 THEN BEGIN
        IF Length(S) > 0 THEN BEGIN
            { implement a backspace }
            Delete(S, Length(S), 1);
            fVideo.ClearEol
        END
        ELSE
        { prevent cursor from moving back to the
          prompt string }
                fCursor.GotoXYC(PosX, fCursor.WhereYC);
    END
```

```
                    ELSE
                        S := S + C;
                    C := fText.GetKey(TRUE)
                END;
                IF UseDefault THEN
                    S := DEF_STRING;
                fText.NewLine(2);
                fText.WriteText('You typed "');
                fText.WriteText(S);
                fText.WriteText('"');
                fText.NewLine(2);
                Delay(WAIT3);
            END;
        END.
```

Nesting objects can be viewed as a technique for implementing pseudo-multiple inheritance: the host class is able to access the various attributes of the encapsulated objects. Nested objects are also more robust than multiple-inheritance objects.

6 | File Objects

Anyone who uses a computer, any kind of computer, comes across files. Files are typically stored on a magnetic medium (floppy or hard disk) with the zeros and ones making up the logical contents. In a way, files are container types of data (I am using the word *data* here in a very broad sense). Some of the data is interpreted as programs (the machine language code) by your computers. Other data describes information stored by an application program. This chapter looks at samples of classes and objects modeling DOS files.

The Basics

DOS supports files of various types and for different purposes. Figure 6.1 is a tree diagram depicting the various genres of files and their hierarchy. At the root of the tree is the generic file, representing the common attributes that all DOS files share. They are:

- Filename
- Size
- Date and time stamp
- Archive bits

Files fall into one of two classes, based on their makeup: ASCII or binary. Figure 6.1 shows the family of ASCII files as split between executable DOS batch files and nonexecutable ASCII files. The latter sub-category is made up of text files that represent the plain text or the source code for a program written for a language compiler or interpreter.

Binary files, on the other side of the tree in Figure 6.1, include executable programs (.COM and .EXE files) as well as data stored in binary form.

Generic File Class

In the last section I presented a general hierarchy of file classes. Let's look at how a subset is implemented. The root class should describe the attributes and methods applicable to all types of files. As stated earlier, the data attributes include the filename, size, date/time stamp, and archive attributes. These attributes are associated with all DOS files:

- File mode. This includes the input, output, append, and execution modes. These modes cover all of the types of common file-related activities.
- File existence status. This attribute accounts for the fact that a text or binary file will be created and/or opened for input.
- Status flag for updating file information. This is used to signal that the size and date/time stamp attributes of an output file need an update.
- File I/O error flag.

In general, the methods associated with files perform either file management or query. In the former category there are the following methods:

FIGURE 6.1. The hierarchy of file classes.

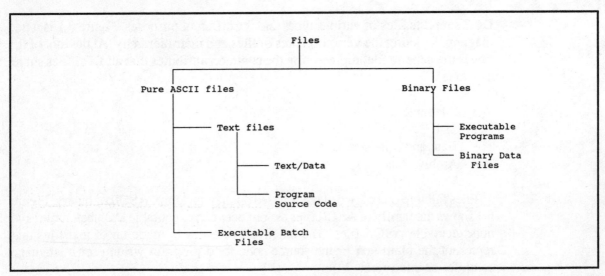

1. Initialize the file attributes listed earlier.
2. Update the file attributes.
3. Rename a file.
4. Delete a file.

The category of query methods includes those that return various attributes, such as size, date stamp, time stamp, I/O error status, and file existence status.

The following is the declaration of a class of general files (Listing 6.1 has the source code for the methods of this class, as well as the declarations and code for other subclasses):

```
GenFileObj = OBJECT
    Filename : STRING;
    FileInfo : SearchRec; { from Unit Dos }
    FileExists : BOOLEAN;
    Mode : IOMode;
    IOError,
    UpdateFileInfo : BOOLEAN;
    FileSize : LONGINT;
    DateTimeStamp : DateTime; { from Unit Dos }
    PROCEDURE Init ( Name      : STRING; { input }
                     FileMode  : IOMode  { input });
    PROCEDURE UpdateInfo;
    FUNCTION AnyIOerror : BOOLEAN;
    FUNCTION Exists : BOOLEAN;
    FUNCTION GetSize : LONGINT;
    PROCEDURE GetDate (VAR  Year,                { output }
                            Month,               { output }
                            Day     : INTEGER    { output });
    PROCEDURE GetTime (VAR  Hour,                { output }
                            Minute,              { output }
                            Second  : INTEGER    { output });
    PROCEDURE RenameIt (NewName : STRING { input });
    PROCEDURE DeleteIt;
END;
```

The data fields and methods for class GenFileObj are based on the previous discussion. You may add a few more methods, such as file-attribute query and control methods. The IOMode type is an enumerated type, declared as follows:

```
IOMode = (input_mode, output_mode, append_mode, execute_mode);
```

The method Init is utilized to initialize the file attributes, including the intended mode of operation. The mode of operation prepares the file for any transaction made by objects that are subclasses of GenFileObj.

Text File Class

A text file stores and retrieves ASCII text. As a subclass of generic files, the class of text files makes use of all of the inherited data attributes. In addition, this class requires two more data attributes: a file handle and an end-of-file flag.

The methods that implement I/O transactions basically include those that open and close the file, read and write text, and query the end-of-file. The following is the declaration of the TextFile class:

```
TextFile = OBJECT (GenFileObj)
    FileVar : TEXT;
    EndOfFile : BOOLEAN;
    PROCEDURE Open;
    PROCEDURE CloseIt;
    FUNCTION AtEndOfFile : BOOLEAN;
    PROCEDURE WriteString(S : String { input });
    PROCEDURE NewLine;
    PROCEDURE ReadString(VAR S : String { output });
END;
```

FileVar is the required file handle, while EndOfFile is the end-of-file flag. The Open method opens the file using the input, output, or append I/O modes, as specified by the FileMode argument of the inherited Init method. The method CloseIt simply closes the books, so to speak, on the file object.

The methods WriteString and NewLine are used to write a single string and emit a new line, respectively. By contrast, the method ReadString reads a string until a new line is encountered. I have limited the methods for text file I/O handling single strings for the sake of simplicity. You may very well expand on these methods to enable I/O of various basic types and in different combinations per single method. Right now, all the information flows in and out of the text file objects in batches of single strings.

Text files may be compressed to reduce their sizes. The simplest form of text compression replaces long words with shorter ones. Decompressing a file involves the reverse process. Compressed text files are essentially text files with the contents rewritten. Whether or not compressed files deserve a separate class is still open to debate. I chose to create a subclass CompressedTextFile out of class TextFile to reflect the basic difference between compressed and uncompressed text files. You are welcome to see it otherwise. The following is the declaration of class CompressedTextFile:

```
CompressedTextFile = OBJECT (TextFile)
  FUNCTION Compress (
                Source        : CompressedTextFile;  { input }
                KeyFile       : TextFile;            { input }
                CompressFile  : BOOLEAN              { input })
                              : BOOLEAN;
    END;
```

This subclass has just one method, namely, Compress. It is responsible for both compressing and decompressing a text file. The Source argument is the object providing source text (either uncompressed or compressed). The KeyFile is a TextFile object containing the compression data, stored in the following format:

```
<find string #1>
<replace string #1>
<find string #2>
<replace string #2>
...............
<find string #n>
<replace string #n>
```

The CompressFile parameter signals a request for compression when TRUE and for decompression when FALSE. Implementing both processes is quite easy: the value of CompressFile determines how each pair of find/replace strings is read.

I have not neutralized the inherited I/O methods with dummy overriding methods. This allows you to read, write, and append to a compressed text file. I saw no reason to prevent you from doing so, although it is a good idea, in general, to exclude compressed text files from direct I/O.

Binary File Class

Binary files are repertoires of data usually storing a copy of a memory image. They are more efficient than text files, especially when storing numbers. Structures are customarily stored in binary files. The subclass of binary files makes full use of the inherited data attributes and methods. The added data attributes are the file handle and an end-of-file flag, just as with the text file subclass. The methods involved with binary file I/O include opening and closing the file, reading and writing data (usually in blocks of bytes), and seeking a specific byte in the binary file. Specifications for these data attributes and methods appear in the following declaration of the ByteFile class:

```
ByteFile = OBJECT (GenFileObj)
    FileVar : FILE;
    EndOfFile : BOOLEAN;
    PROCEDURE Open;
    PROCEDURE CloseIt;
    FUNCTION AtEndOfFile : BOOLEAN;
    PROCEDURE ByteWrite(VAR Buffer;                 { input  }
                            Count   : WORD;         { input  }
                        VAR Result : WORD           { output });
    PROCEDURE ByteRead(VAR  Buffer;                 { output }
                            Count   : WORD;         { input  }
                        VAR Result : WORD           { output });
    PROCEDURE SeekByte(RecNo : WORD { input });
END;
```

The Open method opens the file using the input, output, or append I/O mode, as specified by the FileMode argument of the inherited Init method. The method CloseIt simply closes the file object.

The ByteWrite and ByteRead methods utilize the block I/O routines in Turbo Pascal. It is important to recognize that they use external buffers, represented by the parameter Buffer. This enables an application program to better manage the buffer space in the following ways:

1. It minimizes the number of buffers, by possibly having fewer buffers than the number of binary file objects. These external buffers are used only when needed.
2. It makes the external buffers large, to foster faster binary file I/O.
3. It allows the application program to have a single buffer or multiple buffers with a uniform or nonuniform buffer space. This gives maximum flexibility of buffer management to the application program.

Program File Class

Executable programs are binary files containing machine instructions. Often, programs employ command-line arguments to fine-tune their execution. The command line will be input to the program class's Run procedure. No new data attributes are required for this class. An optional data field keeps track of the value of the DosError variable, exported by unit Dos, after the program is invoked. The methods associated with the class are simple: run the program and return the value of DosError. The following declaration implements these data attributes and methods:

```
ProgramFile = OBJECT (GenFileObj)
    DosErrorStatus : INTEGER;
    PROCEDURE Run (CommandLine : STRING { input });
    FUNCTION SayDosError : INTEGER;
END;
```

The method Run verifies that (a) the mode specified with the inherited method Init is the enumerated executed_mode value, and (b) the program file exists.

LISTING 6.1. The source code for library unit FileObj.

```
Unit FileObj;

{═══════════════════════════════════════════════════════════

                Copyright (c) 1989, 1990  Namir Clement Shammas

    LIBRARY NAME: FileObj

    VERSION 1.0 FOR TURBO PASCAL                    DATE 6/21/1989

    PURPOSE: Exports file objects.

═════════════════════════════════════════════════════════════}

{****************************************************************}
{***********************} INTERFACE {***************************}
{****************************************************************}

Uses Dos;

TYPE

IOMode = (input_mode, output_mode, append_mode, execute_mode);

GenFileObj = OBJECT
```

```
        Filename : STRING;
        FileInfo : SearchRec; { from Unit Dos }
        FileExists : BOOLEAN;
        Mode : IOMode;
        IOError,
        UpdateFileInfo : BOOLEAN;
        FileSize : LONGINT;
        DateTimeStamp : DateTime; { from Unit Dos }
        PROCEDURE Init ( Name       : STRING; { input  }
                         FileMode   : IOMode  { input });
        PROCEDURE UpdateInfo;
        FUNCTION AnyIOerror : BOOLEAN;
        FUNCTION Exists : BOOLEAN;
        FUNCTION GetSize : LONGINT;
        PROCEDURE GetDate (VAR  Year,                { output }
                                Month,               { output }
                                Day     : INTEGER    { output });
        PROCEDURE GetTime (VAR  Hour,                { output }
                                Minute,              { output }
                                Second  : INTEGER    { output });
        PROCEDURE RenameIt (NewName : STRING { input });
        PROCEDURE DeleteIt;
    END;


TextFile = OBJECT (GenFileObj)
    FileVar : TEXT;
    EndOfFile : BOOLEAN;
    PROCEDURE Open;
    PROCEDURE CloseIt;
    FUNCTION AtEndOfFile : BOOLEAN;
    PROCEDURE WriteString (S : String { input });
    PROCEDURE NewLine;
    PROCEDURE ReadString (VAR S : String { output });
END;


CompressedTextFile = OBJECT (TextFile)
    FUNCTION Compress (
                Source          : CompressedTextFile; { input  }
                KeyFile         : TextFile
                CompressFile    : BOOLEAN            { input })
                                : BOOLEAN;
END;


ByteFile = OBJECT (GenFileObj)
```

```
                    FileVar : FILE;
                    EndOfFile : BOOLEAN;
                    PROCEDURE Open;
                    PROCEDURE CloseIt;
                    FUNCTION AtEndOfFile : BOOLEAN;
                    PROCEDURE ByteWrite(VAR Buffer;            { input  }
                                            Count   : WORD;    { input  }
                                        VAR Result  : WORD     { output });
                    PROCEDURE ByteRead(VAR  Buffer;            { output }
                                            Count   : WORD;    { input  }
                                        VAR Result  : WORD     { output });
                  PROCEDURE SeekByte(RecNo : WORD { input });
                END;

                ProgramFile = OBJECT(GenFileObj)
                    DosErrorStatus : INTEGER;
                    PROCEDURE Run(CommandLine : STRING { input });
                    FUNCTION SayDosError : INTEGER;
                END;

                {*****************************************************************}
                {*********************} IMPLEMENTATION {************************}
                {*****************************************************************}

                PROCEDURE ReplaceString(   FindStr,                { input  }
                                           ReplaceStr  : STRING;   { input  }
                                      VAR Strng         : STRING   { in/out });

                VAR find_strlen, repl_strlen,
                    strlen, match_pos : BYTE;

                BEGIN
                    IF (FindStr = '') OR (Strng = '') THEN EXIT;

                    strlen := Length(Strng);
                    find_strlen := Length(FindStr);
                    repl_strlen := Length(ReplaceStr);

                    {- - - - - - - Main body of the procedure - - - - - - - - -}
                    match_pos := POS(FindStr, Strng);
                    WHILE match_pos > 0 DO BEGIN
                        { remove string found }
                        Delete(Strng, match_pos, find_strlen);
                        { replace it with new ReplaceStr }
```

```
            IF repl_strlen > 0 THEN Insert (ReplaceStr, Strng, match_pos);
            { find next matching strings }
            match_pos := POS (FindStr, Strng);
        END; { WHILE }

END; { ReplaceString }


PROCEDURE AlterText (   CodeFile  : STRING;    { input  }
                   VAR  InFile,               { input  }
                        OutFile   : TEXT;      { input  }
                        Compress  : BOOLEAN    { input  });


VAR Line, FindStr, ReplaceStr : STRING;
    CodeFileVar : TEXT;


BEGIN
    Assign(CodeFileVar, CodeFile);
    WHILE NOT EOF(InFile) DO BEGIN
        Reset(CodeFileVar);
        READLN(InFile, Line);
        WHILE NOT EOF(CodeFileVar) DO BEGIN
            IF Compress THEN BEGIN
                READLN(CodeFileVar, FindStr);
                READLN(CodeFileVar, ReplaceStr)
            END
            ELSE BEGIN
                READLN(CodeFileVar, ReplaceStr);
                READLN(CodeFileVar, FindStr)
            END;
            ReplaceString(FindStr, ReplaceStr, Line);
        END;
        WRITELN(OutFile, Line)
    END;
    Close(CodeFileVar);
END;


PROCEDURE GenFileObj.Init ( Name      : STRING; { input  }
                            FileMode  : IOMode  { input  });
BEGIN
    Filename := Name;
    Mode := FileMode;
    FindFirst(Name, Archive, FileInfo);
    IOError := DosError <> 0;
```

```
                    UpdateFileInfo := FALSE;
                    FileExists := DosError = 0;
                    WITH FileInfo DO BEGIN
                        IF FileExists THEN
                            FileSize := Size
                        ELSE
                            FileSize := 0;
                        UnpackTime (Time, DateTimeStamp)
                    END;
                END;


PROCEDURE GenFileObj.UpdateInfo;
BEGIN
  FindFirst (Filename, Archive, FileInfo);
  IOError := DosError <> 0;
  UpdateFileInfo := FALSE;
  FileExists := DosError = 0;
  WITH FileInfo DO BEGIN
      IF FileExists THEN
          FileSize := Size
        ELSE
          FileSize := 0;
    UnpackTime (Time, DateTimeStamp)
  END;
END;


FUNCTION GenFileObj.AnyIOerror : BOOLEAN;
BEGIN
    AnyIOerror := IOError
END;


FUNCTION GenFileObj.Exists : BOOLEAN;
BEGIN
    Exists := FileExists
END;


FUNCTION GenFileObj.GetSize : LONGINT;
BEGIN
    GetSize := FileSize
END;


PROCEDURE GenFileObj.GetDate (VAR   Year,              { output }
                                    Month,             { output }
                                    Day  : INTEGER  { output });
```

```
BEGIN
    Year  := DateTimeStamp.Year;
    Month := DateTimeStamp.Month;
    Day   := DateTimeStamp.Day
END;

PROCEDURE GenFileObj.GetTime(VAR   Hour,                 { output }
                                   Minute,               { output }
                                   Second : INTEGER      { output });
BEGIN
    Hour   := DateTimeStamp.Hour;
    Minute := DateTimeStamp.Min;
    Second := DateTimeStamp.Sec
END;

PROCEDURE GenFileObj.RenameIt(NewName : STRING { input });

VAR FileHandle : FILE;

BEGIN
    IF Exists THEN BEGIN
        Assign(FileHandle, Filename);
        Rename(FileHandle, NewName);
    END;
END;

PROCEDURE GenFileObj.DeleteIt;

VAR FileHandle : FILE;

BEGIN
    IF Exists THEN BEGIN
        Assign(FileHandle, Filename);
        Erase(FileHandle);
    END;
END;

PROCEDURE TextFile.Open;

VAR ModeError : BOOLEAN;

BEGIN
    ModeError := FALSE;
    Assign(FileVar, Filename);
```

```
                        {$I-}
                        CASE Mode OF
                            input_mode  : BEGIN
                                             Reset (FileVar);
                                             EndOfFile := EOF (FileVar)
                                          END;
                            output_mode : Rewrite (FileVar);
                            append_mode : Append (FileVar);
                            ELSE ModeError := TRUE;
                        END;
                        {$I+}
                        IF NOT ModeError THEN
                            IOError := IOResult <> 0
                        ELSE
                            IOError := TRUE;
                END;


                PROCEDURE TextFile.CloseIt;
                BEGIN
                    {$I-} Close (FileVar); {$I+}
                END;


                FUNCTION TextFile.AtEndOfFile : BOOLEAN;
                BEGIN
                    AtEndOfFile := EndOfFile;
                END;


                PROCEDURE TextFile.WriteString (S : String { input });
                BEGIN
                    UpdateFileInfo := TRUE;
                    WRITE (FileVar, S)
                END;


                PROCEDURE TextFile.NewLine;
                BEGIN
                    UpdateFileInfo := TRUE;
                    WRITELN (FileVar)
                END;


                PROCEDURE TextFile.ReadString (VAR S : String { output });
                BEGIN
                    EndOfFile := EOF (FileVar);
                    IF NOT EndOfFile THEN
                        READLN (FileVar, S)
```

```
              ELSE
                  S := '';
   END;

   FUNCTION CompressedTextFile.Compress(
                      Source          : CompressedTextFile;  { input }
                      KeyFile         : TextFile;            { input }
                      CompressFile    : BOOLEAN              { input })
                                      : BOOLEAN;
   BEGIN
       Assign(Source.FileVar, Source.Filename);
       {$I-} Reset(Source.FileVar); {$I+}

       IF (IOResult <> 0) THEN BEGIN
           Compress := FALSE;
           EXIT
       END;

       Assign(FileVar, Filename);
       {$I+} Rewrite(FileVar); {$I+}
       IF (IOResult <> 0) THEN BEGIN
           Compress := FALSE;
           Source.CloseIt;
           EXIT
       END;

       AlterText( KeyFile.Filename, Source.FileVar,
                  FileVar, CompressFile);
       Close(Source.FileVar);
       Close(FileVar);
       Compress := TRUE
   END;


   PROCEDURE ByteFile.Open;


   VAR ModeError : BOOLEAN;


   BEGIN
       ModeError := FALSE;
       Assign(FileVar, Filename);
       {$I-}
       CASE Mode OF
           input_mode : BEGIN
                           Reset(FileVar, 1);
```

```
                                    EndOfFile := EOF (FileVar)
                          END;
              output_mode : Rewrite (FileVar, 1);
              ELSE ModeError := TRUE;
          END;
          {$I+}
          IF NOT ModeError THEN
              IOError := IOResult <> 0
          ELSE
              IOError := TRUE;
      END;


      PROCEDURE ByteFile.CloseIt;
      BEGIN
          {$I-} Close (FileVar); {$I+}
      END;


      FUNCTION ByteFile.AtEndOfFile : BOOLEAN;
      BEGIN
          AtEndOfFile := EndOfFile;
      END;


      PROCEDURE ByteFile.ByteWrite(VAR    Buffer;              { input  }
                                          Count    : WORD; { input  }
                                   VAR    Result   : WORD  { output });
      BEGIN
          UpdateFileInfo := TRUE;
          BlockWrite (FileVar, Buffer, Count, Result)
      END;


      PROCEDURE ByteFile.ByteRead(VAR    Buffer;              { output }
                                         Count    : WORD; { input  }
                                  VAR    Result   : WORD  { output });
      BEGIN
          BlockRead (FileVar, Buffer, Count, Result)
      END;


      PROCEDURE ByteFile.SeekByte(RecNo : WORD { input });
      BEGIN
          Seek (FileVar, RecNo)
      END;


      PROCEDURE ProgramFile.Run (CommandLine : STRING { input });
      BEGIN
```

```
        IF (Mode = execute_mode) AND FileExists THEN
            Exec(Filename, CommandLine);
        DosErrorStatus := DosError
    END;


    FUNCTION ProgramFile.SayDosError : INTEGER;
    BEGIN
        SayDosError := DosErrorStatus
    END;


    END.
```

I took a divide-and-conquer approach in demonstrating the various file classes of unit FileObj. Each class is tested in a separate program.

Listing 6.2 contains a program to test general file objects. The program prompts you for a filename and returns its existence status. If the file exists, then its size, date stamp, and time stamp are also reported. A REPEAT loop enables you to examine the size and date/time stamps of different files. Pressing the [Enter] key at the prompt terminates the program.

LISTING 6.2. Program TSFILE1.PAS to test general file objectives.

```
    Program Test_General_File_Objects;

    {
     Program tests GenFileObj class. The user is prompted for a
     filename. The program reports whether or not the file
     exists. The size and date/time stamp of an existing file
     are displayed.
    }


    Uses Crt, Dos, FileObj;


    PROCEDURE WriteNum(I : INTEGER { input });
    BEGIN
        IF I < 10 THEN
            WRITE('0',I:1)
        ELSE
            WRITE(I:2);
    END;


    VAR AnyFile : GenFileObj;
        TheFileName : STRING;
```

```
              Year, Month, Day,
              Hour, Minute, Second : INTEGER;
              AKey : CHAR;

          BEGIN
          REPEAT
              ClrScr;
              WRITE ('Enter a filename (press [Enter] to exit) -> ');
              READLN (TheFileName); WRITELN;
              IF TheFilename <> '' THEN BEGIN
                AnyFile.Init (TheFileName, input_mode);
                IF AnyFile.Exists THEN BEGIN
                    WRITELN ('File size = ', AnyFile.GetSize, ' bytes');
                    AnyFile.GetDate (Year, Month, Day);
                    WRITE ('Date stamp is ');
                    WriteNum (Month); WRITE ('/');
                    WriteNum (Day); WRITELN ('/', Year);
                    AnyFile.GetTime (Hour, Minute, Second);
                    WRITE ('Time stamp is ');
                    WriteNum (Hour); WRITE (':');
                    WriteNum (Minute); WRITE (':');
                    WriteNum (Second); WRITELN;
                END
                ELSE
                    WRITELN ('File ', TheFilename, ' does not exist');
                WRITELN;
                WRITE ('Press any key to continue ...');
                Akey := ReadKey
              END;
          UNTIL TheFileName = '';
          END.
```

A sample session with TSFILE1.PAS is shown following:

```
Enter a filename (press [Enter] to exit) -> tsfile1.pas

File size = 1393 bytes
Date stamp is 05/18/1989
Time stamp is 09:51:18

Press any key to continue ...


Enter a filename (press [Enter] to exit) -> <[Enter]>
```

Listing 6.3 contains a program to test text file objects. The program creates a text file object and allows you to type in as many lines as you wish (and as long as disk space is available). By entering a blank line, you signal to the program that you are finished typing text. The program closes the text file and reopens it for reading. The lines you typed are slowly displayed on the screen.

While the program prompts you for the text filename, it handles setting the I/O mode for writing and reading text lines. In addition, the AnyIOError message is used to verify the validity of the text file before attempting to write to it. The AtEndOfFile message is sent to the file object when reading the text lines back. The AtEndOfFile message is used in a WHILE loop just like the predefined Eof function with ordinary files.

LISTING 6.3. Program TSFILE2.PAS to test text file objects.

```
Program Test_Text_File_Objects;

{
Program tests the TexFile class.  The program enables you to
write to a text file and then reads its lines back.
}

Uses Crt, Dos, FileObj;

PROCEDURE ShowSlow(S : STRING { input });

VAR I : BYTE;

BEGIN
    FOR I := 1 TO Length(S) DO BEGIN
        WRITE(S[I]);
        Delay(100);
    END;
    WRITELN;
END;

VAR AnyFile : TextFile;
    TheFileName, TextLine : STRING;
    AKey : CHAR;

BEGIN
    REPEAT
        ClrScr;
        WRITE('Enter output filename -> ');
```

```
                READLN (TheFilename); WRITELN;
                AnyFile.Init (TheFilename, output_mode);
                AnyFile.Open;
                IF AnyFile.AnyIOerror THEN BEGIN
                    WRITELN ('Cannot open file ', TheFilename);
                    WRITELN;
                    WRITE ('Press any key to continue ...');
                    AKey := ReadKey;
                END;
            UNTIL NOT AnyFile.AnyIOError;

            WRITELN ('Enter sequence of line, ending it with a blank line');
            REPEAT
                READLN (TextLine);
                AnyFile.WriteString (TextLine);
                AnyFile.NewLine;
            UNTIL TextLine = '';
            AnyFile.CloseIt;
            ClrScr;
            Delay (1000);
            WRITELN ('Reading back the lines from the text file');
            WRITELN; WRITELN;

            AnyFile.Init (TheFileName, input_mode);
            AnyFile.Open;
            WHILE NOT AnyFile.EndOfFile DO BEGIN
                AnyFile.ReadString (TextLine);
                ShowSlow (TextLine);
            END;
        END.
```

A sample session with program TSFILE2.PAS is shown below:

```
Enter output filename -> text.doc

Enter sequence of lines, ending it with a blank line
line 1
line 2
line 3

Reading back the lines from the text file

line 1
line 2
line 3
```

Listing 6.4 shows a program to test compressed text file objects. The program compresses a text file. It prompts you for the name of the input file, output compressed file, and the compression data file. The message "Done" is displayed when the compression is finished. I have omitted file checking to make the program a bit shorter.

LISTING 6.4. Program TSFILE3.PAS to test compressed text file objects.

```pascal
Program Test_Compressed_Text_File_Objects;

{
Program tests the CompressedFile class.  The program enables you
to copy a file from one drive/directory into another.
}

Uses Crt, Dos, FileObj;

CONST BUFFER_SIZE = 1024;

VAR InputFile, OutputFile : CompressedTextFile;
    KeyFile : TextFile;
    SourceFilename, TargetFilename, KeyFilename : STRING;
    AKey : CHAR;

BEGIN
    ClrScr;
    WRITE ('Enter input filename -> ');
    READLN (SourceFilename); WRITELN;
    WRITE ('Enter output filename -> ');
    READLN (TargetFilename); WRITELN;
    WRITE ('Enter compression data file -> ');
    READLN (Keyfilename); WRITELN;
    WRITE ('Compress file ? (Y/N) ');
    READLN (Akey); WRITELN;
    Akey := UpCase (Akey);
    InputFile.Init (SourceFilename, input_mode);
    OutputFile.Init (TargetFilename, output_mode);
    KeyFile.Init (KeyFilename, input_mode);
    IF OutputFile.Compress (InputFile, KeyFile, Akey = 'Y') THEN
BEGIN
        WRITELN;
        WRITELN ('Done');
    END;
END.
```

Listing 6.5 contains the dummy SOURCE.PAS program that is compressed by TSFILE3.PAS using the compression data shown in Figure 6.2. Listing 6.6 has the compressed output file.

LISTING 6.5. Dummy SOURCE.PAS program to be compressed.

```
Program Dummy;

PROCEDURE DonNothing
BEGIN
    WRITELN('Hello')
END;

FUNCTION Pie : REAL;
BEGIN
    Pie := Pi
END;

VAR I : WORD;

BEGIN
    I := 1;
    WHILE I < 1000 DO BEGIN
        IF I < 500 THEN
            WRITELN(I*I)
        ELSE
            WRITELN(I*I div 2);
    END;
END.
```

The contents of file KEYFILE.DAT, shown in Figure 6.2, represent a small subset of Pascal keywords that are compressed. More keywords can be added to the list. In addition, frequently occurring sequences of keywords, such as DO BEGIN, form excellent compression list members.

A sample session with program TSFILE3.PAS follows, with SOURCE.PAS, TARGET.PAS, and KEYFILE.DAT as the input, output, and data compression files, respectively:

```
Enter input filename -> SOURCE.PAS

Enter output filename -> TARGET.PAS
```

FIGURE 6.2. The contents of the compression data file KEYFILE.DAT.

```
                              WHILE
                              @W
                              THEN
                              @T
                              ELSE
                              @E
                              PROCEDURE
                              @P
                              FUNCTION
                              @F
                              BEGIN
                              @B
```

```
      Enter compression data file -> KEYFILE.DAT

      Compress file ? (Y/N) y


      Done
```

LISTING 6.6. Compressed text file TARGET.PAS.

```
      Program Dummy;

      @P DonNothing
      @B
          WRITELN('Hello')
      END;

      @F Pie : REAL;
      @B
          Pie := Pi
      END;

      VAR I : WORD;

      @B
          I := 1;
          @W I < 1000 DO @B
```

```
                    IF I < 500 @T
                        WRITELN (I*I)
                @E
                        WRITELN (I*I div 2);
            END;
        END.
```

Listing 6.7 shows a program to test binary file objects. The program copies a single file of any type (ASCII or binary). You are prompted for the filename, the source directory, and the destination directory. The program displays a message containing the source and target files. In addition, dots are emitted to the screen by the program while copying the file. The program uses a small buffer (1024 bytes) to copy the file. Employing larger buffers speeds up the copy process considerably.

LISTING 6.7. Program TSFILE4.PAS to test binary file objects.

```
Program Test_Binary_File_Objects;

{
Program tests the ByteFile class.  The program enables you to
copy a file from one drive/directory into another.
}

Uses Crt, Dos, FileObj;

CONST BUFFER_SIZE = 1024;

PROCEDURE CheckPath (VAR DosDir : STRING { in/out });
BEGIN
    IF DosDir[Length(DosDir)] <> '\' THEN
        DosDir := DosDir + '\';
END;

VAR InputFile, OutputFile : ByteFile;
    TheFileName, SourceDir, TargetDir : STRING;
    Buffer : ARRAY [1..BUFFER_SIZE] OF BYTE;
    NumRead, NumWrite : WORD;
    AKey : CHAR;

BEGIN
    REPEAT
        ClrScr;
        WRITE ('Enter input filename -> ');
```

```
                        READLN (TheFilename) ; WRITELN;
                        WRITE ('Enter input directory -> ');
                        READLN (SourceDir) ; WRITELN;
                        CheckPath (SourceDir) ;
                        WRITE ('Enter output directory -> ');
                        READLN (TargetDir) ; WRITELN;
                        CheckPath (TargetDir) ;
                        InputFile.Init (SourceDir+TheFilename, input_mode) ;
                        OutputFile.Init (TargetDir+TheFilename, output_mode) ;
                        InputFile.Open;
                        OutputFile.Open;
                        IF InputFile.AnyIOerror THEN BEGIN
                            WRITELN ('Cannot open file ', SourceDir + TheFilename) ;
                            WRITELN;
                            WRITE ('Press any key to continue ...') ;
                            AKey := ReadKey;
                        END;
                    UNTIL NOT InputFile.AnyIOError;
                    WRITELN ('Copying ',  SourceDir + TheFilename,' to ',
                                          TargetDir + TheFilename) ;
                     WRITELN;

                     REPEAT
                         WRITE ('.') ;
                         InputFile.ByteRead (Buffer, BUFFER_SIZE, NumRead) ;
                         OutputFile.ByteWrite (Buffer, NumRead, NumWrite)
                         UNTIL (NumRead = 0) OR (NumRead <> NumWrite) ;
                         InputFile.CloseIt;
                         OutputFile.CloseIt;
                         WRITELN; WRITELN; WRITELN ('Done') ;
                END.
```

A sample session with program TSFILE4.PAS is shown below:

```
Enter input filename -> tsfile4.pas

Enter input directory -> \qp1

Enter output directory -> \

Copying \qp1\tsfile4.pas to \tsfile4.pas

...

Done
```

Listing 6.8 shows a program to test program file objects. The program prompts you for the complete program file name and its command-line arguments. The test program verifies the existence of the program file before attempting to run it. Any DOS error is reported by sending the SayDosError message.

LISTING 6.8. Program TSFILE5.PAS to test program file objects.

```
Program Test_Program_File_Objects;

{
 Program tests the ProgramFile class.
}

Uses Crt, Dos, FileObj;

{$M 8417, 0, 0}

VAR AnyFile : ProgramFile;
    TheFileName, ComLine : STRING;
    AKey : CHAR;

BEGIN
    REPEAT
        ClrScr;
        WRITE ('Enter full program name -> ');
        READLN (TheFilename); WRITELN;
        AnyFile.Init (TheFilename, execute_mode);
        IF NOT AnyFile.Exists THEN BEGIN
            WRITELN ('Cannot open file ', TheFilename);
            WRITELN;
            WRITE ('Press any key to continue ...');
            AKey := ReadKey;
        END;
    UNTIL AnyFile.Exists;
    WRITE ('Enter command line -> ');
    READLN (ComLine); WRITELN;
    AnyFile.Run (ComLine);
    IF AnyFile.SayDosError <> 0 THEN BEGIN
        WRITELN ('Dos error in attempting to run the program');
        WRITELN ('Dos error # ', AnyFile.SayDosError);
    END;
    Akey := ReadKey;
END.
```

A sample session with this program follows. The program invokes the DOS command processor to execute the interal DOS command DIR *.EXE:

```
Enter full program name -> C:\COMMAND.COM

Enter command line -> /C DIR *.EXE


 Volume in drive C is NCR HD020 A
 Directory of C:\

AUTOASK  EXE     5584  10-31-88   5:39p
CLS2     EXE     2896   9-16-88   4:46p
DM       EXE    75616   4-01-88  12:00p
DS       EXE    25638   3-01-87   4:00p
FILEPEEK EXE     6449   2-16-86   3:48p
VL       EXE     7456   3-01-87   4:00p
WHEREIS  EXE     7924   3-01-87   4:00p
        7 File(s)   4481024 bytes free
```

7 | String Objects

Strings are among the most extensively used data structures in interactive applications. This chapter looks at how a hierarchy of string objects is created, depending on the context in which the string is employed.

We use strings for various purposes. To begin with, a string may be regarded as a raw array of characters. In this case, there is no part of the string that has a special meaning or significance. Turbo Pascal provides a number of intrinsics to manipulate strings, such as Length, Delete, Insert, and Pos. These routines are used for general-purpose string manipulation. To build a class of general-purpose strings, the data and methods fields must be defined. A single data field is needed to store the array of characters. You may add a field to store the length of the string; however, such a field must be constantly updated as characters are inserted, deleted, or assigned. Using a method to report the current string length is perhaps more appropriate.

The choice of methods for the class of general strings varies according to needs. At the very least, there should be the following:

1. A method to assign a string variable or literal to the string object
2. A method to return the string length
3. A battery of methods that implement some or all of the Turbo Pascal intrinsics

Other methods can be included, such as lower-case and upper-case conversion, character translation, character trimming, and character padding, to name just a few.

Based on the foregoing, I define a class of general-purpose strings as follows:

```
CONST MAXLEN = 80;
      SPACE = ' ';
```

127

```
           COMMA = ',';
      TYPE
        MSTRING = STRING[MAXLEN];

        TString = OBJECT
             fString : MSTRING;
             PROCEDURE Init(S : MSTRING { input });
             FUNCTION SLength : BYTE;
             PROCEDURE SInsert( SubStr : MSTRING;   { input }
                                Index  : BYTE        { input });
             PROCEDURE SDelete( Index,             { input }
                                Count  : BYTE { input });
             FUNCTION SCopy( Index,              { input }
                             Count  : BYTE { input }) : MSTRING;
             FUNCTION Get(Index : BYTE { input }) : MSTRING;
             FUNCTION SPos(   SubStr : MSTRING;   { input }
                              Index  : BYTE         { input }) : BYTE;
             PROCEDURE UpperCase;
             PROCEDURE LowerCase;
        END;
```

The Init procedure is used to store characters in the fString field without directly accessing the field. The methods SLength, SInsert, SDelete, and SCopy are simple shells of code that invoke their analogous Turbo Pascal intrinsics. The method SCopy can be used to return parts or all of the characters in the string object. Method SPos implements a version of the Pos function that includes an index specifying the number of leading characters not involved in the substring search. Methods UpperCase and LowerCase convert the character case of a string object. Listing 7.1 contains the source code for library unit StrObj, wherein the class TString is coded along with other string classes.

It's Only Words

English sentences are made of space-delimited words. Thus, the space character has a special relevance in a string. Characters surrounded by spaces form words. This is also true for the DOS command line and its arguments. The Turbo Pascal ParamCount and ParamStr functions return the number of words as well as the words themselves. A new class of words is born of the general-purpose string class, TString. The data structure of the subclass of words is basically the inherited one. No special accommodations need to be made for the word delimiter since it is always the space character. The functionality of word objects varies with the application requirement. Methods that count, retrieve, insert, delete, and translate words implement common functionality. I will implement only the first two methods in this list, which parallel the built-in ParamCount and ParamStr functions. The subclass TWord is defined as follows:

```
TWord = OBJECT(TString)
    FUNCTION SLength(UseInherited : BOOLEAN { input }) : BYTE;
    FUNCTION Get(Index : BYTE { input }) : MSTRING;
END;
```

The two methods declared here override the inherited ones, allowing objects of class TWord to respond to these messages in a particular way (polymorphism). The Boolean argument of method SLength is used to invoke the inherited method, returning the number of characters.

Items

The comma is another special delimiter used in strings. Certain database formats employ the comma to delimit the various items in a string as well as in text-based data files. Moreover, the Macintosh HyperTalk language employs list structures using comma-delimited strings.

Comma-delimited strings can be used to simulate small arrays, lists, and stacks. Items within such strings may contain spaces, adding to the power and versatility of this class. For example, the string "United Fans,Colorado Springs,Colorado" contains three items, of which the first two contain spaces.

This item subclass of strings resembles the TWord class in most aspects. The definition follows very similar reasoning. Even the coding is similar. In Listing 7.1 I define the item subclass as follows:

```
TItem = OBJECT(TString)
    FUNCTION SLength(UseInherited : BOOLEAN { input }) : BYTE;
    FUNCTION Get(Index : BYTE { input }) : MSTRING;
END;
```

Tokens

The class of words and items can be expanded to a more flexible class of objects, namely, tokens. Unlike words and items, tokens are delimited by multiple user-defined characters. For example, consider the following expression:

```
Y := A + (B + C) / D
```

If the set of token-delimiting characters is ":=+()/-* ", this expression is parsed into the following tokens:

```
Y := A + (B + C) / D

^     ^     ^    ^     ^
|     |     |    |     |
|     |     |    |     +--------- Token # 5
|     |     |    |
|     |     |    +------------- Token # 4
|     |     |
|     |     +----------------- Token # 3
|     |
|     +--------------------- Token # 2
|
+------------------------- Token # 1
```

Tokens may be separated by a sequence of various token delimiters. A tokenized string needs to be accompanied by a string defining the set of delimiters. Moreover, if the set of delimiters varies, the tokens extracted from a string will most likely vary. Thus, the string of delimiters adds to the data fields of the token class. To maintain the "hands-off-fields" rule, a method is needed to assign the contents of the delimiter field.

In other respects, the class of tokens is similar to the classes of words and items. I define the following TToken class in Listing 7.1:

```
TToken = OBJECT (TString)
     fDelim : MSTRING;
     PROCEDURE Init (  S      : MSTRING;   { input }
                       Delim  : MSTRING    { input });
     FUNCTION SLength (UseInherited : BOOLEAN { input }) : BYTE;
     FUNCTION Get (Index : BYTE { input }) : MSTRING;
END;
```

The fDelim data field stores the token delimiters. The procedure Init is used to initialize the fString and fDelim fields. The other two methods work as in classes TWord and TItem.

Your Title Is . . .

Titles and headings in text are words displayed in a special way. Headings are words that are centered, with the option of having the text in upper case. Titles are uncentered headings. The text of titles may all be in upper case, or the first character of each word may be in upper case. From the object-oriented view, titles and headings are a special subclass of words where the emphasis is on how the words are displayed. Hence, titles and headings (I'll refer to them collectively as titles) have the same data structure and consequently the same data fields as the class of words. The difference is in the functionality of title objects—how they are displayed. I have defined a class TTitle in Listing 7.1 as follows:

```
TTitle = OBJECT (TWord)
      PROCEDURE Display; { uncentered }
      PROCEDURE Center (BlankLines : BYTE);
END;
```

The method Display simply displays the text of the inherited field fString in upper case. The Center method centers the upper-case characters of field fString on the current line and emits BlankLines carriage returns.

LISTING 7.1. Source code for the StrObj library unit.

```
UNIT StrObj;

{════════════════════════════════════════════════════════


            Copyright (c) 1989, 1990  Namir Clement Shammas

     LIBRARY NAME: StrObj

     VERSION 1.0 FOR TURBO PASCAL                    DATE 6/21/1989

     PURPOSE: Implements a library of string objects:

                  + TString: general
                    + TWord: string of space-delimited words
                      + TTitle: upper-case titles
                    + TItem: string of comma-delimited items
                    + TTokens: string of tokens


═══════════════════════════════════════════════════════════}
```

```
{******************************************************************}
{************************}INTERFACE{****************************}
{******************************************************************}


Uses Crt;

CONST MAXLEN = 80;
      SPACE = ' ';
      COMMA = ',';
TYPE
   MSTRING = STRING[MAXLEN];
   TString = OBJECT
        fString : MSTRING;
        PROCEDURE Init(S : MSTRING { input });
        FUNCTION SLength : BYTE;
        PROCEDURE SInsert( SubStr  : MSTRING;   { input }
                           Index   : BYTE       { input });
        PROCEDURE SDelete( Index,           { input }
                           Count   : BYTE { input });
        FUNCTION SCopy(  Index,          { input }
                         Count   : BYTE { input }) : MSTRING;
        FUNCTION Get(Index : BYTE { input }) : MSTRING;
        FUNCTION SPos(   SubStr : MSTRING;   { input }
                         Index  : BYTE       { input }) : BYTE;
        PROCEDURE UpperCase;
        PROCEDURE LowerCase;
   END;


   TWord = OBJECT(TString)
      FUNCTION SLength(UseInherited : BOOLEAN { input }) : BYTE;
      FUNCTION Get(Index : BYTE { input }) : MSTRING;
   END;


   TItem = OBJECT(TString)
      FUNCTION SLength(UseInherited : BOOLEAN { input }) : BYTE;
      FUNCTION Get(Index : BYTE { input }) : MSTRING;
   END;


   TToken = OBJECT(TString)
        fDelim : MSTRING;
        PROCEDURE Init(  S      : MSTRING;   { input }
                         Delim  : MSTRING    { input });
```

```
        FUNCTION SLength(UseInherited : BOOLEAN { input }) : BYTE;
        FUNCTION Get (Index : BYTE { input }) : MSTRING;
    END;

    TTitle = OBJECT (TWord)
        PROCEDURE Display; { uncentered }
        PROCEDURE Center(BlankLines : BYTE);
    END;

{*****************************************************************}
{**********************}IMPLEMENTATION {************************}
{*****************************************************************}


{--------------------------- PosMidStr ----------------}

FUNCTION PosMidStr( Strng    : STRING; { input }
                    First,            { input }
                    Last   : BYTE    { input }) : STRING;

BEGIN
    {- - - - - - - - Argument checking - - - - - - - -}
    IF (  Strng = '') OR (Last < First) THEN BEGIN { bad arguments }
        PosMidStr := '';
        EXIT
    END; { IF }
    { return function value }
    PosMidStr := Copy(Strng, First, Last - First + 1)
END;


{--------------------------- Found_Char -------------}

FUNCTION Found_Char (Ch       : CHAR;   { input }
                     Strng  : STRING; { input }
                     Index  : BYTE    { input }) : BOOLEAN;

{ detects the boundary between a Ch char and one that is not }

BEGIN
    IF Index > 1 THEN
        Found_Char := (Strng[Index-1] = Ch) AND
                      (Strng[Index] <> Ch)
    ELSE
      Found_Char := FALSE;
END; { Found_Char }
```

```
{------------------------------ Found_Space ------------}

FUNCTION Found_Space(   Strng : STRING; { input }
                        Index : BYTE    { input }) : BOOLEAN;


{ detects the boundary between a space and one that is not }

BEGIN
  Found_Space := Found_Char(SPACE, Strng, Index);
END; { Found_Space }


{------------------------------ Found_Comma ------------}

FUNCTION Found_Comma(    Strng  : STRING; { input }
                         Index  : BYTE    { input }) : BOOLEAN;


{ detects the boundary between a comma and one that is not }

BEGIN
    Found_Comma := Found_Char(COMMA, Strng, Index);
END; { Found_Comma }


{------------------------------ Found_Token ------------}

FUNCTION Found_Token(    Strng,                    { input }
                         DelimStr : STRING;   { input }
                         Index    : BYTE      { input }) : BOOLEAN;


{detects the boundary between a token delimiter and one that is not}

BEGIN
    IF Index > 1 THEN
        Found_Token :=    (POS(Strng[Index-1], DelimStr) > 0) AND
                          (POS(Strng[Index], DelimStr) = 0)
    ELSE
        Found_Token := FALSE;
END; { Found_Token }


{ --------------- TString functions and procedures ---------}

{------------------------------ TString.Init ------------}
```

```
PROCEDURE TString.Init (S : MSTRING { input });
BEGIN
    fString := S
END;


{-------------------------- TString.SLength --------------}

FUNCTION TString.SLength : BYTE;
BEGIN
    SLength := Length(fString);
END;


{-------------------------- TString.SInsert --------------}

PROCEDURE TString.SInsert ( SubStr  : MSTRING;    { input  }
                            Index   : BYTE        { input });
BEGIN
    Insert(SubStr, fString, Index);
END;


{-------------------------- TString.SDelete --------------}

PROCEDURE TString.SDelete( Index,         { input  }
                           Count : BYTE   { input });
BEGIN
    Delete(fString, Index, Count);
END;


{---------------------------- TString.SCopy --------------}

FUNCTION TString.SCopy( Index,            { input  }
                        Count : BYTE    { input }) : MSTRING;
BEGIN
    SCopy := Copy(fString, Index, Count)
END;


{---------------------------- TString.Get --------------}

FUNCTION TString.Get (Index : BYTE { input }) : MSTRING;
BEGIN
    IF Index <= SLength THEN
        Get := fString[Index]
    ELSE
        Get := '';
END;
```

```
{------------------------------- TString.SPos --------------}


FUNCTION TString.SPos ( SubStr : MSTRING;    { input }
                        Index  : BYTE        { input }) : BYTE;
VAR aString : STRING;
    charpos : BYTE;


BEGIN
    IF NOT (Index IN [2..MAXLEN]) THEN
        SPos := Pos (SubStr, fString)
    ELSE BEGIN
        aString := fString;
        Delete (aString, 1, Index-1);
        charpos := Pos (SubStr, aString);
        IF charpos > 0 THEN
            INC (charpos, Index-1);
        SPos := charpos
    END;
END;


{-------------------------- TString.UpperCase ---------------}


PROCEDURE TString.UpperCase;


VAR I : BYTE;


BEGIN
    FOR I := 1 TO Length (fString) DO
        fString[I] := UpCase (fString[I]);
END;


{-------------- TString.LowerCase --------------------------}


PROCEDURE TString.LowerCase;


CONST ASCII_SHIFT = ORD ('a') - ORD ('A');


VAR I : BYTE;


BEGIN
    FOR I := 1 TO Length (fString) DO
        IF fString[I] IN ['A'..'Z'] THEN
```

```
                        fString[I] := CHR(ORD(fString[I]) +
                                            ASCII_SHIFT);
        END;


        {--------------- TWord functions and procedures -----------}
        {------------------------------- TWord-SLength -----------}


        FUNCTION TWord.SLength(UseInherited : BOOLEAN { input }) : BYTE;


        VAR i, count, strlen : BYTE;
            words : STRING;


        BEGIN
            IF UseInherited THEN BEGIN
                SLength := TString.SLength;
                EXIT
            END;



            words := fString;
            IF words = '' THEN BEGIN
                SLength := 0;
                EXIT
            END;


            words := SPACE + words + SPACE;
            strlen := Length(words);


            count := 0; { initialize word count }


            FOR i := 2 TO strlen DO
                IF Found_Space(words, i) THEN INC(count);


            SLength := count { return function value }
        END;


        {------------------------------------ TWord.Get ------------}


        FUNCTION TWord.Get(Index : BYTE { input }) : MSTRING;


        VAR i, n, strlen, ptr : BYTE;
            words, wordsought : STRING;
```

```
BEGIN
    words := fString;
    IF Index < 1 THEN Index := 1;
    words := SPACE + words + SPACE;
    n := Index;
    strlen := Length(words);
    i := 2;
    { try to locate the Index'th word }
    WHILE (i <= strlen) AND (n > 0) DO BEGIN
        IF Found_Space(words, i) THEN DEC(n);
        IF n > 0 THEN INC(i);
    END; { WHILE }

    IF i > strlen THEN BEGIN
        Get := '';
        EXIT;
    END
    ELSE BEGIN
        ptr := i; { index the first character of the word }
        { find the tail of the word, since a trailing space
          is always present in the main string }
        WHILE (i <= strlen) AND (words[i] <> ' ') DO INC(i);
        DEC(i);
        wordsought := PosMidStr(words,ptr,i);
    END; { IF }
    Get := wordsought
END;


{--------------- TItem functions and procedures ------------}
{------------------------------- TItem.SLength ---------}


FUNCTION TItem.SLength(UseInherited : BOOLEAN { input }) : BYTE;

VAR i, count, strlen : BYTE;
    items : STRING;


BEGIN
    IF UseInherited THEN BEGIN
        SLength := TString.SLength;
        EXIT
    END;

    items := fString;
    IF items = '' THEN BEGIN
```

```
            SLength := 0;
            EXIT
        END;

        items := COMMA + items + COMMA;
        strlen := Length(items);

        count := 0; { initialize item count }

        FOR i := 2 TO strlen DO
            IF Found_Comma(items, i) THEN INC(count);

        SLength := count { return function value }

    END;

    {---------------------------------- TItem.Get -------------}

    FUNCTION TItem.Get(Index : BYTE { input }) : MSTRING;

    VAR i, n, strlen, ptr : BYTE;
        items, itemsought : STRING;
    BEGIN
        items := fString;
        IF Index < 1 THEN Index := 1;
        items := COMMA + items + COMMA;
        n := Index;
        strlen := Length(items);
        i := 2;
        { try to locate the Index'th item }
        WHILE (i <= strlen) AND (n > 0) DO BEGIN
            IF Found_Comma(items, i) THEN DEC(n);
            IF n > 0 THEN INC(i);
        END; { WHILE }

        IF i > strlen THEN BEGIN
            Get := '';
            EXIT;
        END
        ELSE BEGIN
            ptr := i; { index the first character of the item }
            { find the tail of the item, since a trailing space
              is always present in the main string }
            WHILE (i <= strlen) AND (items[i] <> COMMA) DO INC(i);
```

```
        DEC(i);
        itemsought := PosMidStr(items,ptr,i);
    END; { IF }
    Get := itemsought
END;


{---------------- TToken functions and procedures --------------}


{------------------------------- TToken.Init ----------------}


PROCEDURE TToken.Init(S     : MSTRING; { input }
                      Delim : MSTRING { input  });
BEGIN
    fString := S;
    fDelim := Delim;
    IF fDelim = '' THEN fDelim := ' ';
END;


{------------------------------- TToken.SLength ------------}


FUNCTION TToken.SLength(UseInherited : BOOLEAN { input }) : BYTE;

VAR i, count, strlen : BYTE;
    all_tokens, no_tokens, is_token : BOOLEAN;
    tokens : STRING;

BEGIN
    IF UseInherited THEN BEGIN
        SLength := TString.SLength;
        EXIT
    END;

    tokens := fString;
    IF tokens = '' THEN BEGIN
        SLength := 0;
        EXIT
    END;
    IF fDelim = '' THEN fDelim := ' ';
    tokens := fDelim[1] + tokens;
    strlen := Length(tokens);

    { verify whether string contains characters that are all
      tokens or characters that are non-tokens }
    all_tokens := TRUE;
```

```
        no_tokens := TRUE;
        i := 1;
        WHILE (i <= strlen) AND (all_tokens OR no_tokens) DO BEGIN
            is_token := Pos(tokens[i], fDelim) > 0;
            no_tokens := (NOT is_token) AND no_tokens;
            all_tokens := is_token AND all_tokens;
            INC(i)
        END; { WHILE }

        IF all_tokens OR no_tokens THEN BEGIN
            IF no_tokens THEN SLength := 1; {one token in entire string}
            IF all_tokens THEN SLength := 0; {only token chars in string}
            EXIT
        END;

        count := 0; { initialize token count }

        FOR i := 1 TO strlen DO
            IF Found_Token(tokens, fDelim, i) THEN INC(count);

        SLength := count { return function value }

END; { SLength }

{-------------------------------- TToken.Get -------------}

FUNCTION TToken.Get(Index : BYTE { input }) : MSTRING;

VAR i, n, strlen, ptr : BYTE;
    ch : CHAR;
    tokens : STRING;
BEGIN
    tokens := fString;
    IF Index < 1 THEN Index := 1;
    IF fDelim = '' THEN fDelim := ' ';
    ch := fDelim[1];
    tokens := ch + tokens + ch;
    n := Index;
    strlen := Length(tokens);
    i := 1;
    { try to locate the Index'th token }
    WHILE (i <= strlen) AND (n > 0) DO BEGIN
        IF Found_Token(tokens, fDelim, i) THEN DEC(n);
        IF n > 0 THEN INC(i);
```

```
        END; { WHILE }

        IF i > strlen THEN BEGIN
            Get := '';
            EXIT;
        END
        ELSE BEGIN
            ptr := i; { index the first character of the token }
            { find the tail of the token, since a trailing token
              character is always present in the main string }
            WHILE (i <= strlen) AND (Pos(tokens[i],fDelim) = 0 ) DO
                INC(i);
            DEC(i);
            Get := PosMidStr(tokens,ptr,i);
        END; { IF }
    END;


{---------------------- TTitle procedures ---------------}


PROCEDURE TTitle.Display;

VAR i, strlen : BYTE;

BEGIN
    UpperCase;
    WRITE(fString);
END;


PROCEDURE TTitle.Center(BlankLines : BYTE { input });

BEGIN
    UpperCase;
    GotoXY(40 - TWord.SLength(TRUE) div 2, WhereY);
    WRITE(fString);
    WHILE BlankLines > 0 DO BEGIN
        WRITELN;
        DEC(BlankLines)
    END;
END;


END.
```

Listing 7.2 shows a simple Turbo Pascal test program for the StrObj library unit. The program performs the following:

1. Declares objects for the various string classes.
2. Prompts you to enter a string. The length of the string along with the first and last characters are displayed.
3. Prompts you to enter a set of words. The number of words, the number of characters, the first word, and the last word are shown.
4. Prompts you to enter a list of items. The item count and the first and last items, are posted on the screen.
5. Prompts you for a string containing tokens and token characters. The number of tokens, number of characters, the first token, and the last token are displayed.

LISTING 7.2. Source code for the TSSTR1.PAS test program.

```
Program TesT_String_Objects;

{
  Program tests the various string objects exported by
  unit StrObj.

}

Uses Crt, StrObj;

VAR AString, Delim : MString;
    N : BYTE;
    AKey : CHAR;
    { ---- objects ---- }
    ObjString : TString;
    ObjWord : TWord;
    ObjItem : TItem;
    ObjToken : TToken;
    ObjTitle : TTitle;

BEGIN
    ClrScr;
    { use ObjTitle to dislay program title }
    ObjTitle.Init('String-Object Test Program');
    ObjTitle.Center(2);
    { test object ObjString }
    WRITE('Enter a string -> ');
    READLN(Astring);
    ObjString.Init(AString);
```

```
N := ObjString.SLength;
WRITELN('You typed ', N,' characters');
WRITELN('The first character is ', ObjString.Get(1));
WRITELN('The last character is ', ObjString.Get(N));
WRITELN;
{ test object ObjWord }
WRITE('Enter a string with space-delimited words -> ');
READLN(Astring);
ObjWord.Init(AString);
N := ObjWord.SLength(FALSE);
WRITELN('You typed ', N,' words');
WRITELN('You typed ', ObjWord.SLength(TRUE),' characters');
WRITELN('The first word is ', ObjWord.Get(1));
WRITELN('The last word is ', ObjWord.Get(N));
WRITELN;
{ test object ObjItem }
WRITE('Enter a string with comma-delimited items -> ');
READLN(Astring);
ObjItem.Init(AString);
N := ObjItem.SLength(FALSE);
WRITELN('You entered ', N,' items');
WRITELN('You typed', ObjToken.Slength(TRUE),' characters');
WRITELN('The first item is ', ObjItem.Get(1));
WRITELN('The last item is ', ObjItem.Get(N));
WRITELN;
{ test object ObjToken }
WRITE('Enter a string of tokens -> ');
READLN(AString); WRITELN;
WRITE('Enter token delimiters -> ');
READLN(Delim); WRITELN;
ObjToken.Init(AString, Delim);
N := ObjToken.SLength(FALSE);
WRITELN('You entered ', N,' token');
WRITELN('The first token is ', ObjToken.Get(1));
WRITELN('The last token is ', ObjToken.Get(N));
WRITELN;
WRITELN;
WRITE('Press any key to end the program ...');
AKey := ReadKey;
END.
```

I have placed the following WRITELN statement in the above program to display the number of characters in the ObjWord object:

```
WRITELN('You typed ', ObjWord.SLength(TRUE),' characters');
```

Using the argument TRUE with the SLength message makes the compiler use the inherited method TString.SLength.

A sample session with the foregoing program follows:

STRING-OBJECT TEST PROGRAM

```
Enter a string -> 1234567890
You typed 10 characters
The first character is 1
The last character is 0

Enter a string with space-delimited words ->  11 22 33 44
You typed 4 words
You typed 11 characters
The first word is 11
The last word is 44

Enter a string with comma-delimited items ->  11,22,33,44
You entered 4 items
The first item is 11
The last item is 44

Enter a string of tokens -> 11+22-33*44
Enter token delimiters -> +-*
You entered 4 tokens
You typed 11 characters
The first token is 11
The last token is 44


Press any key to end the program . . .
```

Connecting Different String Subclasses

The string classes defined in Listing 7.1 inherit the methods of the foundation class TString. This enables the characters of the diverse string subclasses to have characters inserted, deleted, and so on. However, there may be applications where a string of characters is viewed as words in one instance and as a list of items in another. The conversion between the various string classes is easy. The TString.SCopy and TString.Init methods provide the required tools. SCopy is utilized to return the entire string of an object, while method Init reinserts the same characters into an object of the other class. Consequently, you end up with multiple objects that contain the same data viewed differently. In such cases, there should be a main object whose strings are copied onto secondary objects. Keep in mind that the strings in the secondary objects need to be updated as the characters of the main object are altered.

The following program (Listing 7.3) demonstrates how the characters in a word object can be examined as a list of items. The following statement is responsible for passing the characters of object ObjWord to ObjItem:

```
ObjItem.Init(ObjWord.SCopy(1,80));
```

Once accessed by ObjItem, the comma-delimited items can be counted and extracted. The program performs the following:

1. Declares the objects for the various string classes.
2. Prompts to enter a string containing spaces and commas. The default string, "11 22,33 44,55 66", is used (and displayed) if you simply press the [Enter] key.
3. The program shows the following information:

   • The number of words in the string
   • The first and the last words
   • The number of items in the string
   • The first and last items

LISTING 7.3. Source code for the TSSTR2.PAS test program.

```
Program TesT_String_Objects_2;

{
 Program illustrates the conversion between
 the various string objects exported by unit StrObj.
}

Uses Crt, StrObj;

CONST DEFAULT_INPUT = '11 22,33 44,55 66';

VAR AString : MString;
    N, PosX : BYTE;
```

```
            AKey : CHAR;
            { ---- objects ---- }
            ObjWord : TWord;
            ObjItem : TItem;
            ObjTitle : TTitle;

        BEGIN
            ClrScr;
            { use ObjTitle to dislay program title }
            ObjTitle.Init ('String-Object Test Program #2');
            ObjTitle.Center (2);
            { test object ObjString }
            WRITE ('Enter a string with spaces and commas -> ');
            PosX := WhereX;
            READLN (AString);
            IF AString = '' THEN BEGIN
                AString := DEFAULT_INPUT;
                GotoXY (PosX, WhereY-1);
                WRITELN (AString)
            END;
            ObjWord.Init (AString);
            N := ObjWord.SLength (FALSE);
            WRITELN ('You typed ', N, ' words');
            WRITELN ('The first word is ', ObjWord.Get (1));
            WRITELN ('The last word is ', ObjWord.Get (N));
            WRITELN;
            { test object ObjItem }
            ObjItem.Init (ObjWord.SCopy (1,80));
            N := ObjItem.SLength (FALSE);
            WRITELN ('You entered ', N, ' items');
            WRITELN ('The first item is ', ObjItem.Get (1));
            WRITELN ('The last item is ', ObjItem.Get (N));
            WRITELN;
            WRITE ('Press any key to end the program ...');
            AKey := ReadKey;
        END.
```

The following screen image is obtained when you run the program and press [Enter] when prompted.

STRING-OBJECT TEST PROGRAM #2

Enter a string with spaces and commas -> **11 22,33 44,55 66**
You typed 4 words

```
The first word is 11
The last word is 66

You entered 3 items
The first item is 11 22
The last item is 55 66

Press any key to end the program . . .
```

Using Virtual Methods

The classes declared in Listing 7.1 spawn static objects. Their advantages (this is true for all static objects) are speed and the ability to alter the parameter list of overridden methods. The method SLength is a particular case for the latter aspect. Using virtual methods enables you to employ the heap rather than store the code and data of an object in the program's data/code segments. Listing 7.4 shows the declaration of the string classes with methods SLength and Get declared virtual. This dictates the following changes:

1. The former procedure Init is declared as a constructor.
2. The VIRTUAL; statement is appended after the declarations of the methods SLength and Get.
3. The virtual method SLength has been stripped of its Boolean argument. The price of introducing virtual methods is the loss of the Boolean arguments that enabled a message to instances of classes TWord, TItem, TToken, and TTitle to invoke the TString.SLength method.
4. The instances of class TToken are initialized using the inherited constructor Init in addition to the method InitDelim, which assigns a value to the fDelim data field.

LISTING 7.4. Declaration of the string classes using virtual methods.

```
CONST MAXLEN = 80;
      SPACE = ' ';
      COMMA = ',';

TYPE
   MSTRING = STRING[MAXLEN];
   TString = OBJECT
        fString : MSTRING;
```

```
            CONSTRUCTOR Init (S : MSTRING { input });
            FUNCTION SLength : BYTE; VIRTUAL;
            PROCEDURE SInsert (    SubStr  : MSTRING;   { input }
                                   Index   : BYTE       { input });
            PROCEDURE SDelete (    Index,             { input }
                                   Count : BYTE   { input });
            FUNCTION SCopy ( Index,            { input }
                             Count : BYTE    { input }) : MSTRING;
            FUNCTION Get (Index : BYTE { input }) : MSTRING; VIRTUAL;
            FUNCTION SPos (   SubStr  : MSTRING;    { input }
                              Index   : BYTE { input }) : BYTE;
            PROCEDURE UpperCase;
            PROCEDURE LowerCase;
     END;


     TWord = OBJECT (TString)
          FUNCTION SLength : BYTE; VIRTUAL;
          FUNCTION Get (Index : BYTE { input }) : MSTRING; VIRTUAL;
     END;


     TItem = OBJECT (TString)
          FUNCTION SLength : BYTE; VIRTUAL;
          FUNCTION Get (Index : BYTE { input }) : MSTRING; VIRTUAL;
     END;


     TToken = OBJECT (TString)
          fDelim : MSTRING;
          PROCEDURE InitDelim(Delim : MSTRING { input });
          FUNCTION SLength : BYTE; VIRTUAL;
          FUNCTION Get (Index : BYTE { input }) : MSTRING; VIRTUAL;
     END;


     TTitle = OBJECT (TWord)
          PROCEDURE Display; { uncentered }
          PROCEDURE Center (BlankLines : BYTE);
     END;
```

Most object-oriented programming languages and their implementations support dynamic objects only to foster polymorphism. This is why using Turbo Pascal 5.5 virtual methods is recommended for implementing polymorphism in a more complex hierarchy of classes.

8 | Array Objects

Arrays are among the most popular data structures. Languages such as BASIC, FORTRAN, Pascal, C, Ada, and Modula-2 support arrays of single and multiple dimensions. Arrays are implemented as static or dynamic structures. In this chapter dynamic arrays of strings are involved in building classes related to arrays, lists, and stacks. I chose to use strings as the basic type to simplify things, compared to building dynamic arrays of generic types.

Array Objects

An array is a data structure with multiple members, all having an identical type. The objects of the array class occupy a defined amount of memory. In static arrays, the required space is determined at compile time, while the space for dynamic arrays is resolved at runtime. Typically, arrays are partially occupied with data. Meaningful data is normally placed at the leading elements, with the trailing elements vacant.

In a dynamic array, the current size is the number of array elements containing meaningful data. The current size represents a partition between occupied and vacant array elements, as shown in Figure 8.1.

In a class of dynamic arrays, the list of data fields must include the maximum array size, the current array size, and the array of elements. The functionality associated with classes of arrays varies depending on the context of the application. Typically, the following actions are taken with dynamic arrays:

1. Creating and removing the dynamic array.
2. Storing and retrieving array elements.
3. Sorting the array.

FIGURE 8.1. The dynamic array.

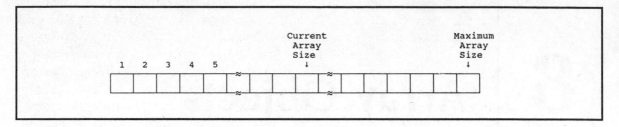

4. Searching for the occurrence of an array element.
5. Reversing the order of the array.

An additional data field is needed to keep track of the status of the array's order. This field is especially important if the search method implements an efficient search algorithm that relies on having the array ordered, such as the binary search.

Listing 8.1 on page 156 contains the source code for the ArrayObj library unit, which exports array-based objects. Based on the preceding discussion, I have defined the StrArray object as follows:

```
CONST STRING_SIZE = 80;

TYPE

LSTRING = STRING[STRING_SIZE];

StrArray = OBJECT
     MaxArraySize,
     VSize { current size } : WORD;
     VData : OneStringPtr;
     SortFlag : BOOLEAN;
     CONSTRUCTOR Init (NumElem : WORD { input });
     DESTRUCTOR Done;
     FUNCTION Store ( Data  : LSTRING; { input }
                      Index : WORD    { input })  : BOOLEAN;
     FUNCTION Recall (VAR Data  : LSTRING;  { output }
                      Index : WORD        { input }) : BOOLEAN;
     FUNCTION GetArSize : WORD;
     PROCEDURE Sort;
     FUNCTION Search (SearchData : LSTRING { input }) : WORD;
     PROCEDURE Reverse;
END;
```

VData is a pointer to a single-array type and is used with GetMem to allocate dynamic arrays. The maximum array size is stored in field MaxArraySize, while the current size is stored in field VSize. The SortFlag field is mainly used to keep track of the status of the array's order. The methods shown implements the functionality of this class, as outlined earlier. The method GetArSize is used to return the current size of the array, to avoid directly accessing the VSize field. The Search method returns the index of the matching element, or zero if no match is found. Using the SortFlag, the Search method is able to detect whether or not the array is in order. If not, it sends a self.Sort message to put the elements in the proper sequence.

I have included the constructor Init and the destructor Done. They are used to create and remove the dynamic array elements, respectively. You can easily add other methods to perform a linear search for unordered arrays or to carry out an insertion sort to maintain the order of the array.

Programming Note

Constructors and destructors are meant to be used with classes that possess virtual methods. A constructor of a class with any virtual method must be invoked as the first message sent to any object of that class. Otherwise the system hangs!

In this chapter I am using the constructor and destructor but no virtual method! I could have used ordinary procedures instead, but I chose to use the constructor and the destructor to highlight the methods that create and remove the dynamic data associated with the objects.

List Objects

Arrays can be used to implement lists. Usually, lists are maintained using pointers to nodes that are individually allocated at runtime. This approach has the advantage of not placing any constraint on the list size, except the availability of heap memory. In the case where you know the maximum list size at runtime, a dynamic array can suitably serve the purpose. The advantage of such an arrangement is that list elements can directly be accessed without having to scroll through the list, starting with the head of the list. Another advantage is that arrays can also implement doubly linked lists by virtue of accessing any element by its index.

Spawning a subclass of lists from a class of arrays enables the former to inherit the data fields and most of the functionality of the parent class. Most notably, sorting arrays yields ordered lists, which also enjoy the use of efficient searching algorithms. The added functionality of a list subclass is the query of empty/full state, insertion of new elements, and the deletion of current elements. The insertion method should implement its own insertion sort algorithm, instead of using the inherited sort method. The following is the declaration of the subclass of ordered lists of strings, StrList:

```
StrList = OBJECT (StrArray)
    FUNCTION IsFull : BOOLEAN;
    FUNCTION IsEmpty : BOOLEAN;
    FUNCTION Insert (Data : LSTRING { input }) : BOOLEAN;
    FUNCTION Delete (Data : LSTRING { input }) : BOOLEAN;
END;
```

The methods Insert and Delete return TRUE if they are successful, and FALSE otherwise. The objects of class StrList rely on the inherited Search method. However, you may be more concerned over the presence (or absence) of the sought element than about its index location. In this case, it is appropriate to compare the result returned by the message Search with zero. By contrast, the index returned by the Search message becomes relevant if you wish to traverse the list starting at the matching element. In this case, the inherited Recall method is also used to access neighboring list elements. Sending Store messages should be avoided since they will most likely overwrite current elements without maintaining an ordered list.

Stack Objects

Arrays may be employed to implement stacks. Usually, stacks are maintained using dynamically linked lists. This approach has the advantage of placing no constraint on the stack size except the availability of heap memory. In the case where you know the maximum stack size at runtime, a dynamic array may be acceptable for this purpose. The advantage of such a design is that stack elements can be directly accessed for operations such as swapping and scrolling. Figure 8.2 illustrates the use of an array to implement a stack.

Propagating a subclass of stacks from a class of arrays enables the former to acquire the data fields and most of the functionality of the parent class. The added functionality of a stack subclass is the query of empty/full state, pushing new

FIGURE 8.2. Using an array to implement a stack.

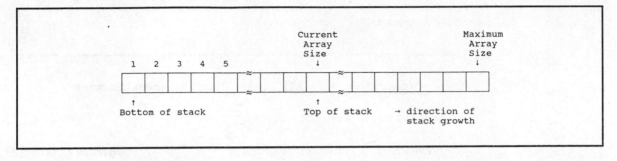

elements onto the stack, popping elements off the stack, swapping the two topmost elements, and scrolling the stack in either up or down directions. The following is the declaration of the subclass of stacked strings, StrStack:

```
StrStack = OBJECT (StrArray)
     FUNCTION IsFull : BOOLEAN;
     FUNCTION IsEmpty : BOOLEAN;
     FUNCTION Push (Data : LSTRING { input }) : BOOLEAN;
     FUNCTION Pop (VAR Data : LSTRING { output }) : BOOLEAN;
     PROCEDURE SwapXY;
     PROCEDURE RollUp;
     PROCEDURE RollDown;
     FUNCTION GetX : LSTRING;
END;
```

The methods Push and Pop return TRUE if they are successful, and FALSE otherwise. The SwapXY method exchanges the two topmost elements. The RollUp and RollDown methods roll the stack upward and downward, respectively. The method GetX returns the topmost stack element without popping it.

The Power of Inheritance

Objects of either class StrList or StrStack enjoy a dual nature due to their inheritance of class StrArray. For example, lists can behave as dynamic arrays of strings when they are sent array-oriented messages, or as lists when the messages of the StrList class are dispatched. A similar comment can be made for the stack objects.

LISTING 8.1. Source code for the ArrayObj library unit.

```pascal
UNIT ArrayObj;

{===============================================================

           Copyright (c) 1989, 1990   Namir Clement Shammas

    LIBRARY NAME: ArrayObj

    VERSION 1.0 FOR TURBO PASCAL                    DATE 6/21/1989

    PURPOSE: Exports arrays-based objects.

    ===============================================================}

{****************************************************************}
{***********************} INTERFACE {***************************}
{****************************************************************}

CONST STRING_SIZE = 80;

TYPE

LSTRING = STRING[STRING_SIZE];
OneString = ARRAY [1..1] OF LSTRING;
OneStringPtr = ^OneString;

StrArray = OBJECT
    MaxArraySize,
    VSize { current size } : WORD;
    VData : OneStringPtr;
    SortFlag : BOOLEAN;
    CONSTRUCTOR Init (NumElem : WORD { input });
    DESTRUCTOR Done;
    FUNCTION Store (Data    : LSTRING;   { input }
                    Index   : WORD       { input }) : BOOLEAN;
     FUNCTION Recall (VAR   Data    : LSTRING;   { output }
                            Index   : WORD       { input }) : BOOLEAN;
    FUNCTION GetArSize : WORD;
    PROCEDURE Sort;
    FUNCTION Search (SearchData : LSTRING { input }) : WORD;
    PROCEDURE Reverse;
END;
```

```
StrList = OBJECT (StrArray)
    FUNCTION IsFull : BOOLEAN;
    FUNCTION IsEmpty : BOOLEAN;
    FUNCTION Insert (Data : LSTRING { input }) : BOOLEAN;
    FUNCTION Delete (Data : LSTRING { input }) : BOOLEAN;
END;

StrStack = OBJECT (StrArray)
    FUNCTION IsFull : BOOLEAN;
    FUNCTION IsEmpty : BOOLEAN;
    FUNCTION Push (Data : LSTRING { input }) : BOOLEAN;
    FUNCTION Pop (VAR Data : LSTRING { output }) : BOOLEAN;
    PROCEDURE SwapXY;
    PROCEDURE RollUp;
    PROCEDURE RollDown;
    FUNCTION GetX : LSTRING;
END;

{****************************************************************}
{*********************} IMPLEMENTATION {************************}
{****************************************************************}

{$R-}

CONSTRUCTOR StrArray.Init (NumElem : WORD { input });
BEGIN
    GetMem (VData, NumElem * STRING_SIZE);
    MaxArraySize := NumElem;
    VSize := 0;
    SortFlag := FALSE;
    { assign null strings to dynamic array }
    WHILE NumElem > 0 DO BEGIN
        VData^ [NumElem] := '';
        DEC (NumElem)
    END;
END;

DESTRUCTOR StrArray.Done;
BEGIN
    FreeMem (VData, MaxArraySize * STRING_SIZE);
    VData := NIL;
    MaxArraySize := 0;
    VSize := 0;
END;
```

```
PROCEDURE StrArray.Sort;

VAR Offset, I, J : WORD;
    TempStr : LSTRING;

BEGIN
    IF VSize < 2 THEN EXIT;
    Offset := VSize;
    WHILE Offset > 1 DO BEGIN
        Offset := Offset div 2;
        REPEAT
            SortFlag := TRUE;
            FOR J := 1 TO VSize - Offset DO BEGIN
                I := J + Offset;
                IF VData^[I] < VData^[J] THEN BEGIN
                    TempStr := VData^[I];
                    VData^[I] := VData^[J];
                    VData^[J] := TempStr;
                    SortFlag := FALSE
                END; { IF }
            END; { FOR }
        UNTIL SortFlag;
    END; { WHILE }
END;


FUNCTION StrArray.Search(SearchData : LSTRING { input }) : WORD;

VAR Low, High, Median : WORD;
    NotFound : BOOLEAN;

BEGIN
    IF NOT SortFlag THEN { need to be sorted }
        Sort;
    Low := 1;
    High := VSize;
    REPEAT
        Median := (Low + High) div 2;
        IF SearchData < VData^[Median] THEN
            High := Median - 1
        ELSE
            Low := Median + 1;
    UNTIL (SearchData = VData^[Median]) OR (Low > High);
```

```
            IF SearchData = VData^[Median] THEN
                Search := Median
        ELSE
                Search := 0;
    END;


PROCEDURE StrArray.Reverse;

VAR I, J : BYTE;
    TempStr : LSTRING;

BEGIN
    FOR I := 1 TO VSize div 2 DO BEGIN
        J := VSize + 1 - I;
        TempStr := VData^[I];
        VData^[I] := VData^[J];
        VData^[J] := TempStr
    END;
END;


FUNCTION StrArray.Store(  Data    : LSTRING;   { input }
                          Index   : WORD       { input })
                                  : BOOLEAN;
BEGIN
    IF Index <= MaxArraySize THEN BEGIN
        IF Index > VSize THEN
            VSize := Index;
        VData^[Index] := Data;
        SortFlag := FALSE;
        Store := TRUE
    END
    ELSE
        Store := FALSE
END;


FUNCTION StrArray.Recall(VAR  Data    : LSTRING;   { output }
                              Index   : WORD       { input })
                                      : BOOLEAN;
BEGIN
    IF Index <= VSize THEN BEGIN
        Data := VData^[Index];
        Recall := TRUE
    END
```

```
        ELSE
            Recall := FALSE
END;


FUNCTION StrArray.GetArSize : WORD;
BEGIN
    GetArSize := VSize;
END;


FUNCTION StrList.IsFull : BOOLEAN;
BEGIN
    IsFull := VSize = MaxArraySize
END;


FUNCTION StrList.IsEmpty : BOOLEAN;
BEGIN
    IsEmpty := VSize = 0
END;


FUNCTION StrList.Insert (Data  : LSTRING { input })
                                  : BOOLEAN;


VAR Index, I : WORD;
    NotFound : BOOLEAN;


BEGIN
    SortFlag := TRUE;
    IF NOT IsFull THEN BEGIN
        NotFound := TRUE;
        Index := 1;
        WHILE (Index <= VSize) AND NotFound DO
            IF Data < VData^[Index] THEN
                NotFound := FALSE
            ELSE
                INC(Index);

        IF Index <= VSize THEN
            FOR I := VSize DOWNTO Index DO
                VData^[I+1] := VData^[I];
        VData^[Index] := Data;
        INC(VSize);
        Insert := TRUE
    END
```

```
            ELSE
                Insert := FALSE;
    END;


    FUNCTION StrList.Delete(Data  : LSTRING { input })
                                  : BOOLEAN;


    VAR Index, I : WORD;
        NotFound : BOOLEAN;


    BEGIN
        IF NOT IsEmpty THEN BEGIN
            NotFound := TRUE;
            Index := 1;
            WHILE (Index <= VSize) AND NotFound DO BEGIN
                IF Data = VData^[Index] THEN
                    NotFound := FALSE
                ELSE
                    INC(Index);
            END;
            IF NOT NotFound THEN BEGIN
                FOR I := Index TO VSize-1 DO
                    VData^[I] := VData^[I+1];
                DEC(VSize);
                Delete := TRUE
            END
            ELSE
                Delete := FALSE
        END
        ELSE
            Delete := FALSE;
    END;


    FUNCTION StrStack.IsFull : BOOLEAN;
    BEGIN
        IsFull := VSize = MaxArraySize
    END;


    FUNCTION StrStack.IsEmpty : BOOLEAN;
    BEGIN
        IsEmpty := VSize = 0
    END;
```

```
FUNCTION StrStack.Push(Data   : LSTRING { input })
                               : BOOLEAN;
BEGIN
    IF NOT IsFull THEN BEGIN
        INC(VSize);
        VData^[VSize] := Data;
        Push := TRUE
    END
    ELSE
        Push := FALSE;
END;


FUNCTION StrStack.Pop(VAR Data : LSTRING { output }) : BOOLEAN;
BEGIN
    IF NOT IsEmpty THEN BEGIN
        Data := VData^[VSize];
        DEC(VSize);
        Pop := TRUE
    END
    ELSE
        Pop := FALSE;
END;


PROCEDURE StrStack.SwapXY;

VAR TempStr : LSTRING;

BEGIN
    IF VSize >= 2 THEN BEGIN
        TempStr := VData^[VSize];
        VData^[VSize] := VData^[VSize-1];
        VData^[VSize-1] := TempStr
    END;
END;


PROCEDURE StrStack.RollDown;

VAR TempStr : LSTRING;
    I : WORD;

BEGIN
    IF VSize < 2 THEN
        EXIT;
    TempStr := VData^[1];
```

```
            FOR I := 1 TO VSize -1 DO
                VData^[I] := VData^[I+1];
            VData^[VSize] := TempStr
        END;


    PROCEDURE StrStack.RollUp;


    VAR TempStr : LSTRING;
        I : WORD;


    BEGIN
        IF VSize < 2 THEN
            EXIT;
        TempStr := VData^[VSize];
        FOR I := VSize DOWNTO 2 DO
            VData^[I] := VData^[I-1];
        VData^[1] := TempStr
    END;


    FUNCTION StrStack.GetX : LSTRING;
    BEGIN
        IF VSize > 0 THEN
            GetX := VData^[VSize]
        ELSE
            GetX := '';
    END;


    END.
```

Listing 8.2 shows the code for a test program that sends messages to the various types of objects exported by the ArrayObj library unit. The program performs the following steps:

1. Declares the tested objects.
2. Allocates the dynamic space for the array of strings.
3. Prompts you to enter a number of strings.
4. Sorts the strings.
5. Displays the sorted array and prompts you to enter a search string. The outcome of the search is displayed.
6. Repeats step 5 until you press the [Enter] key.
7. Deallocates the dynamic memory for the array of strings.
8. Allocates the dynamic space for the list of strings.

9.   Prompts you to enter a number of strings. The input strings are inserted so that the order of the list is maintained.
10.   Displays the ordered list and prompts you to enter a search string. The outcome of the search is displayed.
11.   Repeats step 10 until you press the [Enter] key.
12.   Deallocates the dynamic memory for the list of strings.
13.   Allocates the dynamic space for the stack of strings.
14.   Prompts you to enter a number of strings. The input strings are pushed onto the stack.
15.   Rolls the stack upward twice.
16.   Pops and displays the stack elements.
17.   Deallocates the dynamic memory for the array of strings.

LISTING 8.2. Source code for test program TSARRAY.PAS.

```
Program Test_Array_Objects;

{
 Program tests the various array-based classes exported by
 library unit ArrayObj:

    + Sorted array of strings.
    + Ordered list of strings.
    + Stack of strings.
}

Uses Crt, ArrayObj;

CONST TEST_SIZE = 5;

VAR AnArray : StrArray;
    AList : StrList;
    AStack : StrStack;
    I : WORD;
    S : LSTRING;
    Akey : CHAR;

BEGIN
    ClrScr;
    { test the AnArray object }
    AnArray.Init(TEST_SIZE);
```

```
FOR I := 1 TO TEST_SIZE DO BEGIN
    WRITE ('Enter array string # ',I:2,' -> ');
    READLN (S);
    IF NOT AnArray.Store (S, I) THEN
        WRITELN ('Out of bound index');
END;

AnArray.Sort; { sort the array }
REPEAT
    ClrScr;
    WRITELN ('Sorted array is:'); WRITELN;
    FOR I := 1 TO TEST_SIZE DO
        IF AnArray.Recall (S, I) THEN
            WRITELN (I:2,' ',S);
    WRITELN;
    WRITE ('Search for string (press [Enter] to exit) -> ');
    READLN (S);
    IF S <> '' THEN BEGIN
        I := AnArray.Search (S);
        IF I > 0 THEN
            WRITELN ('Matches element ', I)
        ELSE
            WRITELN ('has no match');
        WRITELN;
        WRITE ('Press space bar to continue ...');
        AKey := ReadKey;
    END;
    WRITELN;
UNTIL S = '';
AnArray.Done; { deallocate dynamic memory }

{ test the AList object }
AList.Init (TEST_SIZE);
FOR I := 1 TO TEST_SIZE DO BEGIN
    WRITE ('Enter list string # ',I:2,' -> ');
    READLN (S);
    IF NOT AList.Insert (S) THEN
        WRITELN ('List is full');
END;

REPEAT
    ClrScr;
    WRITELN ('Ordered list is'); WRITELN;
```

```
        FOR I := 1 TO TEST_SIZE DO
            IF AList.Recall(S, I) THEN
                WRITELN(I:2,' ',S);
        WRITELN;
        WRITE('Search for string (press [Enter] to exit) -> ');
        READLN(S);
        IF S <> '' THEN BEGIN
            I := AList.Search(S);
            IF I > 0 THEN
                WRITELN('Matches element ', I)
            ELSE
                WRITELN('has no match');
            WRITELN;
            WRITE('Press space bar to continue ...');
            AKey := ReadKey;
        END;
        WRITELN;
    UNTIL S = '';
    AList.Done; { deallocate dynamic memory }

    { test the AStack object }
    AStack.Init(TEST_SIZE);
    FOR I := 1 TO TEST_SIZE DO BEGIN
        WRITE('Enter stack string # ',I:2,' -> ');
        READLN(S);
        IF NOT AStack.Push(S) THEN
            WRITELN('Stack is full');
    END;
    WRITELN;
    WRITELN('Popping the stack after rolling it up twice');
    AStack.RollUp;
    AStack.RollUp;
    WHILE AStack.Pop(S) DO
        WRITELN(S);
    WRITELN;
    AStack.Done; { deallocate dynamic memory }
    WRITELN;
    WRITE('Press any key to end the program ...');
    AKey := ReadKey;
END.
```

A sample run is shown next. The session includes the following:

1. The names of five capitals stored in the AnArray object.

2.   The names of five states stored in the AList object.
3.   The names of five colors stored in the AStack object.

```
Enter array string # 1 -> Paris
Enter array string # 2 -> London
Enter array string # 3 -> Berlin
Enter array string # 4 -> Rome
Enter array string # 5 -> Madrid

Sorted array is:

1  Berlin
2  London
3  Madrid
4  Paris
5  Rome

Search for string (press [Enter] to exit )-> London
Matches element 2

Press space bar to continue ...

Search for string (press [Enter] to exit )-> <[Enter] key>

Enter list string # 1 -> California
Enter list string # 2 -> Virginia
Enter list string # 3 -> Michigan
Enter list string # 4 -> Alaska
Enter list string # 5 -> New York

Ordered list is

1  Alaska
2  California
3  Michigan
4  New York
5  Virginia

Search for string (press [Enter] to exit )-> New York
Matches element 4

Press space bar to continue ...

Search for string (press [Enter] to exit )-> <[Enter] key>
```

```
Enter stack string #  1 -> Red
Enter stack string #  2 -> White
Enter stack string #  3 -> Blue
Enter stack string #  4 -> Green
Enter stack string #  5 -> Yellow

Popping the stack after rolling it up twice
Blue
White
Red
Yellow
Green
```

9 | Vector and Matrix Objects

This chapter looks at classes and objects that model floating-point vectors (*vector* is a mathematically oriented synonym for array) and matrices. Such objects are related data structures popular in number-crunching applications. The chapter also presents subclasses that take the general-purpose matrix classes one step further.

The Basic Ingredients

Vectors and matrices may be considered collections of data arranged in single and multiple dimensions, respectively. Vectors and matrices may be either static or dynamic. The static type has its space preallocated at compile time, while the dynamic type offers tailor-fit sixes at runtime. If you use static vectors and matrices, and you want to use a single data type for vectors and a single type for matrices, you will have to choose a size big enough to meet maximum requirements. This often leaves you with extra unused space. Dynamic vectors and matrices are sized more flexibly. Since they are accessed using pointers, no vector or matrix data type needs to be declared. If your data fits in the dynamic vectors or matrices and does not increase in size, then the allocated size and the working size are the same. You can still dynamically allocate a bit more space then the initial requirement. Unlike static vectors and matrices, the extra space is also tailor-fit and may vary between different vectors or matrices.

Vector Class

The dynamic vectors allocate a maximum space and also keep track of the working size, usually close to the maximum space. The maximum and working sizes are data fields in the dynamic vector class. The other data component is the pointer to the allocated memory. These data fields are involved in almost all vector classes. By contrast, the methods reflecting the functionality of the vector class depend very much on the client applications. A few fundamental methods are always employed, like creating and removing the dynamic space for the vector's data, and storing and recalling individual elements. Other methods are left to the software engineer's own discretion. The following is how I declared the class of vectors RealVector:

```
RealVector = OBJECT
    MaxVectorSize,
    VSize : WORD;
    VecPtr : OneRealPtr;
    VectorOpStatus : BOOLEAN;
    CONSTRUCTOR Init (MaxElem : WORD { input });
    DESTRUCTOR Done;
    PROCEDURE Store ( Index   : WORD; { input   }
                        X      : REAL { input   });
    PROCEDURE Recall ( Index  : WORD; { input   }
                    VAR X      : REAL { output  });
    FUNCTION CurrentSize : WORD;
    PROCEDURE Fill (  FillValue : REAL; { input  }
                      NumElem   : WORD  { input });
    PROCEDURE AddScalar (Scalar : REAL { input });
    PROCEDURE MultScalar (Scalar : REAL { input });
    PROCEDURE AddVector (VectB : RealVector { input } );
    FUNCTION MultVector (VectB : RealVector { input }) : REAL;
END;
```

The first three data fields implement the items that were discussed. The Boolean VectorOpStatus is used to report any error detected by a method within this class. An alternate route is to eliminate VectorOpStatus and make all the methods Boolean functions that return the error status. As it stands, VectorOpStatus is assigned TRUE if a message is executed successfully, and FALSE if otherwise.

The constructor, destructor, and the next two methods correspond to the four fundamental methods that I described earlier. The other methods are the ones that I chose to implement. The CurentSize method is used to query the working size. I chose not to implement a similar method to query the maximum size, since that attribute must be supplied by the client applications and is therefore already known. The method Fill fills the first NumElem elements of the vector object with FillValue and is used to quickly initialize all or part of a vector. The AddScalar and MultScalar methods add a scalar to and multiply a scalar with the elements of a vector. The elements affected are in the range of indexes MultVector 1..VSize. The AddVector

---

Programming Note

Constructors and destructors are meant to be used with classes that possess virtual methods. A constructor of a class with any virtual method must be invoked as the first message sent to any object of that class. Otherwise the system hangs!

In this chapter I am using the constructor and destructor but no virtual method! I could have used ordinary procedures instead, but I chose to use the constructor and the destructor to highlight the methods that create and remove the dynamic data.

---

and MultVector methods add and multiply vectors, respectively. The vector object receiving and AddVector or MultVector message must have the same VSize value as the argument vector object. In the case of AddVector, the elements of the object receiving the message are altered. In the case of MultVector, the result is a single value, returned as a function value. The methods AddVector and Vector demonstrate how two RealVector objects interact.

Matrix Class

Building a class of matrices follows a logic similar to that of the vector class. The maximum number of rows and columns, the number of working rows and columns, and the pointer to the matrix are the required data fields. The elements of the dynamic matrix are stored contiguously and are accessed as an unwrapped single-dimension array. The minimal set of methods includes a constructor and a destructor for the creation and removal of the dynamic space, respectively; a method for mapping matrix coordinates onto the single-dimension dynamic array; and methods for storing and recalling data from individual elements. Again, other methods depend on the applied functionality of this class. The following is the declaration of the RealMatrix class:

```
RealMatrix = OBJECT
    NRow, NCol,
    Rows, Cols : WORD;
    MatPtr : OneRealPtr;
    { Determinant : REAL; }
```

```
       MatOpStatus : BOOLEAN;
       FUNCTION Loc (    Row,            { input  }
                         Col : WORD   { input }) : WORD;
       CONSTRUCTOR Init ( NumRows,          { input  }
                          NumCols : WORD { input });
       DESTRUCTOR Done;
       PROCEDURE Store (  Row,             { input  }
                          Col : WORD;   { input  }
                          X   : REAL     { input });
       PROCEDURE Recall (    Row,              { input   }
                             Col  : WORD;  { input    }
                      VAR    X        : REAL  { output });
       PROCEDURE QuerySize (VAR   NumRows,           { output }
                                  NumCols : WORD   { output });
       PROCEDURE Fill ( FillValue : REAL; { input  }
                        RowCount,         { input  }
                        ColCount  : WORD { input });
       PROCEDURE AddScalar (Scalar  : REAL { input });
       PROCEDURE MultScalar (Scalar : REAL { input });
       PROCEDURE MultVector (
                    InVect    : RealVector;   { input  }
                 VAR OutVect : RealVector    { output });
       PROCEDURE MultMatrix(  InMat   : RealMatrix; { input }
                         VAR  OutMat  : RealMatrix   { output });
  {
       PROCEDURE Invert;
        PROCEDURE Solve (    MatA    : RealMatrix; { input  }
                             VectB   : RealVector   { input });
  }
     END;
```

I have commented the Determinant data field as a strong candidate for inclusion if you are doing matrix inversion. The MatOpStatus is used to report the success status of this class's methods and is used in the same manner as VectorOpStatus.

The first five methods implemented the minimal set of methods that I mentioned earlier. The rest of the methods represent a collection I felt to be suitable for this chapter. The QuerySize method supplies its parameters with the working row and column sizes. The Fill method enables you to assign FillValue to the upper left submatrix defined by [I..RowCount, 1..ColCount]. The AddScalar and MultScalar methods add and multiply the elements of the working submatrix area by Scalar, respectively.

FIGURE 9.1. Matrix multiplication rule.

$$
\overset{\text{4 by 3 matrix}}{
\begin{bmatrix}
a_{11} & a_{12} & a_{13} \\
a_{21} & a_{22} & a_{23} \\
a_{31} & a_{32} & a_{33} \\
a_{41} & a_{42} & a_{43}
\end{bmatrix}}
\;\times\;
\overset{\text{3 by 4 matrix}}{
\begin{bmatrix}
b_{11} & b_{12} & b_{13} & b_{14} \\
b_{21} & b_{22} & b_{23} & b_{43} \\
b_{31} & b_{32} & b_{33} & b_{43}
\end{bmatrix}}
\;=\;
\overset{\text{3 by 3 matrix}}{
\begin{bmatrix}
c_{11} & c_{12} & c_{13} \\
c_{21} & c_{22} & c_{23} \\
c_{31} & c_{32} & c_{33}
\end{bmatrix}}
$$

The MultVector method multiplies a matrix and a vector, yielding a vector. This is a rather unusual method—it enables the matrix object receiving a MultVector message to interact with a RealVector object and creat a new RealVector object, passed by reference. The resulting vector may be dynamically created by the message, if needed.

The MultMatrix method multiplies two matrices, yielding a new matrix. This new matrix may be dynamically created by the message, if necessary. The method verifies that the number of columns in the matrix object and the number of rows in the argument InMat are equal. This is required by the mathematical definition of matrix multiplication, illustrated in Figure 9.1.

The methods Invert and Solve are not implemented here due to their length. However, since they are popular matrix operations, I inserted them as comments to emphasize their importance. Their implementation is left as an exercise to the reader.

SpreadSheet Class

Spreadsheets are powerful and sophisticated data structures composed of a matrix of data and formulas. This matrix and a battery of commands are the ingredients of popular applications such as Lotus 1-2-3.

I present the SpreadSheet class as a special subclass of RealMatrix (see Figure 9.2). I limited the features of this new subclass to the following simple matrix column manipulations:

1. Filling a column with a fixed value.
2. Obtaining the total or subtotal of a column.
3. Adding and multiplying column elements with a scalar.

FIGURE 9.2. The SpreadSheet object.

```
                             SpreadSheet object

           column # 1     2     3                                   n
                    ↓     ↓     ↓                                   ↓

               ⎡ a₁₁   a₁₂   a₁₃ ··································· a₁n ⎤
               ⎢                                                       ⎥
               ⎢ a₂₁   a₂₂   a₂₃ ··································· a₂n ⎥
               ⎢                                                       ⎥
               ⎢ a₃₁   a₃₂   a₃₃ ··································· a₃n ⎥
               ⎢                                                       ⎥
               ⎢ a₄₁   a₄₂   a₄₃ ··································· a₄n ⎥
               ⎢                                                       ⎥
               ⎢ ·····················································  ⎥
               ⎢                                                       ⎥
               ⎣ aₘ₁   aₘ₂   aₘ₃ ··································· aₘn ⎦
```

4. Adding two columns and placing the results in a separate column.
5. Multiplying two columns and assigning the results to a third column.

The following is the declaration of the SpreadSheet class:

```
SpreadSheet = OBJECT (RealMatrix)
      PROCEDURE FillColumn (  ColIndex  : WORD; { input }
                              Scalar    : REAL { input });
      FUNCTION SumUp ( ColIndex,              { input }
                       FirstRow,              { input }
                       LastRow  : WORD { input }) : REAL;
      PROCEDURE AddToColumn ( ColIndex  : WORD; { input }
                              Scalar    : REAL { input });
      PROCEDURE MultColumn (  ColIndex  : WORD; { input }
                              Scalar    : REAL { input });
      PROCEDURE AddColumns (  ColA,              { input }
                              ColB,              { input }
                              ColC : WORD   { input });
      PROCEDURE MultColumns ( ColA,              { input }
                              ColB,              { input }
                              ColC : WORD   { input });
      END;
```

All of the data fields required by the SpreadSheet class are inherited. The various methods presented manipulate the data within the matrix-typed object. You are welcome to expand on this class and develop a class with a versatile set of methods.

Statistics Matrix Class

Spreadsheets are good repositories for financial and statistical data. I will focus on the statistical method of performing linear regression between two columns in a matrix. The statistical matrix object is pictured in Figure 9.3.

To build a subclass for linear regression, there are two sets of data fields to consider. The first set is made up of fields that store information necessary to perform the statistical number crunching. They are the column indices, the various statistical summations, and the regression results (slope, intercept, and coefficient of correlation). The second group of data fields is optional, consisting of data fields that store intermediate results and sequence-monitoring fields. The latter fields are used to ensure that the proper sequence of messages has been issued. The following is the declaration of class StatMatrix:

```
StatMatStatus = (no_operation, select_columns, calc_sums);

StatMatrix = OBJECT (SpreadSheet)
    ColX,
    ColY : WORD;
    Sum,
    SumX,
    SumXX,
    SumY,
    SumYY,
    SumXY,
    MeanX,
    SdevX,
    MeanY,
```

FIGURE 9.3. The statistical matrix object.

column of X's ↓ column of Y's ↓

$$\begin{bmatrix} a_{11} & \cdots & a_{1j} & \cdots & a_{1k} & \cdots & a_{1n} \\ a_{21} & \cdots & a_{2j} & \cdots & a_{2k} & \cdots & a_{2n} \\ a_{31} & \cdots & a_{3j} & \cdots & a_{3k} & \cdots & a_{3n} \\ a_{41} & \cdots & a_{4j} & \cdots & a_{4k} & \cdots & a_{4n} \\ \cdots & \cdots & \cdots & \cdots & \cdots & \cdots & \cdots \\ a_{m1} & \cdots & a_{mj} & \cdots & a_{mk} & \cdots & a_{mn} \end{bmatrix}$$

```
        SdevY,
        fSlope,
        fIntercept,
        fRSqr : REAL;
        CalcStatus : StatMatStatus;
        PROCEDURE SelectColumns( X,          { input }
                                 Y : WORD  { input });
        PROCEDURE CalcSums;
        FUNCTION Slope : REAL;
        FUNCTION Intercept : REAL;
        FUNCTION Rsqr : REAL;
        FUNCTION NumData : REAL;
    END;
```

where StatMatStatus is an enumerated type for ensuring the correct sequence of messages:

```
        StatMatStatus = (no_operation, select_columns, calc_sums);
```

The method SelectColumns is used to pick columns for the regression analysis. The method CalcSum performs all of the statistical computations—initializing the statistical summations, updating them, and calculating the regression statistics. The methods Slope, Intercept, Rsqr, and NumData are used to query the results of the regression.

LISTING 9.1. The source code for the VecMatOb library unit.

```
        UNIT VecMatOb;


{===================================================================


           Copyright (c) 1989, 1990  Namir Clement Shammas

           LIBRARY NAME: VecMatOb

           VERSION 1.0 FOR TURBO PASCAL                    DATE 6/21/1989

           PURPOSE: exports classes of vectors, matrices,
                    statistical matrices, and simple spreadsheets


====================================================================}
```

```
{*****************************************************************}
{***********************} INTERFACE {**************************}
{*****************************************************************}
{$R-}

TYPE

OneReal = ARRAY [1..1] OF REAL;
OneRealPtr = ^OneReal;


RealVector = OBJECT
    MaxVectorSize,
    VSize : WORD;
    VecPtr : OneRealPtr;
    VectorOpStatus : BOOLEAN;
    CONSTRUCTOR Init (MaxElem : WORD { input });
    DESTRUCTOR Done;
    FUNCTION CurrentSize : WORD;
    PROCEDURE Store ( Index    : WORD; { input }
                      X        : REAL { input });
    PROCEDURE Recall ( Index   : WORD; { input }
                  VAR X        : REAL { output });
    PROCEDURE Fill (   FillValue : REAL; { input }
                      NumElem   : WORD { input });
    PROCEDURE AddScalar (Scalar : REAL { input });
    PROCEDURE MultScalar (Scalar : REAL { input });
    PROCEDURE AddVector (VectB : RealVector { input } );
    FUNCTION MultVector (VectB : RealVector { input }) : REAL;
END;


RealMatrix = OBJECT
    NRow, NCol,
    Rows, Cols : WORD;
    MatPtr : OneRealPtr;
    Determinant : REAL;
    MatOpStatus : BOOLEAN;
    FUNCTION Loc (  Row,              { input }
                    Col : WORD   { input }) : WORD;
    CONSTRUCTOR Init (   NumRows,         { input }
                      NumCols : WORD    { input });
    DESTRUCTOR Done;
    PROCEDURE QuerySize (VAR  NumRows,           { output }
                        NumCols : WORD   { output });
    PROCEDURE Store (  Row,             { input }
```

```
                          Col : WORD;  { input  }
                          X   : REAL   { input });
        PROCEDURE Recall(     Row,          { input  }
                              Col  : WORD; { input  }
                        VAR X    : REAL  { output });
        PROCEDURE Fill(       FillValue : REAL; { input  }
                             RowCount,          { input  }
                             ColCount  : WORD  { input });
        PROCEDURE AddScalar(Scalar : REAL { input });
        PROCEDURE MultScalar(Scalar : REAL { input });
        PROCEDURE MultVector(
                   InVect : RealVector;  { input  }
              VAR  OutVect : RealVector   { output });
        PROCEDURE MultMatrix( InMat   : RealMatrix;  { input  }
                        VAR OutMat  : RealMatrix    { output });
    {
        PROCEDURE Invert;
        PROCEDURE Solve(     MatA    : RealMatrix;  { input  }
                             VectB   : RealVector   { input });
    }
    END;


    SpreadSheet = OBJECT (RealMatrix)
        PROCEDURE FillColumn(  ColIndex  : WORD; { input  }
                               Scalar    : REAL { input });
        FUNCTION SumUp(   ColIndex,           { input  }
                          FirstRow,           { input  }
                          LastRow  : WORD { input }) : REAL;
        PROCEDURE AddToColumn( ColIndex  : WORD; { input  }
                               Scalar    : REAL { input });
        PROCEDURE MultColumn(  ColIndex  : WORD; { input  }
                               Scalar    : REAL { input });
        PROCEDURE AddColumns(  ColA,            { input  }
                               ColB,            { input  }
                               ColC : WORD   { input });
        PROCEDURE MultColumns( ColA,            { input  }
                               ColB,            { input  }
                               ColC : WORD   { input });

    END;

    StatMatStatus = (no_operation, select_columns, calc_sums);

    StatMatrix = OBJECT (SpreadSheet)
```

```
            ColX,
            ColY : WORD;
            Sum,
            SumX,
            SumXX,
            SumY,
            SumYY,
            SumXY,
            MeanX,
            SdevX,
            MeanY,
            SdevY,
            fSlope,
            fIntercept,
            fRSqr : REAL;
            CalcStatus : StatMatStatus;
            PROCEDURE SelectColumns ( X,          { input }
                                      Y : WORD  { input });
            PROCEDURE CalcSums;
            FUNCTION Slope : REAL;
            FUNCTION Intercept : REAL;
            FUNCTION Rsqr : REAL;
            FUNCTION NumData : REAL;
        END;


{*********************************************************************}
{*********************} IMPLEMENTATION {*********************}
{*********************************************************************}


CONSTRUCTOR RealVector.Init (MaxElem : WORD { input });
BEGIN
    MaxVectorSize := MaxElem;
    VSize := 0;
    GetMem (VecPtr, MaxElem * SizeOf (REAL));
    VectorOpStatus := TRUE;
END;

DESTRUCTOR RealVector.Done;
BEGIN
    MaxVectorSize := 0;
    VSize := 0;
    FreeMem (VecPtr, MaxVectorSize * SizeOf (REAL));
```

```
        VecPtr := NIL;
        VectorOpStatus := TRUE;
END;

FUNCTION RealVector.CurrentSize : WORD;
BEGIN
        VectorOpStatus := TRUE;
        CurrentSize := VSize
END;

PROCEDURE RealVector.Store(   Index    : WORD; { input  }
                              X        : REAL  { input });
BEGIN
        IF Index > MaxVectorSize THEN BEGIN
            VectorOpStatus := FALSE;
            EXIT
        END;
        VecPtr^[Index] := X;
        IF Index > VSize THEN
            VSize := Index;
        VectorOpStatus := TRUE
END;

PROCEDURE RealVector.Recall( Index    : WORD; { input  }
                             VAR X     : REAL  { output });
BEGIN
        IF Index > VSize THEN BEGIN
            VectorOpStatus := FALSE;
            X := 0;
            EXIT
        END;
        X := VecPtr^[Index];
        VectorOpStatus := TRUE
END;

PROCEDURE RealVector.Fill( FillValue : REAL;   { input  }
                           NumElem    : WORD    { input });

VAR I : WORD;

BEGIN
        IF NumElem > MaxVectorSize THEN
            NumElem := MaxVectorSize;
        VSize := NumElem;
```

```
        FOR I := 1 TO NumElem DO
            VecPtr^[I] := FillValue;
        VectorOpStatus := TRUE
END;


PROCEDURE RealVector.AddScalar(Scalar : REAL { input });

VAR I : WORD;

BEGIN
    FOR I := 1 TO VSize DO
        VecPtr^[I] := VecPtr^[I] + Scalar;
    VectorOpStatus := TRUE
END;


PROCEDURE RealVector.MultScalar(Scalar : REAL { input });

VAR I : WORD;

BEGIN
    FOR I := 1 TO VSize DO
        VecPtr^[I] := VecPtr^[I] * Scalar;
    VectorOpStatus := TRUE
END;


PROCEDURE RealVector.AddVector(VectB : RealVector { input } );

VAR I : WORD;

BEGIN
    IF VSize <> VectB.VSize THEN BEGIN
        VectorOpStatus := FALSE;
        EXIT;
    END;
    FOR I := 1 TO VSize DO
        VecPtr^[I] := VecPtr^[I] +
                        VectB.VecPtr^[I];
    VectorOpStatus := TRUE
END;


FUNCTION RealVector.MultVector(VectB : RealVector { input }) : REAL;

VAR I : WORD;
    Sum : REAL;
```

```
BEGIN
    IF VSize <> VectB.VSize THEN BEGIN
        VectorOpStatus := FALSE;
        MultVector := 0;
        EXIT;
    END;
    Sum := 0;
    FOR I := 1 TO VSize DO
        Sum := Sum + VecPtr^[I] * VectB.VecPtr^[I];
    VectorOpStatus := TRUE;
    MultVector := Sum { return function value }
END;



FUNCTION RealMatrix.Loc(    Row,            { input }
                            Col : WORD { input }) : WORD;
BEGIN
    Loc := (Col - 1) * NRow + Row
END;



CONSTRUCTOR RealMatrix.Init( NumRows,            { input }
                             NumCols : WORD  { input });
BEGIN
    NCol := NumCols;
    NRow := NumRows;
    Rows := 0;
    Cols := 0;
    GetMem(MatPtr, NumCols * NumRows * SizeOf(REAL));
    MatOpStatus := TRUE;
END;



DESTRUCTOR RealMatrix.Done;
BEGIN
    NCol := 0;
    NRow := 0;
    Rows := 0;
    Cols := 0;
    FreeMem(MatPtr, NRow * NCol * SizeOf(REAL));
    MatPtr := NIL;
    MatOpStatus := TRUE;
END;
```

```
PROCEDURE RealMatrix.QuerySize(VAR NumRows,              { output }
                                  NumCols : WORD { output });
BEGIN
    NumRows := Rows;
    NumCols := Cols;
    MatOpStatus := TRUE
END;

PROCEDURE RealMatrix.Store( Row,          { input }
                            Col : WORD; { input }
                            X   : REAL { input });
BEGIN
    IF  (Row > NRow) OR
        (Col > NCol) THEN BEGIN
            MatOpStatus := FALSE;
            EXIT
    END;
    IF Row > Rows THEN
        Rows := Row;
    IF Col > Cols THEN
        Cols := Col;
    MatPtr^[Loc(Row,Col)] := X;
    MatOpStatus := TRUE
END;

PROCEDURE RealMatrix.Recall( Row,          { input }
                             Col : WORD; { input }
                         VAR X   : REAL { output });
BEGIN
    IF  (Row > Rows) OR
        (Col > Cols) THEN BEGIN
            MatOpStatus := FALSE;
            X := 0;
            EXIT
    END;
    X := MatPtr^[Loc(Row,Col)];
    MatOpStatus := TRUE
END;

PROCEDURE RealMatrix.Fill( FillValue : REAL; { input }
                           RowCount,         { input }
                           ColCount  : WORD { input });

VAR I, J : WORD;
```

```
BEGIN
    IF RowCount > NRow THEN
        RowCount := NRow;
    IF ColCount > NCol THEN
        ColCount := NCol;
    Rows := RowCount;
    Cols := ColCount;
    FOR I := 1 TO RowCount DO
        FOR J := 1 TO ColCount DO
            MatPtr^[Loc(I,J)] := FillValue;
    MatOpStatus := TRUE
END;

PROCEDURE RealMatrix.AddScalar(Scalar : REAL { input });

VAR I, J, K : WORD;

BEGIN
    FOR I := 1 TO Rows DO
        FOR J := 1 TO Cols DO BEGIN
            K := Loc(I,J);
            MatPtr^[K] := MatPtr^[K] + Scalar;
        END;
    MatOpStatus := TRUE
END;

PROCEDURE RealMatrix.MultScalar(Scalar : REAL { input });

VAR I, J, K : WORD;

BEGIN
    FOR I := 1 TO Rows DO
        FOR J := 1 TO Cols DO BEGIN
            K := Loc(I,J);
            MatPtr^[K] := MatPtr^[K] * Scalar;
        END;
    MatOpStatus := TRUE
END;

PROCEDURE RealMatrix.MultVector(
                  InVect  : RealVector;  { input }
            VAR   OutVect : RealVector   { input });

VAR I, J : WORD;
```

```
          BEGIN
              IF InVect.VSize <> NCol THEN BEGIN
                  MatOpStatus := FALSE;
                  EXIT
              END;
              IF OutVect.VecPtr = NIL THEN
                  OutVect.Init(InVect.VSize);
              OutVect.Fill(0, InVect.VSize);
              FOR I := 1 TO Rows DO
                  FOR J := 1 TO Cols DO
                      OutVect.VecPtr^[I] := OutVect.VecPtr^[I] +
                                            InVect.VecPtr^[J] *
                                            MatPtr^[Loc(I,J)];

              MatOpStatus := TRUE
          END;


          PROCEDURE RealMatrix.MultMatrix(
                          InMat   : RealMatrix;  { input  }
                      VAR OutMat  : RealMatrix   { output });


          VAR I, J, K, L : WORD;


          BEGIN
              IF ( Cols <> InMat.Rows) THEN BEGIN
                  MatOpStatus := FALSE;
                  EXIT
              END;
              IF OutMat.MatPtr = NIL THEN
                  OutMat.Init(Rows, InMat.Cols);
              OutMat.Rows := Rows;
              OutMat.Cols := InMat.Cols;
              FOR I := 1 TO Rows DO
                  FOR J := 1 TO InMat.Cols DO BEGIN
                      L := OutMat.Loc(I,J);
                      OutMat.MatPtr^[L] := 0.0;
                      FOR K := 1 TO Cols DO
                      OutMat.MatPtr^[L] := OutMat.MatPtr^[L] +
                              MatPtr^[Loc(I,K)] *
                              InMat.MatPtr^[InMat.Loc(K,J)];
                  END;
              MatOpStatus := TRUE
          END;
```

```
PROCEDURE SpreadSheet.FillColumn(  ColIndex  : WORD; { input }
                                   Scalar    : REAL  { input });
VAR I, Offset : WORD;

BEGIN
    IF ColIndex > NCol THEN BEGIN
        MatOpStatus := FALSE;
        EXIT
    END;
    IF ColIndex > Cols THEN
        Cols := ColIndex;
    Offset := Loc(1,ColIndex)-1;
    FOR I := Offset+1 TO Offset+Rows DO
        MatPtr^[I] := Scalar;
    MatOpStatus := TRUE
END;


FUNCTION SpreadSheet.SumUp(  ColIndex,         { input }
                             FirstRow,         { input }
                             LastRow  : WORD   { input }) : REAL;
VAR Sum : REAL;
    I, Offset : WORD;


BEGIN
    IF (ColIndex > Cols) OR
       (FirstRow > Rows) OR
       (LastRow > Rows) THEN BEGIN
       MatOpStatus := FALSE;
       SumUp := 0;
       EXIT
    END;
    Sum := 0;
    Offset := Loc(1, ColIndex) - 1;
    FOR I := Offset + FirstRow TO Offset + LastRow DO
        Sum := Sum + MatPtr^[I];
    MatOpStatus := TRUE;
    SumUp := Sum { return function value }
END;

PROCEDURE SpreadSheet.AddToColumn(   ColIndex  : WORD; { input }
                                     Scalar    : REAL  { input });


VAR I, Offset : WORD;
```

```
BEGIN
    IF ColIndex > NCol THEN BEGIN
        MatOpStatus := FALSE;
        EXIT
    END;
    IF ColIndex > Cols THEN
        Cols := ColIndex;
    Offset := Loc(1,ColIndex)-1;
    FOR I := Offset+1 TO Offset+Rows DO
        MatPtr^[I] := MatPtr^[I] + Scalar;
    MatOpStatus := TRUE
END;


PROCEDURE SpreadSheet.MultColumn( ColIndex  : WORD; { input }
                                  Scalar    : REAL  { input });


VAR I, Offset : WORD;


BEGIN
    IF ColIndex > NCol THEN BEGIN
        MatOpStatus := FALSE;
        EXIT
    END;
    IF ColIndex > Cols THEN
        Cols := ColIndex;
    Offset := Loc(1,ColIndex)-1;
    FOR I := Offset+1 TO Offset+Rows DO
        MatPtr^[I] := MatPtr^[I] * Scalar;
    MatOpStatus := TRUE
END;


PROCEDURE SpreadSheet.AddColumns( ColA,            { input }
                                  ColB,            { input }
                                  ColC : WORD      { input });

VAR I : WORD;


BEGIN
    IF (ColA > Cols) OR
       (ColB > Cols) OR
       (ColC > NCol) THEN BEGIN
        MatOpStatus := FALSE;
        EXIT
    END;
```

```
        IF ColC > Cols THEN
            Cols := ColC;
        FOR I := 1 TO Rows DO
            MatPtr^[Loc(I,ColC)] := MatPtr^[Loc(I,ColA)] +
                                        MatPtr^[Loc(I,ColB)];
        MatOpStatus := TRUE
END;


PROCEDURE SpreadSheet.MultColumns(    ColA,           { input  }
                                      ColB,           { input  }
                                      ColC : WORD     { input  });


VAR I : WORD;

BEGIN
    IF  (ColA > Cols) OR
        (ColB > Cols) OR
        (ColC > NCol) THEN BEGIN
        MatOpStatus := FALSE;
        EXIT
    END;
    IF ColC > Cols THEN
        Cols := ColC;
    FOR I := 1 TO Rows DO
        MatPtr^[Loc(I,ColC)] := MatPtr^[Loc(I,ColA)] *
                                    MatPtr^[Loc(I,ColB)];
    MatOpStatus := TRUE
END;


PROCEDURE StatMatrix.SelectColumns(  X,           { input  }
                                     Y : WORD     { input  });
BEGIN
    MatOpStatus :=  (X > 0) AND (Y > 0) AND
                    (X <= Cols) AND (Y <= Cols);
    IF MatOpStatus THEN BEGIN
        ColX := X;
        ColY := Y;
        CalcStatus := select_columns
    END
    ELSE BEGIN
        ColX := 0;
        ColY := 0;
        CalcStatus := no_operation
    END;
END;
```

```
PROCEDURE StatMatrix.CalcSums;

VAR I : WORD;
    X, Y : REAL;

BEGIN
    IF CalcStatus = no_operation THEN BEGIN
      MatOpStatus := FALSE;
       EXIT
    END;
    Sum := 0;
    SumX := 0;
    SumXX := 0;
    SumY := 0;
    SumYY := 0;
    SumXY := 0;
    FOR I := 1 TO Rows DO BEGIN
        X := MatPtr^[Loc(I,ColX)];
        Y := MatPtr^[Loc(I,ColY)];
        Sum := Sum + 1;
        SumX := SumX + X;
        SumXX := SumXX + X * X;
        SumY := SumY + Y;
        SumYY := SumYY + Y * Y;
        SumXY := SumXY + X * Y
    END;
    MeanX := SumX / Sum;
    MeanY := SumY / Sum;
    SdevX := SQRT((SumXX - SQR(SumX)/Sum)/(Sum-1));
    SdevY := SQRT((SumYY - SQR(SumY)/Sum)/(Sum-1));
    fSlope := (SumXY - Sum * MeanX * MeanY) / SQR(SdevX) / (Sum-1);
    fIntercept := MeanY - fSlope * MeanX;
    fRsqr := SQR(SdevX / SdevY * fSlope);
    CalcStatus := calc_sums;
END;

FUNCTION StatMatrix.Slope : REAL;
BEGIN
    Slope := fSlope
END;

FUNCTION StatMatrix.Intercept : REAL;
BEGIN
    Intercept := fIntercept
END;
```

```
FUNCTION StatMatrix.Rsqr : REAL;
BEGIN
    Rsqr := fRsqr
END;


FUNCTION StatMatrix.NumData : REAL;
BEGIN
    NumData := Sum
END;


END.
```

I have elected to apply a divide-and-conquer approach in testing unit VecMatOb. Each exported class is demonstrated in a separate program.

The first program, shown in Listing 9.2, tests the RealVector class. The program includes a procedure to display the elements of a RealVector object. Notice that it is a non-OOP approach to write this additional routine outside the declaration of class RealVector. The program tests the targeted class in the following ways:

1. Three instances of the RealVEctor class are initialized: objects V1, V2, and V3. The test is set to 5 elements.
2. Object V1 is sent the message Fill(1.0, TEST_SIZE), and the vector is displayed.
3. A scalar of 2 is added to object V1, and the contents of the updated object are shown.
4. All elements of Object V1 are multiplied by 10 by sending the MultScalar (10) message. The new values of the V1 object are posted.
5. The object V2 is filled with 2s and displayed.
6. The contents of object V1 are copied onto object V3 using a loop instead of an object assignment. This technique is used when the copy (object V3 in this case) is to be manipulated, keeping he original (object V1) intact. If object assignment were used, the dynamic pointer of V3 would point to the same address of V1, making object V3 an equivalent alias to V1. Consequently, all changes to object V3 would automatically be reflected on object V1. After the copying operation, vector V3 is displayed.
7. The message AddVector(V2) is sent to object V3, adding the elements of V2 to those of V3. This message and step 6 together constitute the vector operation V3 = V1 + V2. The contents of V3 are displayed.
8. The elements of object V1 are assigned 0.1. The new vector is shown along with the scalar result of multiplying vectors V1 and V3.

LISTING 9.2. Program TSVMAT1.PAS to test the RealVector class.

```pascal
Program Test_RealVectors;

{ Program tests the various methods of RealVector objects }

Uses Crt, VecMatOb;

CONST TEST_SIZE = 5;

VAR V1, V2, V3 : RealVector;
    X : REAL;
    I : WORD;
    AKey : CHAR;

PROCEDURE DisplayVector (V : RealVector);

VAR J : WORD;
    X : REAL;

BEGIN
    FOR J := 1 TO V.CurrentSize DO BEGIN
     V.Recall (J, X);
     WRITE (X:4:1, ' ');
    END;
    WRITELN; WRITELN;
END;

BEGIN
    { allocate dynamic array space }
    V1.Init (TEST_SIZE);
    V2.Init (TEST_SIZE);
    V3.Init (TEST_SIZE);
    ClrScr;
    V1.Fill (1.0, TEST_SIZE);
    WRITE ('Vector V1 is : ');
    DisplayVector (V1);
    V1.AddScalar (2.0);

    WRITELN ('After adding 2.0 to each element, vector V1 is : ');
    DisplayVector (V1);
    V1.MultScalar (10);
    WRITELN ('After multiplying each element by 10, vector V1 is : ');
    DisplayVector (V1);
```

```
V2.Fill(2.0, TEST_SIZE);
WRITE('Vector V2 is : ');
DisplayVector(V2);
{ copy elements of V1 onto V3, one at a time }
FOR I := 1 TO V1.CurrentSize DO BEGIN
  V1.Recall(I, X);
  V3.Store(I, X);
END;
WRITE('Vector V1 is copied onto V3 : ');
DisplayVector(V3);
V3.AddVector(V2);
WRITE('V3 = V1 + V2 gives : ');
DisplayVector(V3);

V1.Fill(0.1, TEST_SIZE);
WRITE('The elements of V1 are assigned 0.1 : ');
DisplayVector(V1);
WRITELN('V1 * V3 = ', V1.MultVector(V3):4:1);

{ deallocate dynamic array space }
V3.Done;
V2.Done;
V1.Done;
WRITELN;
WRITE('Press any key to end the program ...');
AKey := ReadKey;
END.
```

The screen output of running this program is as follows:

```
Vector V1 is :  1.0   1.0   1.0   1.0   1.0

After adding 2.0 to each element, vector V1 is :
 3.0   3.0   3.0   3.0   3.0

After multiplying each element by 10, vector V1 is :
30.0 30.0 30.0 30.0 30.0

Vector V2 is :  2.0   2.0   2.0   2.0   2.0

Vector V1 is copied onto V3 : 30.0  30.0  30.0  30.0  30.0

V3 = V1 + V2 gives : 32.0  32.0  32.0  32.0  32.0
```

```
The elements of V1 are assigned 0.1 :  0.1   0.1   0.1   0.1   0.1

V1 * V3 = 16.0

Press any key to end the program . . .
```

The next program, shown in Listing 9.3, tests the RealMatrix class. The program includes routines to display RealVector and RealMatrix objects. The program performs as follows:

1. Three instances of the RealMatrix class are declared: M1, M2, and M3. In addition, two instances of the class RealVector, V1 and V2, are created to be included in some of the tested methods. Objects M1, M2, and V1 are allocated dynamic arrray/matrix space.
2. Object M1 is sent the message Fill(1.0, TEST_SIZE, TEST_SIZE) to fill its elements with 1s. These elements are displayed using the local procedure DisplayMatrix.
3. The elements of object M1 are incremented by 4 through the message AddScalar(4.0). The contents of the updated matrix are shown on the screen.
4. The elements of M1 are multiplied by 10 via the message MultScalar(10) and are posted on the screen.
5. The vector V1 is filled with 0.1s and its contents displayed prior to sending the MultVector(V1, V2) message to object M1. The result of multiplying matrix M1 and vector V1 is placed in the newly created vector V2. The contents of V2 are displayed.
6. The elements of matrix object M2 are filled with 0.1s. The program displays objects M1 and M2 before sending M1 the MultMatrix(M2, M3) message. The Boolean value of M1.MatOpStatus is examined in an IF statement to query the success of the matrix multiplication. The resulting matrix, M3, is displayed if the Boolean flag returns TRUE.

LISTING 9.3. Program TSVMAT2.PAS to test the RealMatrix class.

```
Program Test_RealMatrix;

{ Program tests the various methods of RealMatrix objects }

Uses Crt, VecMatOb;

CONST TEST_SIZE = 3;
```

```
VAR V1, V2 : RealVector;
    M1, M2, M3 : RealMatrix;
    AKey : CHAR;

PROCEDURE Wait;

VAR AKey : CHAR;

BEGIN
    WRITELN;
    WRITE('Press any key to continue ...');
    AKey := ReadKey; WRITELN;
    WRITELN
END;

PROCEDURE DisplayVector(V : RealVector);

VAR J : WORD;
    X : REAL;

BEGIN
    FOR J := 1 TO V.CurrentSize DO BEGIN
      V.Recall(J, X);
      WRITE(X:4:1, ' ');
    END;
    WRITELN; WRITELN;
END;

PROCEDURE DisplayMatrix(M : RealMatrix);

VAR I, J, NRows, NCols : WORD;
    X : REAL;

BEGIN
    M.QuerySize(NRows, NCols);
    FOR I := 1 TO NRows DO BEGIN
      FOR J := 1 TO NCols DO BEGIN
          M.Recall(I, J, X);
          WRITE(X:4:1, ' ')
      END;
      WRITELN;
    END;
    WRITELN;
END;
```

```
BEGIN
    { allocate dynamic array space }
    V1.Init (TEST_SIZE);
    M1.Init (TEST_SIZE, TEST_SIZE);
    M2.Init (TEST_SIZE, TEST_SIZE);
    ClrScr;
    M1.Fill (1.0, TEST_SIZE, TEST_SIZE);
    WRITELN ('Matrix M1 is :');
    DisplayMatrix (M1);
    M1.AddScalar (4.0);
    WRITELN ('Matrix M1 is, after adding 4 to each element:');
    DisplayMatrix (M1);
    M1.MultScalar (10);
    WRITELN ('Matrix M1 is, after multiplying each element by 10:');
    DisplayMatrix (M1);
    V1.Fill (0.1, TEST_SIZE);
    WRITE ('Vector V1 is : ');
    DisplayVector (V1);
    M1.MultVector (V1, V2);
    WRITE ('M1 * V1 yields the vector ');
    DisplayVector (V2);
    Wait;
    M2.Fill (0.1, TEST_SIZE, TEST_SIZE);
    WRITELN ('Matrix M1 is :');
    DisplayMatrix (M1);
    WRITELN ('Matrix M2 is :');
    DisplayMatrix (M2);
    M1.MultMatrix (M2, M3);
    IF M1.MatOpStatus THEN BEGIN
      WRITELN ('M1 * M2 yields the following matrix:');
      DisplayMatrix (M3);
    END;


    { deallocate dynamic array space }
    M3.Done;
    M2.Done;
    M1.Done;
    V1.Done;
    V2.Done;
    WRITELN;
    WRITE ('Press any key to end the program ...');
    AKey := ReadKey;
END.
```

The screen output of running the program is shown here:

```
Matrix M1 is :
 1.0  1.0  1.0
 1.0  1.0  1.0
 1.0  1.0  1.0

Matrix M1 is, after adding 4 to each element :
 5.0  5.0  5.0
 5.0  5.0  5.0
 5.0  5.0  5.0

Matrix M1 is, after multiplying each element by 10:
50.0 50.0 50.0
50.0 50.0 50.0
50.0 50.0 50.0

Vector V1 is :  0.1   0.1   0.1

M1 * V1 yields the vector 15.0  15.0  15.0

Press any key to continue ...

Matrix M1 is :
50.0 50.0 50.0
50.0 50.0 50.0
50.0 50.0 50.0

Matrix M2 is :
 0.1  0.1  0.1
 0.1  0.1  0.1
 0.1  0.1  0.1

M1 * M2 yields the following matrix:
15.0 15.0 15.0
15.0 15.0 15.0
15.0 15.0 15.0

Press any key to end the program . . .
```

The program shown in Listing 9.4 tests the SpreadSheet class. The program performs the following tasks (the elements of the updated matrix object are displayed after each step):

1. A single instance, object M1, of class SpreadSheet is declared.
2. The elements of object M1 are assigned 1.0.
3. The elements at index [1, 1] and [TEST_SIZE, TEST_SIZE] are assigned 50 and 5, respectively.
4. The first column of the object is filled with 10s by sending the Fill-Column(1, 10) message to object M1.
5. The sums of columns 1 and 2 are displayed by sending SumUp messages to M1.
6. The message AddToColumn(2, 4) is sent to M1 to increment the elements of the second column by 4.
7. The message MultColumn is sent to object M1 to multiply the second column by 0.1.
8. The message AddColumns(1, 2, 3) is sent to add the first two columns, placing the results in the third one.
9. The message MultColumns(1, 2, 3) is sent to M1 to multiply the first two columns, placing the results in the third one.

LISTING 9.4. Program TSVMAT3.PAS to test the SpreadSheet class.

```
Program Test_SpreadSheet;

{ Program tests the various methods of SpreadSheet objects }

Uses Crt, VecMatOb;

CONST TEST_SIZE = 3;

VAR M1 : SpreadSheet;
    AKey : CHAR;

PROCEDURE Wait;
BEGIN
    WRITELN;
    WRITE('Press any key to continue ...');
    AKey := ReadKey; WRITELN;
    WRITELN
END;

PROCEDURE DisplayMatrix(M : SpreadSheet);

VAR I, J, NRows, NCols : WORD;
    X : REAL;
```

```
BEGIN
    M.QuerySize(NRows, NCols);
    FOR I := 1 TO NRows DO BEGIN
      FOR J := 1 TO NCols DO BEGIN
        M.Recall(I, J, X);
        WRITE(X:4:1,' ')
      END;
      WRITELN;
    END;
    WRITELN;
END;

BEGIN
    { allocate dynamic array space }
    M1.Init(TEST_SIZE, TEST_SIZE);
    ClrScr;
    M1.Fill(1.0, TEST_SIZE, TEST_SIZE);
    WRITELN('Matrix M1 is:');
    DisplayMatrix(M1);
    WRITELN('After assigning 50 and 5 to extreme elements, matrix is:');
    M1.Store(1,1,50);
    M1.Store(TEST_SIZE, TEST_SIZE, 5);
    DisplayMatrix(M1);
    M1.FillColumn(1, 10);
    WRITELN('After filling column 1 with 10''s, Matrix M1 is:');
    DisplayMatrix(M1);
    WRITELN('Sum of column 1 = ', M1.SumUp(1, 1, TEST_SIZE):4:1);
    WRITELN('Sum of column 2 = ', M1.SumUp(2, 1, TEST_SIZE):4:1);
    WRITELN;
    Wait;
    M1.AddToColumn(2, 4);
    WRITELN('After adding 4''s to column 2, matrix is:');
    DisplayMatrix(M1);
    M1.MultColumn(2, 0.1);
    WRITELN('After multiplying column 2 by 0.1, matrix is:');
    DisplayMatrix(M1);
    M1.AddColumns(1, 2, 3);
    WRITELN('After Col3 = Col1 + Col2, matrix is:');
    DisplayMatrix(M1);
    M1.MultColumns(1, 2, 3);
    WRITELN('After Col3 = Col1 * Col3, matrix is:');
    DisplayMatrix(M1);
    { deallocate dynamic array space }
    M1.Done;
```

```
            WRITELN;
            WRITE('Press any key to end the program ...');
            AKey := ReadKey;
      END.
```

The screen output of running this program is as follows:

```
Matrix M1 is:
 1.0  1.0  1.0
 1.0  1.0  1.0
 1.0  1.0  1.0

After assigning 50 and 5 to extreme elements, matrix is:
50.0 1.0  1.0
 1.0  1.0  1.0
 1.0  1.0  5.0

After filling column 1 with 10's, Matrix M1 is:
10.0  1.0  1.0
10.0  1.0  1.0
10.0  1.0  5.0

Sum of column 1 = 30.0
Sum of column 2 =  3.0


Press any key to continue ...

After adding 4's to column 2, matrix is:
10.0  5.0  1.0
10.0  5.0  1.0
10.0  5.0  5.0

After multiplying column 2 by 0.1, matrix is:
10.0  0.5  1.0
10.0  0.5  1.0
10.0  0.5  5.0

After Col3 = Col1 + Col2, matrix is:
10.0  0.5 10.5
10.0  0.5 10.5
10.0  0.5 10.5
```

```
After Col3 = Col1 * Col3, matrix is:
10.0  0.5  5.0
10.0  0.5  5.0
10.0  0.5  5.0
```

```
Press any key to end the program . . .
```

The last test program, shown in Listing 9.5, tests the StatMatrix class. The program carries out the following tasks:

1. Declares a single instance, object M1, of the class StatMatrix.
2. Assigns the dynamic matrix the dimensions of ten rows and two columns.
3. Fills the matrix with data based on the equation relating the Celsius and the Fahrenheit temperature scales.

$$F^\circ = 32 + 1.8\ C^\circ$$

The first column is assigned the Celsius degrees, starting at 25° and in increments of 5°. The second column is assigned the Fahrenheit degrees using the Random function to introduce a bit of random deviation (or noise).

4. Displays the matrix and carries out the column selection by sending the message SelectColumns(1, 2) to object M1.
5. Performs the statistical computations by sending the CalcSums message to M1, and displays the regression results.

LISTING 9.5. Program TSVMAT4.PAS to test the StatMatrix class.

```
Program Test_StatMatrix;

{ Program tests the various methods of StatMatrix objects }

Uses Crt, VecMatOb;

CONST MAX_COL = 2;
      MAX_ROW = 10;

VAR M1 : StatMatrix;
    X : REAL;
    I : WORD;
    AKey : CHAR;
```

```
                    PROCEDURE Wait;
                    BEGIN
                        WRITELN;
                        WRITE('Press any key to continue ...');
                        AKey := ReadKey; WRITELN;
                        WRITELN
                    END;


                    PROCEDURE DisplayMatrix(M : StatMatrix);

                    VAR I, J, NRows, NCols : WORD;
                        X : REAL;

                    BEGIN
                        M.QuerySize(NRows, NCols);
                        FOR I := 1 TO NRows DO BEGIN
                          FOR J := 1 TO NCols DO BEGIN
                                M.Recall(I, J, X);
                                WRITE(X:5:1,' ')
                          END;
                          WRITELN;
                        END;
                        WRITELN;
                    END;

                    BEGIN
                        { allocate dynamic array space }
                        M1.Init(MAX_ROW, MAX_COL);
                        ClrScr;
                        { store data in the two columns }
                        Randomize;
                        FOR I := 1 TO MAX_ROW DO BEGIN
                          X := 20 + 5 * I;
                          M1.Store(I, 1, X);
                          X := 32 + 1.8 * (20 + 5 * I) + 2*(0.5-Random);
                          M1.Store(I, 2, X);
                        END;
                        WRITELN('Matrix M1 is:');
                        DisplayMatrix(M1);
                        M1.SelectColumns(1, 2);
                        M1.CalcSums;
                        WRITELN('Number of data points = ', M1.NumData:3:0);
                        WRITELN('R-square = ', M1.Rsqr);
                        WRITELN('Col2 = ',M1.Intercept:4:1,' + ', M1.Slope:4:1,' * Col1');
```

```
                    { deallocate dynamic array space }
                    M1.Done;
                    WRITELN;
                    WRITE ('Press any key to end the program ...');
                    AKey := ReadKey;
            END.
```

The screen output of this program is shown here:

```
Matrix M1 is:
25.0  76.5
30.0  85.5
35.0  95.8
40.0 103.3
45.0 112.4
50.0 122.9
55.0 130.2
60.0 140.2
65.0 149.2
70.0 157.4

Number of data points = 10
R-square = 9.99458805275026E-0001
Col2 = 31.7 + 1.8 * Col1

Press any key to end the program . . .
```

10 | Polynomial Objects

This chapter looks at mathematical polynomials as objects. Polynomials are special, popular functions that exhibit great flexibility and possess interesting features. To simplify matters, I will discuss real, single-variable polynomials with real coefficients and exclude other types (such as polynomials with complex coefficients and polynomials with multiple variables).

The Basics

Simple real polynomials have the following general form:

$$P_n(X) = a_0 + a_1X + a_2X^2 + \cdots + a_nX^n$$

A polynomial is a summation of power terms. Each power term contributes to the polynomial its value multiplied by a coefficient. The order of a polynomial is the power of the highest-power term having a nonzero coefficient.

As an object, a polynomial has certain attributes and functionalities. Its order and coefficients are its defining attributes. On the functionality side, polynomials can be evaluated, added, subtracted, multiplied, divided, integrated, differentiated, and so on. Some of these polynomial operations, including integration and differentiation, can be performed using numerical analysis techniques. Another set of operations attempts to determine specific types of loci on a polynomial, such as points where the polynomial values are at a minimum, maximum, or zero (that is, root).

Classifying polynomials is a rather abstract process, and it depends on how you are looking at them. The general class, call it Polynomial, is perhaps the most common ground where one would start. The Polynomial class defines the data fields associated with a polynomial object and a few very basic methods. The methods include the assignment and query of the polynomial order and coefficients, as well as the evaluation of the polynomial at a given argument.

The next step is to spawn a subclass of polynomials that are involved in calculus-type operations. Let's call this subclass CalculusPoly. The methods associated with this subclass manipulate the values of the individual coefficients rather than the values of the polynomial. Typical methods for the CalculusPoly class are polynomial math (adding, subtracting, multiplying, and dividing), integration, and differentiation. Such methods derive new polynomials from existing ones. They are not focused on the value of a polynomial for any given argument.

A subclass, call it NumAnalPoly, can be derived from the class of CalculusPoly by introducing methods that implement numerical analysis algorithms. These methods determine various types of mathematical loci and values associated with a polynomial. Unlike the inherited methods of class CalculusPoly, these methods do not create new polynomials by altering the coefficients of existing ones. Rather, they yield numerical values that describe certain properties of a polynomial. These include the roots of the polynomial, the minimum/maximum points, the slope at a specific argument, the area under the curve between two points, and so on. The mathematical values determined by the methods of class NumAnalPoly may or may not be stored in dedicated fields. This depends on the type of client application that will use the polynomial objects. The general design intuition is to rely on methods that simply return the desired results. You may include a set of fields that keep often-needed values.

Listing 10.1 on page 206 contains the source code for the PolyObj library unit. The unit contains Turbo Pascal implementation of the polynomial classes. The unit exports the MAX_ORDER constant, set to 20, as the upper limit for polynomial orders. You should increase this constant if you might be handling polynomials of orders exceeding 20. The library unit also exports a real-typed array to manage the array of polynomial coefficients:

```
TYPE CoeffArray = ARRAY [0..MAX_ORDER] OF REAL;
```

The Polynomial class is declared as follows:

```
Polynomial = OBJECT
    Coeff : CoeffArray;
    Order : BYTE;
    PROCEDURE Initialize(   PolyOrder : BYTE;        { input }
                            PolyCoeff : CoeffArray   { input });
```

```
                  PROCEDURE QueryPoly( VAR PolyOrder  : BYTE;          { output }
                                       VAR PolyCoeff   : CoeffArray  { output });
                  FUNCTION PolyVal(X : REAL { input }) : REAL;
            END;
```

The data fields store the polynomial coefficients and order of the polynomial. The accompanying methods serve very basic purposes: initializing the data fields, retrieving the data fields, and evaluating the polynomial at a specific argument value.

The CalculusPoly subclass is declared as follows:

```
CalculusPoly = OBJECT (Polynomial)
   PolyError : BOOLEAN;
   PROCEDURE AddCoeff(PolyB : CalculusPoly { input });
   FUNCTION MultCoef(   PolyA,                 { input }
                        PolyB : CalculusPoly  { input }) : BOOLEAN;
   PROCEDURE Integrate(   PassInX,           { input }
                          ValueAtX : REAL   { input });
END;
```

This subclass adds only a few new methods to the data fields and methods inherited from class Polynomial. The method AddCoeff adds the coefficients of the argument polynomial to those of the target object. The MultCoef method cross-multiplies the coefficients of the two polynomial arguments to determine the coefficients of their object. The Boolean result serves to indicate whether or not the multiplication actually occurred. A FALSE value indicates that the operation was aborted because the order of the resulting polynomial would have exceeded MAX_ORDER. The Integrate method performs a calculus integration on the polynomial coefficients. Integrating an nth order polynomial:

$$p_n(X) = a_0 + a_1 X + a_2 X^2 + \cdots + a_n X^n$$

yields a polynomial with an order of $n + 1$:

$$P_n(X) = A_0 + a_0 X + a_1 X^2/2 + a_2 X^3/3 + \cdots + a_n X^{n+1}/(n + 1)$$

where A_0 is the new constant term coefficient. This is calculated by method Integrate using the supplied value for the integrated polynomial at a specific argument value.

The CalculusPoly class incorporates a few methods that are typical. You can include other polynomial operations, such as subtraction, division, and differentiation.

The third subclass is NumAnalPoly, declared as a subclass of CalculusPoly:

```
NumAnalPoly = OBJECT(CalculusPoly)
   FUNCTION PolyRoot(VAR   Guess      : REAL; { input }
                            Tolerance : REAL; { input }
                            MaxIter   : BYTE  { input }) : BOOLEAN;
   FUNCTION Area(A, B : REAL) : REAL;
END;
```

This subclass incorporates methods for performing two typical numerical analysis algorithms. PolyRoot solves for a real root of a polynomial, given a guess for the root, a tolerance level (that is, a small positive number that determines the accuracy of the solution), and the maximum number of iterations to prevent infinite looping. The method returns TRUE if a solution is found within MaxIter iterations; otherwise, a FALSE value is returned. The method uses Newton's iterative algorithm to refine the submitted guess for the root. Other methods (like the Lin-Bairstow method) are able to return all of the real and imaginary roots of a polynomial, but coding such a method requires an additional data structure to handle an array of results.

The Area method computes the area under the polynomial between points A and B, using Simpson's rule. The Area method creates an array of discrete polynomial values by repeatedly sending PolyVal messages.

LISTING 10.1. The source code of the PolyObj library unit.

```
Unit PolyObj;

{===========================================================


          Copyright (c) 1989, 1990   Namir Clement Shammas

     LIBRARY NAME: PolyObj

     VERSION 1.0 FOR TURBO PASCAL                    DATE 4/27/1989

     PURPOSE: creates and exports polynomial classes.

     ========================================================}


{*****************************************************************}
{***********************} INTERFACE {***************************}
{*****************************************************************}
```

```
CONST MAX_ORDER = 20;

TYPE CoeffArray = ARRAY [0..MAX_ORDER] OF REAL;

Polynomial = OBJECT
    Coeff : CoeffArray;
    Order : BYTE;
    PROCEDURE Initialize(   PolyOrder : BYTE;            { input }
                            PolyCoeff : CoeffArray   { input });
   PROCEDURE QueryPoly(     VAR PolyOrder  : BYTE;           { output }
                            VAR PolyCoeff  : CoeffArray    { output });
   FUNCTION PolyVal(X : REAL { input }) : REAL;
END;

CalculusPoly = OBJECT (Polynomial)
    PolyError : BOOLEAN;
    PROCEDURE AddCoeff(  PolyB : CalculusPoly  { input });
    FUNCTION MultCoef(    PolyA,                      { input }
                         PolyB : CalculusPoly  { input }) : BOOLEAN;
    PROCEDURE Integrate( PassInX,          { input }
                         ValueAtX : REAL   { input });

END;

NumAnalPoly = OBJECT (CalculusPoly)
    FUNCTION PolyRoot (VAR   Guess      : REAL; { input }
                             Tolerance : REAL; { input }
                             MaxIter    : BYTE { input }) : BOOLEAN;
    FUNCTION Area (A, B : REAL) : REAL;
END;

{****************************************************************}
{*********************} IMPLEMENTATION {************************}
{****************************************************************}


PROCEDURE Polynomial.Initialize(
                    PolyOrder : BYTE;      { input }
                    PolyCoeff : CoeffArray { input });

VAR I : BYTE;

BEGIN
    IF PolyOrder IN [1..MAX_ORDER] THEN
```

```
                Order := PolyOrder
        ELSE
            Order := 0;

        FOR I := 0 TO PolyOrder DO
            Coeff[I] := PolyCoeff[I];

        IF PolyOrder < MAX_ORDER THEN
            FOR I := PolyOrder+1 TO MAX_ORDER DO
                Coeff[I] := 0.0;
    END;

    PROCEDURE Polynomial.QueryPoly(
                        VAR PolyOrder   : BYTE;          { output }
                        VAR PolyCoeff   : CoeffArray     { output });

    VAR I : BYTE;

    BEGIN
        PolyOrder := Order;

        FOR I := 0 TO PolyOrder DO
            PolyCoeff[I] := Coeff[I]
    END;

    FUNCTION Polynomial.PolyVal(X : REAL { input }) : REAL;

    VAR Sum : REAL;
        I : BYTE;

    BEGIN
        Sum := Coeff[Order];
        FOR I := Order - 1 DOWNTO 0 DO
            Sum  := Sum * X + Coeff[I];
        PolyVal  := Sum { return function value }
    END;

    PROCEDURE CalculusPoly.AddCoeff(PolyB : CalculusPoly { input });

    VAR BigOrder, I : BYTE;

    BEGIN
        IF Order > PolyB.Order THEN
            BigOrder := Order
```

```
        ELSE
            BigOrder := PolyB.Order;

        FOR I := 0 TO BigOrder DO
            Coeff[I] := Coeff[I] + PolyB.Coeff[I];

        { update polynomial order }
        Order := BigOrder;
        { check order of polynomial }
        WHILE (Order > 0) AND
               (Coeff[Order] = 0) DO
               DEC(Order);
END;

FUNCTION CalculusPoly. MultCoef(
                        PolyA,                  { input  }
                        PolyB : CalculusPoly { input }) : BOOLEAN;

VAR I, J, K : BYTE;

BEGIN
    IF ( PolyA.Order + PolyB.Order) > MAX_ORDER THEN BEGIN
        MultCoef := FALSE;
        EXIT;
    END;
    { assign order of object }
    Order := PolyA.Order + PolyB.Order;
    { initialize Coeff field of self }
    FOR I := 0 TO MAX_ORDER DO
        Coeff[I] := 0.0;
    FOR I := 0 TO PolyA.Order DO
        FOR J := 0 TO PolyB.Order DO BEGIN
            K := I + J;
            Coeff[K] := Coeff[K] +
                        PolyA.Coeff[I] * PolyB.Coeff[J];
        END;
    MultCoef := TRUE
END;

PROCEDURE CalculusPoly.Integrate( PassInX,          { input  }
                                  ValueAtX : REAL   { input });

VAR I : BYTE;
    Sum : REAL;
```

```
BEGIN
    IF Order >= MAX_ORDER THEN EXIT;

    FOR I := Order DOWNTO 0 DO
        Coeff[I+1] := Coeff[I] / (I+1);
    INC(Order);
    { determine the value of the new C[0] }
    Sum := Coeff[Order];
    FOR I := Order - 1 DOWNTO 1 DO
        Sum := Sum * PassInX + Coeff[I];
    Sum := Sum * PassInX;
    Coeff[0] := ValueAtX - Sum;
END;

FUNCTION NumAnalPoly.PolyRoot(
                    VAR Guess       : REAL; { input  }
                        Tolerance   : REAL; { input  }
                        MaxIter     : BYTE  { input }) : BOOLEAN;

VAR Iter : BYTE;
    Incr, Diff : REAL;
    Diverge : BOOLEAN;

BEGIN
    Diverge := FALSE;
    Iter := 0;
    REPEAT
        Incr := 0.01;
        IF ABS(Guess) > 1 THEN
        Incr := Incr * Guess;
            Diff := 2 * Incr * PolyVal(Guess) /
                (PolyVal(Guess+Incr) - PolyVal(Guess-Incr));
        Guess := Guess - Diff;
        INC(Iter);
        IF Iter > MaxIter THEN Diverge := TRUE;
    UNTIL (ABS(Diff) < Tolerance) OR Diverge;

    PolyRoot := NOT Diverge { return function value }
END;

FUNCTION NumAnalPoly.Area( A,        { input  }
                        B : REAL  { input }) : REAL;

CONST MAX_POINTS = 20;
```

```
TYPE DiscreteArray = ARRAY [0..MAX_POINTS] OF REAL;

VAR Y : DiscreteArray;
    DeltaX, X, SumEven, SumOdd : REAL;
    I : BYTE;

BEGIN
    DeltaX := (B - A) / MAX_POINTS;
    X := A;
    FOR I := 0 TO MAX_POINTS DO BEGIN
        Y[I] := PolyVal(X);
        X := X + DeltaX
    END;

    SumOdd := Y[1];
    SumEven := Y[2];
    I := 3;
    WHILE I <= MAX_POINTS DO BEGIN
        SumOdd := SumOdd + Y[I];
        SumEven := SumEven + Y[I+1];
        INC(I, 2)
    END;

    Area := DeltaX / 3 *
            (Y[0] + 4*SumOdd + 2*SumEven - Y[MAX_POINTS])

END;

END.
```

I wrote the test program TSPOLY.PAS, shown in Listing 10.2, to exercise the exported classes of the PolyObj library unit. The program defines three CalculusPoly-class objects and one NumAnalPoly object. Once the order and coefficients of the objects are assigned, the program sends various messages to them:

1. Objects PolyC and PolyB are added and the new coefficients, assigned to PolyC, are displayed.
2. Objects PolyA and PolyB are multiplied and the resulting polynomial is assigned to object PolyC. The coefficients of the result are displayed.
3. The PolyA polynomial object is integrated, and the result is used to determine the area under the original PolyA object between 0 and 1. The area is computed by taking the difference between the integrated polynomial values at 1 and 0. The program displays the result 0.33333.

4. The root of the QuadPoly object is calculated, starting with a guess value of 3. The program displays the result 1, which is the solution for the polynomial $1 - 2X + X^2$ (which is also $(X - 1)^2$).

5. The area under the QuadPoly polynomial between 0 and 1 is calculated by sending the message Area to object QuadPoly. The program displays the result 0.33333.

LISTING 10.2. The source code for the test program TSPOLY.PAS.

```
Program Test_PolyObjects;

{
 Program to manipulate polynomial object exported by
 PolyObj unit. The program performs the following:

 1.  Assigns polynomial coefficients.
 2.  Adds polynomials and displays the result.
 3.  Multiplies polynomials and displays the result.
 4.  Calculates the analytical area under a polynomial.
 5.  Calculates the root of a polynomial.
 6.  Calculates the area under a polynomila, using a
     merical method.
}


Uses Crt, PolyObj;

VAR C : CoeffArray;
    Guess : REAL;
    I, AnOrder : BYTE;
    PolyA, PolyB, PolyC : CalculusPoly;
    QuadPoly : NumAnalPoly;
    AKey : CHAR;

BEGIN
    ClrScr;
    AnOrder := 2;
    C[0] := 1.0;
    C[1] := -2.0;
    C[2] := 1.0;
    PolyA.Initialize(AnOrder, C);
    PolyC.Initialize(AnOrder, C); { or use PolyC := PolyA }
```

```
C[0] := 1.0;
C[1] := -1.0;
C[2] := 1.0;
PolyB.Initialize(AnOrder, C);

PolyC.AddCoeff(PolyB);
PolyC.QueryPoly(AnOrder, C);
WRITELN('The sum of Y1 = 1 - X + X^2 and Y2 = 1 - 2X + X^2');
WRITELN('is : ');
WRITE('Y3 = ', C[0]:6:1);
FOR I := 1 TO AnOrder DO BEGIN
    WRITELN(' +');
    WRITE(' (':5,C[I]:6:1,') * X^', I:-2);
END;
WRITELN;
WRITELN;

IF PolyC.MultCoef(PolyA,PolyB) THEN BEGIN
    PolyC.QueryPoly(AnOrder, C);
    WRITE('The product of Y1 = 1 - X + X^2 ');
    WRITELN('and Y2 = 1 - 2X + X^2');
    WRITELN('is : ');
    WRITE('Y3 = ', C[0]:6:1);
    FOR I := 1 TO AnOrder DO BEGIN
        WRITELN(' +');
        WRITE(' (':5,C[I]:6:1,') * X^', I:-2);
    END;
    WRITELN;
    WRITELN;
END;
PolyA.Integrate(0.0, 0.0);
WRITELN('Area under PolyA between 0 and 1 = ',
        PolyA.PolyVal(1.0) - PolyA.PolyVal(0.0));
WRITELN;

AnOrder := 2;
C[0] := 1;
C[1] := -2.0;
C[2] := 1;
QuadPoly.Initialize(AnOrder, C);
Guess := 3.0;
IF QuadPoly.PolyRoot(Guess, 0.0001, 30) THEN
```

```
     WRITELN;
     WRITELN('Area under QuadPoly between 0 and 1 = ',
             QuadPoly.Area(0.0,1.0));
     WRITELN;
     WRITE('Press any key to end the program ...');
     AKey := ReadKey;
     WRITELN;
  END.
```

When you run the test program, the following screen image appears:

```
The sum of Y1 = 1 - X + X^2 and Y2 = 1 - 2X + X^2
is :
Y3 =    2.0 +
     ( -3.0) * X^1 +
     (  2.0) * X^2

The product of Y1 = 1 - X + X^2 and Y2 = 1 - 2X + X^2
is :
Y3 =    1.0 +
     ( -3.0) * X^1 +
     (  4.0) * X^2 +
     ( -3.0) * X^3 +
     (  1.0) * X^4

Area under PolyA between 0 and 1 = 3.33333333333030E-0001

Root of Y = 1 - 2X + X^2 is   1.000

Area under QuadPoly between 0 and 1 = 3.33333333333030E-0001

Press any key to end the program ...
```

Suggested Extensions

The polynomial classes given so far can be further extended. For example, you can add data fields and methods that enable you to plot a polynomial over a range of values. The added data fields enable you to define the X and Y axes for curve plotting, number of tick marks, and so on. The plotting method(s) would draw the sought polynomial. Adding graphics-related methods to the Polynomial class also provides its subclasses with the same benefits.

New classes of polynomials can be introduced to model other types of polynomials:

1. The extended polynomial with terms having negative powers. A class declaration of such a polynomial might look like this:

```
TYPE CoeffArray = ARRAY [-MAX_ORDER..MAX_ORDER] OF REAL;

ExtPolynomial = OBJECT
    Coeff : CoeffArray;
    PosOrder, NegOrder : BYTE;
    PROCEDURE Initialize(  PlusOrder,                    { input  }
                           MinusOrder   : BYTE;          { input  }
                           PolyCoeff    : CoeffArray     { input });
    PROCEDURE QueryPoly( VAR PlusOrder,                  { output }
                             MinusOrder   : BYTE;        { output }
                         VAR PolyCoeff    : CoeffArray   { output });
    FUNCTION PolyVal(X : REAL { input }) : REAL;
END;
```

where the data fields take into account separate orders for the positive and negative powers. The arguments of methods Initialize and QueryPoly also reflect the new dual-order scheme.

2. The complex polynomial class. This class employs coefficients that are complex numbers and returns complex numbers when evaluated. Even the polynomial arguments are complex numbers. The declaration of a complex polynomial class might look like this:

```
TYPE Complex = RECORD
                   Reel,
                   Imag : REAL
               END;
     CoeffArray = ARRAY [0..MAX_ORDER] OF Complex;

ComplexPolynomial = OBJECT
    Coeff : CoeffArray;
    Order : BYTE;
    PROCEDURE Initialize(  PolyOrder : BYTE;         { input  }
                           PolyCoeff : CoeffArray    { input });
```

```
        PROCEDURE QueryPoly(   VAR PolyOrder  : BYTE;         { output }
                               VAR PolyCoeff  : CoeffArray  { output });
        PROCEDURE PolyVal(       X        : Complex;  { input  }
                           VAR   Result : Complex     { output });
    END;
```

3. The class of bivariate polynomials, which employs two variables, call them *X* and *Y*. This class has two order fields, one for each variable. A matrix of coefficients must be used to accommodate cross product terms. For example, the coefficient of the cross product of *X* and *Y* is at index [1. 1], that of *X* squared and *Y* cubed is at [2, 3], and so on. The declaration of a bivariate polynomial class might look like this:

```
TYPE CoeffMatrix = ARRAY [0..MAX_ORDER,0..MAX_ORDER] OF REAL;


BivariatePolynomial = OBJECT
    Coeff : CoeffMatrix;
    OrderX, OrderY : BYTE;
    PROCEDURE Initialize(  PolyOrderX,                  { input  }
                           PolyOrderY  : BYTE;          { input  }
                           PolyCoeff   : CoeffMatrix  { input });
    PROCEDURE QueryPoly(   VAR  PolyOrderX,                 { output }
                                PolyOrderY  : BYTE;         { output }
                           VAR  PolyCoeff   : CoeffMatrix { output });
    FUNCTION PolyVal(X, Y : REAL { input }) : REAL;
END;
```

11 | Linear Regression Objects

The classes and objects in object-oriented languages model a wide spectrum of real-world objects. In this chapter I will present an example that deals with a more abstract object (one that is not tangible), namely, the statistics of linear regression. Such statistics describe the relationship between two variables. I will demonstrate how to build classes and subclasses for various cases of linear and linearized regression.

The Basics

Linear regression is a statistical technique for relating the variations of two variables—X the independent variable and Y the dependent variable. The linear regression model is represented by the following simple equation:

$$Y = A + B * X \qquad (1)$$

where A and B are the intercept and the slope of the straight line passing through the set of (X, Y) data or observations (see Figure 11.1). The regression line is calculated such that it minimizes the sum of squared vertical distances (better known as errors) between the line and each value of Y. This is considered the best straight-line fit through a set of (X, Y) data. The correlation coefficient, R^2, is a statistic that indicates the goodness of fit, or the ability of the regression slope and intercept to explain the relationship between X and Y. Its values range between 0 and 1. A 0 (zero) indicates a total lack of fit, meaning that the regression slope and intercept are totally insignificant. By contrast, a value of 1 indicates a perfect fit, which means that the regression line is able to explain all of the observed relationship between Y and X.

FIGURE 11.1. Typical linear regression fit.

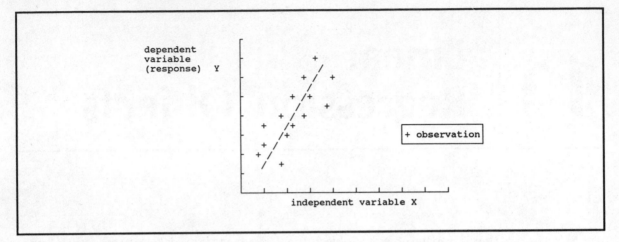

The regression calculations involve the number of observations and the summations of X_i, Y_i, X_i^2, Y_i^2, and $(X_i * Y_i)$. Every time a new set of observations is processed, these summations must be cleared first. At least two observations must be available for the summations to be eligible for processing. An enumerated variable is useful in monitoring the correct sequence of computational phases—clearing the summations, updating the summations, and calculating the regression statistics. The intercept is calculated using the following equation:

$$A = \frac{\Sigma Y \ \Sigma X^2 - \Sigma X \ \Sigma XY}{N \ \Sigma X^2 - (\Sigma X)^2} \tag{2}$$

where N is the number of observations. The intercept is calculated using:

$$B = \frac{N \ \Sigma XY - \Sigma X \ \Sigma Y}{N \ \Sigma X^2 - (\Sigma X)^2} \tag{3}$$

Once the regression slope and intercept are found, Equation (1) can be used to calculate the value of either X or Y, given the other. This is also known as projecting X on Y or projecting Y on X.

Extended Precision

The statistical summations may suffer from lost accuracy when dealing with numbers that vary in magnitude. To enhance to precision, some statisticians have recommended that the observed X and Y values be shifted by quasi-average values. A focal point, (X_0, Y_0), is the reference point for the shifts in the X and Y values. This shift affects the regression equation as follows:

$$Y - Y_0 = A' + B * (X - X_0) \tag{4}$$

The shift in data affects the calculated value of the intercept, but not the slope. The following equation converts A' into A:

$$A = Y_0 + A' - B * X_0 \tag{5}$$

Linearized Regression

The linear regression model is the simplest model, assuming a straightforward linear relation between two variables. In many cases, however, a linear relation exists not between the observed variables, but among functions (or transformations) of them. Thus, the regression model for a general transformation is written as:

$$F(Y) = A'' + B'' * G(X) \tag{6}$$

where a straight line is fitted through the set of $(G(X), F(Y))$ data instead of (X, Y). The intercept is calculated using the following equation:

$$A = \frac{\Sigma F(Y)\ \Sigma G(X)^2 - \Sigma G(X)\ \Sigma G(X)F(Y)}{N\ \Sigma G(X)^2 - (\Sigma G(X))^2} \tag{7}$$

The intercept is calculated using:

$$B = \frac{N\ \Sigma G(X)F(Y) - \Sigma G(X)\ \Sigma F(Y)}{N\ \Sigma G(X)^2 - (\Sigma G(X))^2} \tag{8}$$

In projections of X on Y or Y on X, the input, and the result must be inverse transformed.

Regression Classes

In constructing a class for linear regression, there are two sets of data fields to consider. The first are fields that store information necessary to perform the statistical number crunching. They are the various statistical summations and the regression results (slope, intercept, and coefficient of correlation). The second group of data fields are optional, consisting of fields that store intermediate results and sequence-monitoring fields. The latter fields are used to ensure that the proper sequence of messages has been issued. The following is the declaration of class LinearRegression:

```
LinearRegression = OBJECT
    Sum,
    SumX,
    SumXX,
    SumY,
    SumYY,
    SumXY,
    MeanX,
    MeanY,
    SdevX,
    SdevY,
    fSlope,
    fIntercept,
    fRSqr : REAL;
    LRStatus : LRStatusEnum;
    LRerrorMessage : STRING;
    FUNCTION SayLRerror : STRING;
    CONSTRUCTOR ClearSums;
    PROCEDURE AddData ( X,          { input  }
                        Y : REAL { input }); VIRTUAL;
    PROCEDURE DelData ( X,          { input  }
                        Y : REAL { input }); VIRTUAL;
    PROCEDURE CalcLR;
    FUNCTION Rsqr : REAL;
    FUNCTION Slope : REAL;
    FUNCTION Intercept : REAL; VIRTUAL;
    FUNCTION NumData : REAL;
    FUNCTION ProjectX (X : REAL { input }) : REAL; VIRTUAL;
    FUNCTION ProjectY (Y : REAL { input }) : REAL; VIRTUAL;
END;
```

The constructor ClearSum and the methods AddData, DelData, and CalcLR are involved in preparing the statistical summations and obtaining the sought results. Notice that I am using scalar arguments in the methods AddData and DelData. This avoids the use and management of either static or dynamic arrays. Such arrays may be implemented in the client applications. The methods Rsqr, Slope, Intercept, and NumData return the sought statistics. The methods ProjectX and ProjectY are used in the optional post-regression projections. The method SayLRerror reports the error message (if none, it returns a null string) associated with the last message. The LinearRegression class contains a number of virtual routines—the procedures and functions that will be overridden by subclasses.

Listing 11.1 on page 223 contains the code for the LinearRegression class and the other subclasses. The exported constant NO_VALUE is assigned to a function's value when such a function is called out of sequence.

Enhanced-Precision Class

The class of enhanced-precision regression may be grafted from the LinearRegression class. All of the data fields of the parent class are required, in addition to the (X, Y) coordinates for the focal point. This dictates the need for a method that stores the focal point coordinates if you want to maintain the rule of avoiding direct access of any data fields. The nature of the computations involved requires that the methods AddData, DelData, Intercept, ProjectX, and ProjectY be overridden. I have chosen to implement an overriding Intercept method that returns an intercept equivalent to that of the parent class, making corrections for the focal point coordinates. If the inherited method Intercept is used, the value returned does not include any adjustments for the focal point coordinates. The following is the declaration of the class EnhancedPrecisionLR:

```
EnhancedPrecisionLR = OBJECT (LinearRegression)
    X0,
    Y0 : REAL;
    CONSTRUCTOR SetFocalPoint (Xref,          { input  }
                               Yref : REAL   { input });
    PROCEDURE AddData ( X,          { input  }
                        Y  : REAL   { input }); VIRTUAL;
    PROCEDURE DelData ( X,          { input  }
                        Y  : REAL   { input }); VIRTUAL;
    FUNCTION Intercept : REAL; VIRTUAL;
    FUNCTION ProjectX (X : REAL { input }) : REAL; VIRTUAL;
    FUNCTION ProjectY (Y : REAL { input }) : REAL; VIRTUAL;
END;
```

Linearized Regression Class

Linearized regression is an extension to simple linear regression. Classes and objects for this type of statistical computation first transform the raw observations before feeding them to the statistical summations. Thanks to the procedural-parameter features in Turbo Pascal, a flexible scheme of user-defined transformations can be supported. Otherwise, a single repertoire-type of function must be used to catalog the various transformations, using a CASE statement. Even then, you would still be limited to the coded transformations, so using procedural parameters is definitely a superior approach! The LinRegOb unit exports the following procedure type:

```
RealFunction = FUNCTION(X : Real) : REAL;
```

A subclass of linearized regression must add procedural-typed fields. A minimum of two such fields are needed to transform the X and Y data. Two additional fields are required to access functions for inverse transformations. Since assigning these procedural fields is vital, an additional Boolean field can be used to detect the needed assignment. There must be a new method to assign the transformation functions and their inverses. The nature of the calculations affects the methods AddData, DelData, ProjectX, and ProjectY, which must be overridden. The methods reporting the regression statistics need not be changed, since converting from Equation (6) to Equation (1) is not always possible. The following is the declaration of the LinearizedRegression subclass:

```
LinearizedRegression = OBJECT (LinearRegression)
    TransformX,
    TransformY,
    InverseTransformX,
    InverseTransformY : RealFunction;
    HaveTransfFunctions : BOOLEAN;
    CONSTRUCTOR SetTransfFunction(FX,                        { input }
                                  FY,                        { input }
                                  INV_FX,                    { input }
                                  INV_FY : RealFunction { input });
    PROCEDURE AddData( X,          { input }
                       Y : REAL    { input }); VIRTUAL;
    PROCEDURE DelData( X,          { input }
                       Y : REAL    { input }); VIRTUAL;
    FUNCTION ProjectX(X : REAL { input }) : REAL; VIRTUAL;
    FUNCTION ProjectY(Y : REAL { input }) : REAL; VIRTUAL;
END;
```

LISTING 11.1. The source code for the LinRegOb library unit.

```
UNIT LinRegOb;


{======================================================================


                Copyright (c) 1989, 1990   Namir Clement Shammas

        LIBRARY NAME: LinRegOb

        VERSION 1.0 FOR TURBO PASCAL                    DATE 6/21/1989

        PURPOSE: Exports classes and objects that model linear(ized)
                 regression statistics.


================================================================}

{******************************************************************}
{***********************} INTERFACE {****************************}
{******************************************************************}

CONST NO_VALUE = -1.0E+20;

TYPE

RealFunction = FUNCTION(X : Real) : REAL;

LRStatusEnum = (clear_sums, update_sums, calc_linreg);

LinearRegression = OBJECT
      Sum,
      SumX,
      SumXX,
      SumY,
      SumYY,
      SumXY,
      MeanX,
      MeanY,
      SdevX,
      SdevY,
      fSlope,
      fIntercept,
```

```
        fRSqr : REAL;
        LRStatus : LRStatusEnum;
        LRerrorMessage : STRING;
        FUNCTION SayLRerror : STRING;
        CONSTRUCTOR ClearSums;
        PROCEDURE AddData ( X,              { input }
                            Y : REAL    { input }); VIRTUAL;
        PROCEDURE DelData ( X,              { input }
                            Y : REAL    { input }); VIRTUAL;
        PROCEDURE CalcLR;
        FUNCTION Rsqr : REAL;
        FUNCTION Slope : REAL;
        FUNCTION Intercept : REAL; VIRTUAL;
        FUNCTION NumData : REAL;
        FUNCTION ProjectX (X : REAL { input }) : REAL; VIRTUAL;
        FUNCTION ProjectY (Y : REAL { input }) : REAL; VIRTUAL;
END;


EnhancedPrecisionLR = OBJECT (LinearRegression)
        X0,
        Y0 : REAL;
        CONSTRUCTOR SetFocalPoint ( Xref,        { input }
                                    Yref : REAL { input });
        PROCEDURE AddData ( X,            { input }
                            Y : REAL   { input }); VIRTUAL;
        PROCEDURE DelData ( X,            { input }
                            Y : REAL   { input }); VIRTUAL;
        FUNCTION Intercept : REAL; VIRTUAL;
        FUNCTION ProjectX (X : REAL { input }) : REAL; VIRTUAL;
        FUNCTION ProjectY (Y : REAL { input }) : REAL; VIRTUAL;
END;


LinearizedRegression = OBJECT (LinearRegression)
        TransformX,
        TransformY,
        InverseTransformX,
        InverseTransformY : RealFunction;
        HaveTransfFunctions : BOOLEAN;
        CONSTRUCTOR SetTransfFunction ( FX,                      { input }
                                        FY,                      { input }
                                        INV_FX,                  { input }
                                        INV_FY : RealFunction { input });
```

```
                    PROCEDURE AddData( X,              { input }
                                       Y   : REAL  { input }); VIRTUAL;
                    PROCEDURE DelData( X,              { input }
                                       Y   : REAL  { input }); VIRTUAL;
                    FUNCTION ProjectX( X   : REAL  { input }) : REAL; VIRTUAL;
                    FUNCTION ProjectY( Y   : REAL  { input }) : REAL; VIRTUAL;
        END;



        {*****************************************************************}
        {*********************} IMPLEMENTATION {*************************}
        {*****************************************************************}


        FUNCTION LinearRegression.SayLRError : STRING;
        BEGIN
            SayLRerror := LRerrorMessage
        END;


        CONSTRUCTOR LinearRegression.ClearSums;
        BEGIN
            Sum := 0;
            SumX := 0;
            SumXX := 0;
            SumY := 0;
            SumYY := 0;
            SumXY := 0;
            LRStatus := clear_sums
        END;


        PROCEDURE LinearRegression.AddData( X,         { input }
                                            Y : REAL  { input });
        BEGIN
            Sum := Sum + 1;
            SumX := SumX + X;
            SumY := SumY + Y;
            SumXX := SumXX + SQR(X);
            SumYY := SumYY + SQR(Y);
            SumXY := SumXY + X * Y;
            IF Sum > 1 THEN
                LRStatus := update_sums;
        END;
```

```
PROCEDURE LinearRegression.DelData( X,          { input }
                                    Y : REAL  { input });
BEGIN
   IF Sum = 0 THEN BEGIN
     LRerrorMessage := 'No data to delete';
       EXIT
   END;
   Sum := Sum - 1;
   SumX := SumX - X;
   SumY := SumY - Y;
   SumXX := SumXX - SQR(X);
   SumYY := SumYY - SQR(Y);
   SumXY := SumXY - X * Y;
   IF Sum < 1 THEN
       LRStatus := clear_sums;
END;

PROCEDURE LinearRegression.CalcLR;
BEGIN
   IF LRstatus < update_sums THEN BEGIN
       LRerrorMessage := 'Insufficient data';
       EXIT
   END;
   MeanX := SumX / Sum;
   MeanY := SumY / Sum;
   SdevX := SQRT((SumXX - SQR(SumX)/Sum)/(Sum-1));
   SdevY := SQRT((SumYY - SQR(SumY)/Sum)/(Sum-1));
   fSlope := (SumXY - Sum * MeanX * MeanY) / SQR(SdevX) / (Sum-1);
   fIntercept := MeanY - fSlope * MeanX;
   fRsqr := SQR(SdevX / SdevY * fSlope);
   LRStatus := calc_linreg;
   LRerrorMessage := '';
END;

FUNCTION LinearRegression.Slope : REAL;
BEGIN
   IF LRstatus = calc_linreg THEN BEGIN
       LRerrorMessage := '';
       Slope := fSlope
   END
   ELSE BEGIN
       LRerrorMessage := 'Incorrect sequence of messages';
       Slope := NO_VALUE
   END;
END;
```

```
                    FUNCTION LinearRegression.Intercept : REAL;
                    BEGIN
                        IF LRstatus = calc_linreg THEN BEGIN
                            LRerrorMessage := '';
                            Intercept := fIntercept
                        END
                        ELSE BEGIN
                            LRerrorMessage := 'Incorrect sequence of messages';
                            Intercept := NO_VALUE
                        END;
                    END;

                    FUNCTION LinearRegression.Rsqr : REAL;
                    BEGIN
                        IF LRstatus = calc_linreg THEN BEGIN
                            LRerrorMessage := '';
                            Rsqr := fRsqr
                        END
                        ELSE BEGIN
                            LRerrorMessage := 'Incorrect sequence of messages';
                            Rsqr := NO_VALUE
                        END;

                    END;


                    FUNCTION LinearRegression.NumData : REAL;
                    BEGIN
                        NumData := Sum
                    END;


                    FUNCTION LinearRegression.ProjectX(X : REAL { input }) : REAL;
                    BEGIN
                        IF LRStatus = calc_linreg THEN BEGIN
                            LRerrorMessage := '';
                            ProjectX := fIntercept + fSlope * X
                        END
                        ELSE BEGIN
                            LRerrorMessage := 'Incorrect sequence of messages';
                            ProjectX := NO_VALUE;
                        END;
                    END;

                    FUNCTION LinearRegression.ProjectY(Y : REAL { input }) : REAL;
```

```
BEGIN
    IF LRStatus = calc_linreg THEN BEGIN
        LRerrorMessage := '';
        ProjectY := (Y - fIntercept) / fSlope
    END
    ELSE BEGIN
        LRerrorMessage := 'Incorrect sequence of messages';
        ProjectY := NO_VALUE;
    END;
END;


CONSTRUCTOR EnhancedPrecisionLR.SetFocalPoint( Xref,         { input }
                                               Yref : REAL { input });
BEGIN
    LinearRegression.ClearSums;
    X0 := Xref;
    Y0 := Yref
END;


PROCEDURE EnhancedPrecisionLR.AddData( X,            { input }
                                       Y : REAL    { input });
BEGIN
    LinearRegression.AddData(X - X0, Y - Y0)
END;


PROCEDURE EnhancedPrecisionLR.DelData( X,            { input }
                                       Y : REAL    { input });
BEGIN
    LinearRegression.DelData(X - X0, Y - Y0)
END;


FUNCTION EnhancedPrecisionLR.Intercept : REAL;
BEGIN
    Intercept := Y0 + fIntercept - fSlope * X0
END;


FUNCTION EnhancedPrecisionLR.ProjectX( X   : REAL { input })
                                        : REAL;
BEGIN
    IF LRstatus = calc_linreg THEN BEGIN
        LRerrorMessage := '';
        ProjectX := Y0 + LinearRegression.ProjectX(X - X0)
    END
    ELSE BEGIN
        LRerrorMessage := 'Incorrect sequence of messages';
```

```
                    ProjectX := NO_VALUE
        END
END;


FUNCTION EnhancedPrecisionLR.ProjectY(Y : REAL { input })
                                    : REAL;
BEGIN
    IF LRstatus = calc_linreg THEN BEGIN
        LRerrorMessage := '';
        ProjectY := X0 + LinearRegression.ProjectX(Y - Y0)
    END
    ELSE BEGIN
        LRerrorMessage := 'Incorrect sequence of messages';
        ProjectY := NO_VALUE
    END
END;


CONSTRUCTOR LinearizedRegression.SetTransfFunction(
                            FX,                     { input }
                            FY,                     { input }
                            INV_FX,                 { input }
                            INV_FY : RealFunction   { input });

BEGIN
    LinearRegression.ClearSums;
    TransformX := FX;
    TransformY := FY;
    InverseTransformX := INV_FX;
    InverseTransformY := INV_FY;
    HaveTransfFunctions := TRUE;
END;


PROCEDURE LinearizedRegression. AddData(
                            X,          { input }
                            Y : REAL { input });

BEGIN
    IF HaveTransfFunctions THEN
        LinearRegression.AddData(TransformX(X), TransformY(Y))
    ELSE
        LRerrorMessage := 'Missing transformation functions';
END;


PROCEDURE LinearizedRegression. DelData(
```

```
                                    X,         { input }
                                    Y : REAL { input });
BEGIN
    IF HaveTransfFunctions THEN
        LinearRegression.DelData(TransformX(X), TransformY(Y))
    ELSE
        LRerrorMessage := 'Missing transformation functions';
END;


FUNCTION LinearizedRegression.ProjectX(X  : REAL { input })
                                            : REAL;
BEGIN
    IF (LRstatus = calc_linreg) AND HaveTransfFunctions THEN BEGIN
        LRerrorMessage := '';
        ProjectX :=  InverseTransformY(
                        LinearRegression.ProjectX(TransformX(X)))
    END
    ELSE BEGIN
        LRerrorMessage := 'Incorrect sequence of messages';
        ProjectX := NO_VALUE
    END
END;


FUNCTION LinearizedRegression.ProjectY(Y : REAL { input })
                                            : REAL;
BEGIN
    IF (LRstatus = calc_linreg) AND HaveTransfFunctions THEN BEGIN
        LRerrorMessage := '';
        ProjectY :=  InverseTransformX(
                        LinearRegression.ProjectY(TransformY(Y)))
    END
    ELSE BEGIN
        LRerrorMessage := 'Incorrect sequence of messages';
        ProjectY := NO_VALUE
    END
END;


END.
```

Listing 11.2 contains a test program for library unit LinRegOb. The program uses the same data to test objects of the three exported classes. The results of the LinearRegression and EnhancedPrecisionLR objects are values of the same statistics. The LinearizedRegression object performs a power fit (that is, fits observed data with the model $Ln(Y)=A+B*Ln(X)$). Consequently, the regression results of this object differ from those of a linear regression (with and without enhanced precision).

The program performs the following:

1. Declares the regression objects LR, XLR, and TLR.
2. Prompts you for the number of observations.
3. Clears the summations of the three objects.
4. Prompts you for the focal point. The coordinates of the focal point are passed to the XLR object by sending it the SetFocalPoint message.
5. Assigns the function MyLn as the transformation function for both X and Y data. In addition, the program assigns the function MyExp as the inverse transformation functions for both X and Y. The functions MyLn and MyExp are shells for the predefined functions Ln and Exp. Such shells are required by Turbo Pascal when using predefined functions as procedural parameters.
6. Prompts you for positive (X, Y) data. The input data is used to update the statistical summations of the three regression objects.
7. Sends CalcLR messages to each of the three objects to obtain regression results.
8. Displays the regression statistics.
9. Prompts you, using a REPEAT loop, for a value of X to be projected onto Y. The program displays the projected values by sending a ProjectX message to the three objects. An input of zero is interpreted as a signal to exit the loop.

LISTING 11.2. Program TSLINREG.PAS to test unit LinRegOb.

```
Program Test_LinRegOb;

{
Program simultaneously tests objects of the three classes
exported by unit LinRegOb.  The same data is processed
through each object.
}

Uses Crt, LinRegOb;

{ the next two functions are "shells" for the Ln and Exp
  functions.  The MyLn and MyExp functions are used in
  the transformation of data.
}
```

```
{$F+}
FUNCTION MyLn (X : REAL { input  }) : REAL;
BEGIN
    MyLn := Ln (X)
END;

FUNCTION MyExp (X : REAL { input  }) : REAL;
BEGIN
    MyExp := Exp (X)
END;
{$F-}


VAR LR : LinearRegression;
    XLR : EnhancedPrecisionLR;
    TLR : LinearizedRegression;

    X, Y, X0, Y0 : REAL;
    I, N : BYTE;
    AKey : CHAR;


BEGIN
    ClrScr;
    REPEAT
        WRITE ('Enter number of data points -> ');
        READLN (N); WRITELN;
    UNTIL N > 2;

    { invoke constructors to initialize summations }
    LR.ClearSums;

    { set focal point for XLR object }
    WRITE ('Enter focal point coordinates X and Y : ');
    READLN (X0, Y0); WRITELN;
    XLR.SetFocalPoint (X0, Y0);
    { set transformations for a log-log curve fit with object TLR }
    TLR.SetTransfFunction (MyLn, MyLn, MyExp, MyExp);
    { get the data }
    FOR I := 1 TO N DO BEGIN
        WRITE ('Enter positive values for X and Y : ');
        READLN (X, Y);
        LR.AddData (X, Y);
        XLR.AddData (X, Y);
```

```
                    TLR.AddData(X,Y);
            END;
            WRITELN; WRITELN;


            { calculate regression statistics for the three objects }
            LR.CalcLR;
            XLR.CalcLR;
            TLR.CalcLR;
            { display results }
            WRITE('An ordinary linear regression gives the following');
            WRITELN(' results:');
            WRITELN('R-square = ', LR.Rsqr);
            WRITELN('Y = (',LR.Intercept,') + (',LR.Slope,') * X');
            WRITELN;
            WRITE('An extended-precision linear regression ');
            WRITELN('gives the following results:');
            WRITELN('R-square = ', XLR.Rsqr);
            WRITELN('Y = (',XLR.Intercept,') + ',XLR.Slope,') * X');
            WRITELN;
            WRITE('A linearized power regression gives the following');
            WRITELN(' results:');
            WRITELN('R-square = ', TLR.Rsqr);
            WRITELN('Y = (', TLR.Intercept,') + (',TLR.Slope,') * X');
            WRITELN;
            { compare projections of X on Y }
            REPEAT
                WRITE('Enter X to project (0 to exit) : ');
                READLN(X); WRITELN;
                IF X > 0 THEN BEGIN
                    WRITE('Y = ', LR.ProjectX(X));
                    WRITELN(' using LR.ProjectX message');
                    WRITE('Y = ',XLR.ProjectX(X));
                    WRITELN(' using XLR.ProjectX message');
                    WRITE('Y = ',TLR.ProjectX(X));
                    WRITELN(' using TLR.ProjectX message');
                    WRITELN;
                END;
            UNTIL X <= 0;
            WRITELN;
            WRITE('Press any key to end the program ...');
            AKey := ReadKey;
        END.
```

For the following data:

X	Y
10	10
30	33
60	58
70	73
80	82

the following screen output is produced by the program. The focal point used is (50, 50) and the projections of X are made at 25, 50, and 75:

```
Enter number of data points -> 5

Enter focal point coordinates X and Y : 50 50

Enter positive values for X and Y :  10 10
Enter positive values for X and Y :  30 33
Enter positive values for X and Y :  60 58
Enter positive values for X and Y :  70 73
Enter positive values for X and Y :  80 82


An ordinary linear regression gives the following results:
R-square = 9.94761229057985E-0001
Y = ( 6.11764705940004E-0001) + ( 1.01176470588143E+0000) * X

An extended-precision linear regression gives the following re-
sults:
R-square = 9.94761229061623E-0001
Y = ( 6.11764705838141E-0001) + 1.01176470588325E+0000) * X

A linearized power regression gives the following results:
R-square = 9.96862273572333E-0001
Y = ( 2.58147816929579E-0002) + ( 9.99945277124425E-0001) * X

Enter X to project (0 to exit) : 25

Y = 2.59058823529631E+0001 using LR.ProjectX message
Y = 2.59058823529049E+0001 using XLR.ProjectX message
Y = 2.56492533085984E+0001 using TLR.ProjectX message

Enter X to project (0 to exit) : 50
```

```
Y = 5.12000000000116E+0001 using LR.ProjectX message
Y = 5.12000000000116E+0001 using XLR.ProjectX message
Y = 5.12965608503437E+0001 using TLR.ProjectX message

Enter X to project (0 to exit) : 75

Y = 7.64941176470602E+0001 using LR.ProjectX message
Y = 7.64941176470602E+0001 using XLR.ProjectX message
Y = 7.69431340256706E+0001 using TLR.ProjectX message


Enter X to project (0 to exit) : 0

Press any key to end the program . . .
```

12 | Electrical Circuit Objects

Our civilization relies heavily on electricity and electronics. The computers you work on are made up of thousands of circuits of various sizes. This chapter looks at modeling very simple DC (direct current) electrical circuits using classes and objects. Electrical circuits are more tangible than the entities modeled in previous chapters. The electrical circuits covered in this chapter are kept at a very simple level to allow all readers to follow the discussion.

The Simplest Circuit

The simplest DC circuit is shown in Figure 12.1. The circuit contains a battery supplying V volts and a resistor of R ohms. The current (measured in amps) flowing through the circuit is calculated using Ohm's law:

$$I = V/R$$

The voltage represents the electrical driving force in the circuit, while the resistance represents the hindrance to the flow of electrons in the circuit.

Series of Resistors

The circuit of Figure 12.1 has a single resistor. In reality, almost all circuits have multiple resistors. What happens if you place more than one resistor in series, one

FIGURE 12.1. The simplest DC circuit.

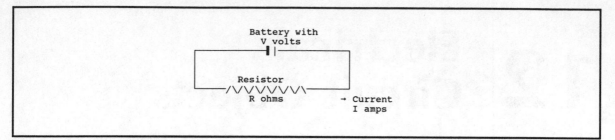

after the other, as shown in Figure 12.2? Chaining resistors in this manner yields a global circuit resistance equal to the sum of the individual resistances:

$$R_T = R_1 + R_2 + R_3$$

This equation can be extended to n resistors:

$$R_T = R_1 + R_2 + ... + R_n$$

The current flowing through the circuit is obtained using the following equation:

$$I = V / R_T$$

Parallel Resistors

Resistors can also be placed in parallel, as shown in Figure 12.3. Each parallel branch offers a conduit to the electrons. How does this influence the overall circuit resistance? To answer this, we consider the reciprocal of the resistance, the conductance. The total conductance of the circuit (that is, the reciprocal of the total

FIGURE 12.2. DC circuit with resistors in series.

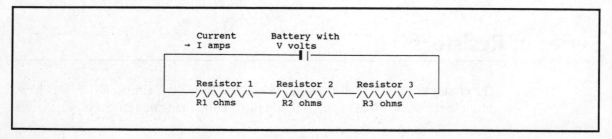

FIGURE 12.3. DC circuit with parallel resistors.

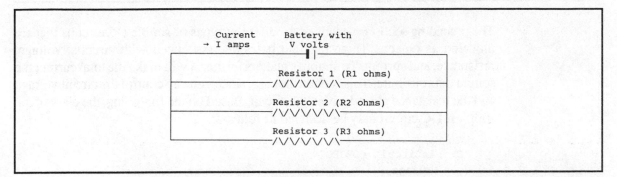

resistance) is the sum of the conductances of each branch (that is, the reciprocals of the resistances for each branch):

$$C_T = C_1 + C_2 + C_3$$

or,

$$1/R_T = 1/R_1 + 1/R_2 + 1/R_3$$

This equation can be extended to n parallel resistors:

$$1/R_T = 1/R_1 + 1/R_2 + \ldots + 1/R_n$$

The current flowing out of the battery is obtained using the following formula:

$$I = V / R_T$$

The current flowing in each parallel resistor is inversely proportional to the branch's resistance. You need not be concerned about calculating the current in each branch, since I am focusing on the total current.

Mixing Series and Parallel Resistors

Most electrical circuits contain resistors connected in various combinations of both series and parallel configurations that meet the design's need. To calculate the total current, the total resistance of each circuit has to be worked out starting with the innermost resistance. This is demonstrated later using a simple example.

Circuit Objects

The preceding sections described the different types of simple DC circuits that are modeled as objects. Three data attributes are associated with circuits: voltage, resistance, and current. To simplify matters further, I will make the total current the sought data attribute. This is often the case, since you can control the circuit voltage and the resistance placed within the circuit. Based on the foregoing, the class of the simplest DC circuit may be declared as follows:

```
SimpleCircuit = OBJECT
    Voltage,
    Resistance : REAL;
    PROCEDURE GetVoltage(Volts : REAL { input });
    PROCEDURE GetResistance(Ohms : REAL { input });
    FUNCTION CalcCurrent : REAL;
END;
```

Voltage and Resistance are the only data fields defined within the SimpleCircuit class. I chose not to include the current as a data field, but to make it the result returned by the method CalcCurrent. The other two methods simply set the voltage and the resistance. Listing 12.1 contains the source code for the Circuit library unit, where the detailed code of the methods is found.

A class of circuits with series resistors can draw from the SimpleCircuit class. The voltage and resistance attributes are also ingredients of this new class. The GetVoltage method is also needed. The CalcCurrent method can also be used with this class if the Resistance field is used to keep track of the sum of resistances. This dictates the implementation of a new method to obtain the trailing resistances. The following is the declaration of the SeriesCircuit subclass:

```
SeriesCircuit = OBJECT(SimpleCircuit)
    PROCEDURE GetNextResistance(Ohms : REAL { input });
END;
```

The inherited method GetResistance sets the first resistance, while method Get-NextResistance is used to add the other resistances in the circuit. Thus, the GetResistance message acts as an initialization or a reset for the value in the Resistance field.

A subclass of parallel resistors can be similarly modeled and declared:

```
ParallelCircuit = OBJECT(SimpleCircuit)
    PROCEDURE GetNextResistance(Ohms : REAL { input });
END;
```

The method ParallelCircuit.GetNextResistance is applied just like method SeriesCircuit.GetNextResistance, though coded differently to obtain the total resistance of parallel resistors.

What about mixed circuits? To implement a simple manual model, a new subclass of mixed circuits can be derived from the class of series circuits. The data fields and the methods GetResistance and CalcCurrent are inherited from class SimpleCircuit. All that is needed is to declare a method that handles the parallel or series connection. I declare the MixedCircuit class as follows:

```
MixedCircuit = OBJECT (SeriesCircuit)
    PROCEDURE GetOtherResistance (
                Ohms      : REAL;    { input }
                InSeries : BOOLEAN { input });
END;
```

The method GetOtherResistance checks the value of the Boolean parameter to decide the type of resistance connection. If TRUE, a GetNextResistance message is sent; otherwise, parallel resistance computations are carried out within the method GetOtherResistance.

LISTING 12.1. Source code for the Circuit library unit.

```
UNIT Circuit;

{===============================================================


            Copyright (c) 1989, 1990   Namir Clement Shammas


    LIBRARY NAME: Circuit


    VERSION 1.0 FOR TURBO PASCAL              DATE 6/21/1989


    PURPOSE: Exports objects that represent simple DC circuits.


    ===========================================================}


{******************************************************************}
{***********************} INTERFACE {***************************}
{******************************************************************}
```

```
TYPE

SimpleCircuit = OBJECT
    Voltage,
    Resistance : REAL;
    PROCEDURE GetVoltage(Volts : REAL { input });
    PROCEDURE GetResistance(Ohms : REAL { input });
    FUNCTION CalcCurrent : REAL;
END;

SeriesCircuit = OBJECT (SimpleCircuit)
    PROCEDURE GetNextResistance(Ohms : REAL { input });
END;

ParallelCircuit = OBJECT (SimpleCircuit)
    PROCEDURE GetNextResistance(Ohms : REAL { input });
END;

MixedCircuit = OBJECT (SeriesCircuit)
    PROCEDURE GetOtherResistance(
                Ohms     : REAL;   { input }
                InSeries : BOOLEAN { input });
END;


{*****************************************************************}
{***********************} IMPLEMENTATION {***********************}
{*****************************************************************}

PROCEDURE SimpleCircuit.GetVoltage(Volts : REAL { input });
BEGIN
    Voltage := Volts
END;

PROCEDURE SimpleCircuit.GetResistance(Ohms : REAL { input });
BEGIN
    Resistance := Ohms
END;

FUNCTION SimpleCircuit.CalcCurrent : REAL;
BEGIN
    IF Resistance <> 0 THEN
        CalcCurrent := Voltage / Resistance
    ELSE
        CalcCurrent := 0;
END;
```

```
PROCEDURE SeriesCircuit.GetNextResistance(Ohms : REAL { input });
BEGIN
    Resistance := Resistance + Ohms
END;


PROCEDURE ParallelCircuit.GetNextResistance(Ohms : REAL { input });
BEGIN
    Resistance := 1/(1/Resistance + 1/Ohms);
END;


PROCEDURE MixedCircuit. GetOtherResistance(
                    Ohms        : REAL;     { input  }
                    InSeries    : BOOLEAN { input });
BEGIN
    IF InSeries THEN
        GetNextResistance(Ohms)
    ELSE
        Resistance := 1/(1/Resistance + 1/Ohms)
END;

END.
```

The code in Listing 12.1 is simplified and reduced in length, thanks to the inheritance features of OOP.

Listing 12.2 shows a test program for the Circuit unit. The program tests series, parallel, and mixed circuits, and performs the following tasks:

1. Tests the series-circuit object. The program prompts you for a positive voltage and a positive value for the first resistance using REPEAT-UNITL loops. Another REPEAT=UNTIL loop is employed to query you for additional resistances. A zero value is interpreted by the program as a signal to exit the loop and calculate the electrical current.
2. Tests the parallel-circuit object. As in step 1, the program prompts you for a positive voltage and a positive value for the first resistance using REPEAT-UNTIL loops, and a separate REPEAT-UNTIL loop is used to prompt you for additional resistances. A zero value is again the signal to exit the loop and calculate the current.
3. Tests the mixed object. As before, the program requests a positive voltage and a positive value for the first resistance using REPEAT-UNTIL loops. Another REPEAT-UNTIL loop queries you for added resistances as well as the accompanying connection types. A zero value is the signal to exit the loop and calculate the current.

LISTING 12.2. Test program TSELECTR.PAS.

```pascal
Program Test_Circuits;

{
 Program tests the various circuit objects
 exported by unit Circuit.
}

Uses Crt, Circuit;

VAR Series : SeriesCircuit;
    Parallel : ParallelCircuit;
    Mixed : MixedCircuit;

    Volts,
    Ohms : REAL;
    AKey : CHAR;

BEGIN
    REPEAT
        ClrScr;
        WRITE('Enter circuit voltage : ');
        READLN(Volts); WRITELN;
        Series.GetVoltage(Volts);
    UNTIL Volts > 0;
    REPEAT
        WRITE('Enter first resistance : ');
        READLN(Ohms); WRITELN;
        IF Ohms > 0 THEN
            Series.GetResistance(Ohms);
    UNTIL Ohms > 0;

    REPEAT
        WRITE('Enter additional series resistance (0=exit) : ');
        READLN(Ohms); WRITELN;
        Series.GetNextResistance(Ohms);
    UNTIL Ohms = 0;
    WRITELN('Current in circuit = ', Series.CalcCurrent, ' Amps');
    WRITELN;
    WRITE('Press any key to continue ...');
    AKey := ReadKey;

    REPEAT
```

```
        ClrScr;
        WRITE('Enter circuit voltage : ');
        READLN(Volts); WRITELN;
        Parallel.GetVoltage(Volts);
    UNTIL Volts > 0;
    REPEAT
        WRITE('Enter first resistance : ');
        READLN(Ohms); WRITELN;
        IF Ohms > 0 THEN
            Parallel.GetResistance(Ohms);
    UNTIL Ohms > 0;

    REPEAT
        WRITE('Enter additional parallel resistance (0=exit) : ');
        READLN(Ohms); WRITELN;
        IF Ohms > 0 THEN
            Parallel.GetNextResistance(Ohms);
    UNTIL Ohms = 0;
    WRITELN('Current in circuit = ',Parallel.CalcCurrent,' Amps');
    WRITELN;
    WRITE('Press any key to continue ...');
    AKey := ReadKey;

    REPEAT
        ClrScr;
        WRITE('Enter circuit voltage : ');
        READLN(Volts); WRITELN;
        Mixed.GetVoltage(Volts);
    UNTIL Volts > 0;
    REPEAT
        WRITE('Enter first resistance : ');
        READLN(Ohms); WRITELN;
        Mixed.GetResistance(Ohms);
    UNTIL Ohms > 0;

    REPEAT
        WRITE('Enter additional resistance (0=exit) : ');
        READLN(Ohms); WRITELN;
        IF Ohms > 0 THEN BEGIN
            REPEAT
                WRITE('P)arallel or S)eries -> ');
                READLN(AKey); WRITELN;
                Akey := UpCase(Akey);
            UNTIL AKey IN ['P','S'];
```

```
                    Mixed.GetOtherResistance(Ohms, AKey = 'S');
        END;
    UNTIL Ohms = 0;
    WRITELN('Current in circuit = ',Mixed.CalcCurrent,' Amps');
    WRITELN;

END.
```

Figure 12.4 shows the circuits used for the sample session. The resistances in the mixed circuit are marked to indicate the order of entry in the program. The 5-ohm resistance is entered as the first resistance, then the series 20-ohm, then the parallel 30-ohm, and finally the series 10-ohm resistance. This order must be followed to obtain the correct answer. No such restriction applies to the other two types of circuits.

The sample session with the test program is shown following:

```
Enter circuit voltage : 100

Enter first resistance : 5

Enter additional series resistance (0=exit) :  25

Enter additional series resistance (0=exit) :  20

Enter additional series resistance (0=exit) :  0

Current in circuit = 2.00000000000000E+0000 Amps

Press any key to continue ...

Enter circuit voltage : 50

Enter first resistance : 20

Enter additional parallel resistance (0=exit) :  25

Enter additional parallel resistance (0=exit) :  0

Current in circuit = 4.50000000000000E+0000 Amps

Press any key to continue ...

Enter circuit voltage : 12
```

FIGURE 12.4. Circuits used for sample sessions.

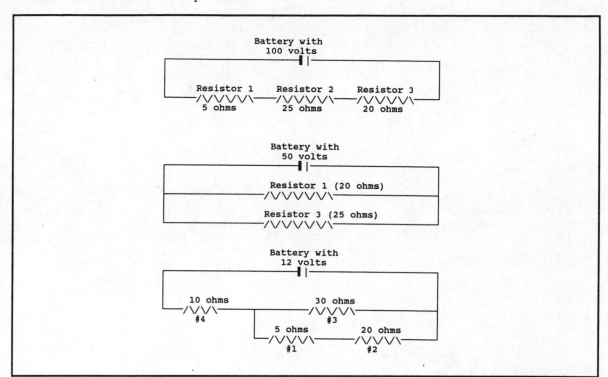

```
Enter first resistance : 5

Enter additional resistance (0=exit) : 20

P)arallel or S)eries -> s

Enter additional resistance (0=exit) : 30

P)arallel or S)eries -> p

Enter additional resistance (0=exit) : 10

P)arallel or S)eries -> s

Enter additional resistance (0=exit) : 0

Current in circuit = 5.07692307692196E-0001 Amps
```

13 | Calculator Objects

This is another chapter that looks at modeling physical objects using OOP classes and objects. The target real-world object is the electronic calculator—specifically, the Reverse Polish Notation calculator. The Hewlett-Packard company is among the manufacturers of various types of RPN calculators: scientific, financial, programmable, and so on.

This chapter also illustrates the creation of subclasses across multiple units. Both the physical calculator and the OOP-emulated calculator comprise interior and exterior components. This chapter presents one library unit that contains the classes and code for the internal portion and a separate unit that spawns additional subclasses to manage the user interface. This is an example of how a programmer can build on and customize classes exported by an existing library unit. Separate units can always be used to implement two levels of functional variation. At the lower level, things can be done in a few different ways, while the higher level is subject to personal preferences and therefore varies widely.

The Basic RPN Calculator

Figure 13.1 is a diagram of the automatic stack for the modeled calculator. The stack has the following characteristics:

1. There are four stack registers: X, Y, Z, and T.
2. The X register is the top of the stack; its value is displayed by the calculator.
3. The T register is the bottom of the stack.
4. Pushing the stack moves data from the X to the Y to the Z to the T registers.
5. Unary operators and functions act on the X register. The stack does not move. The older value of X is stored in a separate register called LastX.

FIGURE 13.1. The automatic stack.

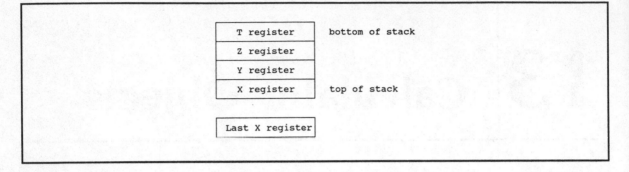

6. Binary operators and functions work on the X and Y registers. The older value of X is stored in the LastX register, while the value of the Y register is lost.

7. When a binary operator or a function is invoked the stack is dropped such that the value in the Z register is copied onto the Y register and the value of the T register is copied onto the Z register.

Operations on the stack include pushing, popping, rolling up, rolling down, and clearing the stack; swapping the X and Y registers; and performing the basic math operations (including change of sign of the X register).

In a class of simple RPN calculators based on this stack, the data fields must accommodate the stack and LastX registers. This can be done by using a collection of scalar fields—one field per register—or by using an array for the stack and a single field for LastX. You can also use an array to accommodate both the stack and the LastX register. I have chosen the second scheme, with the following enumerated type to index the elements of stack registers:

```
StackRegEnum = (Xreg, Yreg, Zreg, Treg);
```

Indexes of this enumerated type are clearer than plain integers. A string-typed field for reporting error messages is optional but highly recommended.

The methods associated with this class are divided into the following groups:

1. An initialization method to reset the stack and LastX registers
2. A collection of methods to access any stack register (this is needed when you wish to view lower registers without resorting to fancy stack pushing and popping), the LastX register, and the internally stored error message

3. A set of methods for stack manipulation, such as rolling up/down, pushing, popping, and swapping registers X and Y

4. A group of stack cleanup methods to clear the entire stack (basically reinitialize) or to clear just the X register

5. A set of methods to perform binary math operations

The class declaration is as follows:

```
Calculator = OBJECT
    Stack : ARRAY [StackRegEnum] OF REAL;
    LastX : REAL;
    ErrorMessage : STRING;
    PROCEDURE Init;
    FUNCTION GetReg(RegIndex : StackRegEnum { input }) : REAL;
    FUNCTION GetLastX : REAL;
    FUNCTION SayError : STRING;
    PROCEDURE Push(X : REAL { input });
    FUNCTION Pop : REAL;
    PROCEDURE Add;
    PROCEDURE Subtract;
    PROCEDURE Multiply;
    PROCEDURE Divide;
    PROCEDURE ClearStack;
    PROCEDURE ClearX;
    PROCEDURE RollUp;
    PROCEDURE RollDown;
    PROCEDURE CHS;
    PROCEDURE Swap;
END;
```

Listing 13.1 on page 254 contains the complete source code for the CalcObj library unit.

The Scientific RPN Calculator

RPN scientific calculators are a subclass of RPN calculators with scientific functions and a set of memory registers. An array-typed field representing the memory registers is needed for this subclass. The array's index range is between 0 and an upper limit assigned to the constant LAST_MEM exported by unit CalcObj.

The methods associated with the subclass of RPN scientific calculators are log, trig, and other transcendental functions. The class of MemCalc is declared as follows:

```
MemCalc = OBJECT (Calculator)
      Memory : ARRAY [0..LAST_MEM] OF REAL;
      PROCEDURE Init;
      PROCEDURE Square;
      PROCEDURE SquareRoot;
      PROCEDURE Reciprocal;
      PROCEDURE Power; { Y^X }
      PROCEDURE Store(MemIndex : BYTE { input });
      PROCEDURE Recall(MemIndex : BYTE { input });
      FUNCTION GetMemory(MemIndex : BYTE { input }) : REAL;
      PROCEDURE Sine;
      PROCEDURE Cosine;
      PROCEDURE Tangent;
      PROCEDURE ArcTangent;
      PROCEDURE Loge;
      PROCEDURE Exponential;
      PROCEDURE AbsVal;
   END;
```

The constructor Init sends a Calculator.Init message and then assigns zeros to the Memory array. The methods implementing math functions are written as parameterless Pascal procedures, since they take their arguments from the RPN stack and return their results to the X register. The Store and Recall methods also move data between the stack and the memory registers. The Recall method pushes the RPN stack with the value taken from a memory register. By contrast, storing the value of the X register into a memory register leaves the RPN stack undisturbed. The GetMemory method is the only method that is written as a Pascal function. It is used to give a client unit or program access to the Memory array without disturbing the RPN stack.

The Financial Calculator Class

Financial calculators perform various financial calculations. Often, these machines include memory registers and some math functions, but no trigonometric functions. In addition, there may be a separate set of registers to store financial variables. The class of financial calculators that I model is a subclass of the scientific calculators.

Therefore, it includes all of the inherited math functions and the memory registers. The modeled class is limited, for the sake of brevity, to solving the following simple financial formula for any of its variables, given the others:

$$FV = PV(1 + I)^N$$

where FV is the future value, PV is the present value, I is the interest rate in fraction, and N is the number of periods.

The desired features dictate the inclusion of an array-typed field to handle the four financial variables. The following enumerated type is declared and is used to access the various financial registers:

```
BusiMemEnum = (PV_, FV_, N_, I_);
```

The methods defined within this class need to carry out the following tasks:

1. Initialize the calculator object and reset the financial memory.
2. Copy the value of the X register into a financial register.
3. Push the value of a financial register onto the RPN stack.
4. Calculate the sought financial variable.

The BusiCalc class is declared as follows:

```
BusiCalc = OBJECT (MemCalc)
    BusiMemory : ARRAY [BusiMemEnum] OF REAL;
    PROCEDURE Init;
    PROCEDURE ResetBusiMem;
    PROCEDURE StorePV;
    PROCEDURE StoreFV;
    PROCEDURE StoreI;
    PROCEDURE StoreN;
    PROCEDURE RecallPV;
    PROCEDURE RecallFV;
    PROCEDURE RecallI;
    PROCEDURE RecallN;
    PROCEDURE CalcPV;
    PROCEDURE CalcFV;
    PROCEDURE CalcI;
    PROCEDURE CalcN;
END;
```

The ResetBusiMem method resets the financial registers by assigning them zeros. This process should be used whenever a new problem is handled to delete old values in the financial registers. The methods that calculate the sought financial results test the given variables for positive values before proceeding with the calculations. This strategy permits these methods to detect missing values. The Storexx methods copy the X register into financial registers. The reverse is performed by the Recallxx family of methods.

LISTING 13.1. Source code for the CalcObj library unit.

```
UNIT CalcObj;

{====================================================================

                    Copyright (c) 1989, 1990  Namir Clement Shammas

       LIBRARY NAME: CalcObj

       VERSION 1.0 FOR TURBO PASCAL                    DATE 6/21/1989

       PURPOSE: Unit exports RPN calculator classes.


====================================================================}

{*******************************************************************}
{************************} INTERFACE {*****************************}
{*******************************************************************}

CONST LAST_MEM = 9;

TYPE

StackRegEnum = (Xreg, Yreg, Zreg, Treg);
BusiMemEnum = (PV_, FV_, N_, I_);

Calculator = OBJECT
    Stack : ARRAY [StackRegEnum] OF REAL;
    LastX : REAL;
    ErrorMessage : STRING;
    PROCEDURE Init;
    FUNCTION GetReg(RegIndex : StackRegEnum { input }) : REAL;
    FUNCTION GetLastX : REAL;
    FUNCTION SayError : STRING;
```

```
                   PROCEDURE Push(X : REAL { input });
                   FUNCTION Pop : REAL;
                   PROCEDURE Add;
                   PROCEDURE Subtract;
                   PROCEDURE Multiply;
                   PROCEDURE Divide;
                   PROCEDURE ClearStack;
                   PROCEDURE ClearX;
                   PROCEDURE RollUp;
                   PROCEDURE RollDown;
                   PROCEDURE CHS;
                   PROCEDURE Swap;
              END;


    MemCalc = OBJECT (Calculator)
              Memory : ARRAY [0..LAST_MEM] OF REAL;
              PROCEDURE Init;
              PROCEDURE Square;
              PROCEDURE SquareRoot;
              PROCEDURE Reciprocal;
              PROCEDURE Power; { Y^X }
              PROCEDURE Store(MemIndex : BYTE { input });
              PROCEDURE Recall(MemIndex : BYTE { input });
              FUNCTION GetMemory(MemIndex : BYTE { input }) : REAL;
              PROCEDURE Sine;
              PROCEDURE Cosine;
              PROCEDURE Tangent;
              PROCEDURE ArcTangent;
              PROCEDURE Loge;
              PROCEDURE Exponential;
              PROCEDURE AbsVal;
         END;


    BusiCalc = OBJECT (MemCalc)
              BusiMemory : ARRAY [BusiMemEnum] OF REAL;
              PROCEDURE Init;
              PROCEDURE ResetBusiMem;
              PROCEDURE StorePV;
              PROCEDURE StoreFV;
              PROCEDURE StoreI;
              PROCEDURE StoreN;
              PROCEDURE RecallPV;
              PROCEDURE RecallFV;
```

```
          PROCEDURE RecallI;
          PROCEDURE RecallN;
          PROCEDURE CalcPV;
          PROCEDURE CalcFV;
          PROCEDURE CalcI;
          PROCEDURE CalcN;
      END;



{********************************************************************}
{**********************} IMPLEMENTATION {**********************}
{********************************************************************}


FUNCTION LocalPower(Base, Exponent : REAL) : REAL;
BEGIN
    IF Base > 0 THEN
        LocalPower := Exp(Exponent * Ln(Base))
    ELSE
        LocalPower := -1;
END;


PROCEDURE Calculator.Init;

VAR RegIndex : StackRegEnum;

BEGIN
    FOR RegIndex := Xreg TO Treg DO
        Stack[RegIndex] := 0;
    ErrorMessage := '';
    LastX := 0;
END;


FUNCTION Calculator.GetReg(RegIndex : StackRegEnum { input }) :
REAL;
BEGIN
    GetReg := Stack[RegIndex]
END;


FUNCTION Calculator.GetLastX : REAL;
BEGIN
    GetLastX := LastX
END;
```

```
FUNCTION Calculator.SayError : STRING;
BEGIN
    SayError := ErrorMessage
END;


PROCEDURE Calculator.Push( X : REAL { input });

VAR RegIndex : StackRegEnum;

BEGIN
    FOR RegIndex := Treg DOWNTO Yreg DO
        Stack[RegIndex] := Stack[Pred(RegIndex)];
    Stack[Xreg] := X;
    ErrorMessage := '';
END;


FUNCTION Calculator.Pop : REAL;

VAR RegIndex : StackRegEnum;

BEGIN
    LastX := Stack[Xreg];
    FOR RegIndex := Xreg TO Zreg DO
        Stack[RegIndex] := Stack[Succ(RegIndex)];
    ErrorMessage := '';
    Pop := LastX;
END;


PROCEDURE Calculator.Add;
BEGIN
    LastX := Stack[Xreg];
    Stack[Xreg] := Stack[Yreg] + Stack[Xreg];
    Stack[Yreg] := Stack[Zreg];
    Stack[Zreg] := Stack[Treg];
    ErrorMessage := '';
END;


PROCEDURE Calculator.Subtract;
BEGIN
    LastX := Stack[Xreg];
    Stack[Xreg] := Stack[Yreg] - Stack[Xreg];
    Stack[Yreg] := Stack[Zreg];
    Stack[Zreg] := Stack[Treg];
```

```
        Stack[Zreg] := Stack[Treg];
        ErrorMessage := '';
    END;


PROCEDURE Calculator.Multiply;
BEGIN
    LastX := Stack[Xreg];
    Stack[Xreg] := Stack[Yreg] * Stack[Xreg];
    Stack[Yreg] := Stack[Zreg];
    Stack[Zreg] := Stack[Treg];
    ErrorMessage := '';
END;


PROCEDURE Calculator.Divide;
BEGIN
    IF Stack[Xreg] <> 0 THEN BEGIN
        LastX := Stack[Xreg];
        Stack[Xreg] := Stack[Yreg] / Stack[Xreg];
        Stack[Yreg] := Stack[Zreg];
        Stack[Zreg] := Stack[Treg];
        ErrorMessage := '';
    END
    ELSE
        ErrorMessage := 'Cannot divide by zero';
END;


PROCEDURE Calculator.ClearStack;
BEGIN
    Init;
    ErrorMessage := '';
END;


PROCEDURE Calculator.ClearX;
BEGIN
    Stack[Xreg] := 0;
    ErrorMessage := '';
END;


PROCEDURE Calculator.RollUp;

VAR TempReg : REAL;
    RegIndex : StackRegEnum;
```

```
BEGIN
    TempReg := Stack[Treg];
    FOR RegIndex := Treg DOWNTO Yreg DO
        Stack[RegIndex] := Stack[Pred(RegIndex)];
    Stack[Xreg] := Tempreg;
    ErrorMessage := '';
END;

PROCEDURE Calculator.RollDown;

VAR TempReg : REAL;
    RegIndex : StackRegEnum;

BEGIN
    TempReg := Stack[Xreg];
    FOR RegIndex := Xreg TO Zreg DO
        Stack[RegIndex] := Stack[Succ(RegIndex)];
    Stack[Treg] := TempReg;
    ErrorMessage := '';
END;

PROCEDURE Calculator.CHS;
BEGIN
    Stack[Xreg] := -Stack[Xreg];
    ErrorMessage := '';
END;

PROCEDURE Calculator.Swap;

VAR TempReg : REAL;

BEGIN
    TempReg := Stack[Xreg];
    Stack[Xreg] := Stack[Yreg];
    Stack[Yreg] := TempReg;
    ErrorMessage := '';
END;

PROCEDURE MemCalc.Init;

VAR I : WORD;

BEGIN
    Calculator.Init;
```

```
        FOR I := 0 TO LAST_MEM DO
            Memory[I] := 0;
END;

PROCEDURE MemCalc.Square;
BEGIN
    LastX := Stack[Xreg];
    Stack[Xreg] := SQR(Stack[Xreg]);
    ErrorMessage := '';
END;

PROCEDURE MemCalc.SquareRoot;
BEGIN
    IF Stack[Xreg] >= 0 THEN BEGIN
        LastX := Stack[Xreg];
        Stack[Xreg] := SQRT(Stack[Xreg]);
        ErrorMessage := '';
    END
    ELSE
        ErrorMessage := 'Error: square root of a negative number';
END;

PROCEDURE MemCalc.Reciprocal;
BEGIN
    IF Stack[Xreg] <> 0 THEN BEGIN
        LastX := Stack[Xreg];
        Stack[Xreg] := 1(Stack[Xreg]);
        ErrorMessage := '';
    END
    ELSE
        ErrorMessage := 'Error: reciprocal of zero';
END;

PROCEDURE MemCalc.Power;

VAR RegIndex : StackRegEnum;

BEGIN
    IF Stack[Yreg] > 0 THEN BEGIN
        LastX := Stack[Xreg];
        Stack[Xreg] := Exp(Stack[Xreg] * Ln(Stack[Yreg]));
        Stack[Yreg] := Stack[Zreg];
        Stack[Zreg] := Stack[Treg];
        ErrorMessage := '';
    END
```

```
        ELSE
            ErrorMessage := 'Error: power of negative number';
    END;


    PROCEDURE MemCalc.Store (MemIndex : BYTE { input });
    BEGIN

        IF MemIndex IN [0..LAST_MEM] THEN BEGIN
            Memory[MemIndex] := Stack[Xreg];
            ErrorMessage := '';
        END
        ELSE
            ErrorMessage := 'Out-of-range memory index';
    END;


    PROCEDURE MemCalc.Recall (MemIndex : BYTE { input });

    VAR RegIndex : StackRegEnum;

    BEGIN
        IF MemIndex IN [0..LAST_MEM] THEN BEGIN
            FOR RegIndex := Treg DOWNTO Yreg DO
                Stack[RegIndex] := Stack[Pred(RegIndex)];
            Stack[Xreg] := Memory[MemIndex];
            ErrorMessage := '';
        END
        ELSE
            ErrorMessage := 'Out-of-range memory index';
    END;


    FUNCTION MemCalc.GetMemory (MemIndex : BYTE { input }) : REAL;
    BEGIN
        IF MemIndex IN [0..LAST_MEM] THEN
            GetMemory := Memory[MemIndex]
        ELSE
            GetMemory := 0;
    END;


    PROCEDURE MemCalc.Sine;
    BEGIN
        LastX := Stack[Xreg];
        Stack[Xreg] := Sin(Stack[Xreg]);
        ErrorMessage := '';
    END;
```

```
PROCEDURE MemCalc.Cosine;
BEGIN
    LastX := Stack[Xreg];
    Stack[Xreg] := Cos(Stack[Xreg]);
    ErrorMessage := '';
END;


PROCEDURE MemCalc.Tangent;
BEGIN
    IF ABS(Stack[XReg]-(Pi/2)) > 0.0001 THEN BEGIN
        LastX := Stack[Xreg];
        Stack[Xreg] := Sin(LastX) / Cos(LastX);
        ErrorMessage := '';
    END
    ELSE
        ErrorMessage := 'Tangent of 90 degrees is infinity';
END;


PROCEDURE MemCalc.ArcTangent;
BEGIN
    LastX := Stack[Xreg];
    Stack[Xreg] := Arctan(Stack[Xreg]);
    ErrorMessage := '';
END;


PROCEDURE MemCalc.Loge;
BEGIN
    IF Stack[XReg] > 0 THEN BEGIN
        LastX := Stack[Xreg];
        Stack[Xreg] := Ln(Stack[Xreg]);
        ErrorMessage := '';
    END
    ELSE
        ErrorMessage := 'Error: invalid argument for Ln';
END;


PROCEDURE MemCalc.Exponential;
BEGIN
    LastX := Stack[Xreg];
    Stack[Xreg] := Exp(Stack[Xreg]);
    ErrorMessage := '';
END;
```

```
PROCEDURE MemCalc.AbsVal;
BEGIN
    Stack[Xreg] := Abs(Stack[Xreg]);
END;


PROCEDURE BusiCalc.Init;

VAR RegIndex : BusiMemEnum;

BEGIN
    MemCalc.Init;
    FOR RegIndex := PV_ TO I_ DO
        BusiMemory[RegIndex] := 0;
    ErrorMessage := '';
END;


PROCEDURE BusiCalc.ResetBusiMem;

VAR RegIndex : BusiMemEnum;

BEGIN
    FOR RegIndex := PV_ TO I_ DO
        BusiMemory[RegIndex] := 0;
    ErrorMessage := '';
END;


PROCEDURE BusiCalc.StorePV;
BEGIN
    BusiMemory[PV_] := Stack[Xreg];
    ErrorMessage := '';
END;


PROCEDURE BusiCalc.StoreFV;
BEGIN
    BusiMemory[FV_] := Stack[Xreg];
    ErrorMessage := '';
END;


PROCEDURE BusiCalc.StoreI;
BEGIN
    BusiMemory[I_] := Stack[Xreg];
    ErrorMessage := '';
END;
```

```
PROCEDURE BusiCalc.StoreN;
BEGIN
    BusiMemory[N_] := Stack[Xreg];
    ErrorMessage := '';
END;


PROCEDURE BusiCalc.RecallPV;

VAR RegIndex : StackRegEnum;

BEGIN
    FOR RegIndex := Treg DOWNTO Yreg DO
        Stack[RegIndex] := Stack[Pred(RegIndex)];
    Stack[Xreg] := BusiMemory[PV_];
    ErrorMessage := '';
END;


PROCEDURE BusiCalc.RecallFV;

VAR RegIndex : StackRegEnum;

BEGIN
    FOR RegIndex := Treg DOWNTO Yreg DO
        Stack[RegIndex] := Stack[Pred(RegIndex)];
    Stack[Xreg] := BusiMemory[FV_];
    ErrorMessage := '';
END;


PROCEDURE BusiCalc.RecallI;

VAR RegIndex : StackRegEnum;

BEGIN
    FOR RegIndex := Treg DOWNTO Yreg DO
        Stack[RegIndex] := Stack[Pred(RegIndex)];
    Stack[Xreg] := BusiMemory[I_];
    ErrorMessage := '';
END;


PROCEDURE BusiCalc.RecallN;

VAR RegIndex : StackRegEnum;
```

```
                    BEGIN
                        FOR RegIndex := Treg DOWNTO Yreg DO
                            Stack[RegIndex] := Stack[Pred(RegIndex)];
                        Stack[Xreg] := BusiMemory[N_];
                        ErrorMessage := '';
                    END;


                    PROCEDURE BusiCalc.CalcFV;


                    VAR RegIndex : StackRegEnum;


                    BEGIN
                        IF (BusiMemory[PV_] > 0) AND (BusiMemory[I_] > 0) AND
                            (BusiMemory[N_] > 0) THEN BEGIN
                            LastX := Stack[Xreg];
                            FOR RegIndex := Treg DOWNTO Yreg DO
                            Stack[RegIndex] := Stack[Pred(RegIndex)];
                            Stack[Xreg] := BusiMemory[PV_] *
                                        LocalPower((1+BusiMemory[I_]), BusiMemory[N_]);
                            ErrorMessage := '';
                        END
                        ELSE
                            ErrorMessage := 'Bad financial arguments';
                    END;


                    PROCEDURE BusiCalc.CalcPV;


                    VAR RegIndex : StackRegEnum;


                    BEGIN
                        IF (BusiMemory[FV_] > 0) AND (BusiMemory[I_] > 0) AND
                            (BusiMemory[N_] > 0) THEN BEGIN
                            LastX := Stack[Xreg];
                            FOR RegIndex := Treg DOWNTO Yreg DO
                                Stack[RegIndex] := Stack[Pred(RegIndex)];
                            Stack[Xreg] := BusiMemory[FV_] /
                                        LocalPower((1+BusiMemory[I_]), BusiMemory[N_]);
                            ErrorMessage := '';
                        END
                        ELSE
                            ErrorMessage := 'Bad financial arguments';
                    END;
```

```
PROCEDURE BusiCalc.CalcI;

VAR RegIndex : StackRegEnum;

BEGIN
    IF (BusiMemory[FV_] > 0) AND (BusiMemory[N_] > 0) AND
        (BusiMemory[PV_] > 0) THEN BEGIN
        LastX := Stack[Xreg];
        FOR RegIndex := Treg DOWNTO Yreg DO
            Stack[RegIndex] := Stack[Pred(RegIndex)];
        Stack[Xreg] := LocalPower(BusiMemory[FV_]/BusiMemory[PV_],
                        (1 / BusiMemory[N_])) - 1;
        ErrorMessage := '';
    END
    ELSE
        ErrorMessage := 'Bad financial arguments';
END;

PROCEDURE BusiCalc.CalcN;

VAR RegIndex : StackRegEnum;

BEGIN
    IF (BusiMemory[FV_] > 0) AND (BusiMemory[I_] > 0) AND
        (BusiMemory[PV_] > 0) THEN BEGIN
        LastX := Stack[Xreg];
        FOR RegIndex := Treg DOWNTO Yreg DO
            Stack[RegIndex] := Stack[Pred(RegIndex)];
        Stack[Xreg] := Ln(BusiMemory[FV_]/BusiMemory[PV_]) /
                        Ln(1 + BusiMemory[I_]);
        ErrorMessage := '';
    END
    ELSE
        ErrorMessage := 'Bad financial arguments';
    END;

    END.
```

The CalcObj library unit handles the internal workings of the various calculator classes. The user interface brings out a vast number of options and alternatives. Listing 13.2 shows the source code for library unit ViewCalc, the user-interface part, which provides the shell for the CalcObj unit. A software developer may provide a unit like CalcObj in complied form (preventing the client programmer from altering it) while offering ViewCalc with its source code for easy customization.

The ViewCalc unit defines two new subclasses. The subclass ViewMemCalc is subclass of MemCalc. It incorporates merely one method: UseIt. This method does everything except allocate/deallocate objects of class ViewMemCalc. The implementation part of the library unit contains all of the local constants and variables used by the library's methods.

```
ViewMemCalc = OBJECT (MemCalc)
    PROCEDURE UseIt;
END;
```

The unit ViewCalc also declares a similar class for viewing the financial RPN calculator:

```
ViewBusiCalc = OBJECT (BusiCalc)
    PROCEDURE UseIt;
END;
```

The local constants and variables (and any data types you defined in the implementation section) cannot be altered by the client programmer. The client program has no access to such constants, types, or variables.

The type of interface implemented in unit ViewCalc is very simple. The screen displays the RPN stack, the memory registers, the last error message, and a menu for operators and commands. A ">" prompt appears at the bottom part of the screen. Your input is captured using the ReadKey function (exported by Crt), and provision is made to correctly deal with the backspace character. If you type a valid arithmetic operator, the operation is performed immediately; you do not have to press the [Enter] key. If the first character you type is not a valid arithmetic operator, your input is collected in a string until you press [Enter]. Your input will be a number specifying the command you want carried out. If a command requires a parameter, an additional prompt will be issued. The program is written to detect bad numeric input and is therefore crash-proof in that area.

LISTING 13.2. The source code for the ViewCalc library unit.

```
UNIT ViewCalc;

{=======================================================

        Copyright (c) 1989, 1990  Namir Clement Shammas

LIBRARY NAME: ViewCalc
```

```
VERSION 1.0 FOR TURBO PASCAL                DATE 6/21/1989

PURPOSE:

================================================================}


{*****************************************************************}
{***********************} INTERFACE {****************************}
{*****************************************************************}


Uses CalcObj;

TYPE

ViewMemCalc = OBJECT (MemCalc)
    PROCEDURE UseIt;
END;

ViewBusiCalc = OBJECT (BusiCalc)
    PROCEDURE UseIt;
END;

{*****************************************************************}
{*********************} IMPLEMENTATION {************************}
{*****************************************************************}

Uses Crt;

CONST FIRST_REG_LINE = 2;
      MEMORY_COLUMN = 40;
      MESSAGE_LINE = 13;
      OP_LINE = 15;
      COM_LINE1 = 16;
      FIRST_REG_COLUMN = 7;
      FIRST_PROMPT_LINE = 22;
      SECOND_PROMPT_LINE = 24;


VAR RPN : MemCalc;
    I, OpCode : BYTE;
    ErrorCode : INTEGER;
    X : REAL;
    AKey : CHAR;
    OpString : STRING[5];
    RegIndex : StackRegEnum;
```

```
PROCEDURE ViewMemCalc.UseIt;
BEGIN
    { initialize calculator and memory }
    Init;

    ClrScr;
    { display memory labels }
    GotoXY(15,1);
    WRITE('Stack');
    GotoXY(50,1);
    WRITE('Memory');
    { display register names }
    GotoXY(1, FIRST_REG_LINE);
    WRITELN('   T');
    WRITELN('   Z');
    WRITELN('   Y');
    WRITELN('   X');
    WRITELN;
    WRITELN('LastX');
    { display memory register numbers }
    FOR I := 0 TO LAST_MEM DO BEGIN
        GotoXY(MEMORY_COLUMN,FIRST_REG_LINE+I);
        WRITE(I:1);
    END;
    { display operators and commands }
    GotoXY(1,OP_LINE);
    WRITE('Operators: + - / *');
    GotoXY(1,COM_LINE1);
    WRITELN(
    'Commands: 0. Exit, 1. Enter, 2. ClearStack, 3. ClearX, 4. CHS');
    WRITELN(
    '          5. Roll up, 6. Roll down, 7. Swap, 8. Pop, 9. Square');
    WRITELN(
    '          10. Square root, 11. Power, 12. Sin, 13. Cos, 14. Tan');
    WRITELN(
    '          15. ArcTan, 16. Ln, 17. Exp, 18. Abs, 19. Store');
    WRITELN(
    '          20. Recall, 21. LastX');
    { main loop }
    REPEAT
        OpString := ''; { reset command string }
        { display stack registers }
        I := 0;
```

```
            FOR RegIndex := TReg DOWNTO Xreg DO BEGIN
                GotoXY(FIRST_REG_COLUMN, FIRST_REG_LINE + I);
                INC(I);
                WRITE(GetReg(RegIndex));
            END;
            { display LastX }
            GotoXY(FIRST_REG_COLUMN, FIRST_REG_LINE + 5);
            WRITE(GetLastX);
            { display memory contents }
            FOR I := 0 TO LAST_MEM DO BEGIN
                GotoXY(MEMORY_COLUMN+2,FIRST_REG_LINE + I);
                WRITE(GetMemory(I));
            END;
            { display error message }
            GotoXY(1, MESSAGE_LINE);
            WRITE('Error Message> ', SayError);
            ClrEol;
            { prompt for operator or command }
            GotoXY(1,FIRST_PROMPT_LINE);
            WRITE('> ');
            ClrEol;
            AKey := ReadKey; WRITE(AKey);
            IF AKey IN ['+','-','*','/'] THEN
                { process operator }
                CASE AKey OF
                    '+' : Add;
                    '-' : Subtract;
                    '*' : Multiply;
                    '/' : Divide;
                END
        ELSE BEGIN { process command number }
            OpString := AKey;
            WHILE AKey <> #13 DO BEGIN
                AKey := ReadKey;
                IF NOT (AKey IN [#13, #8]) THEN BEGIN
                    WRITE(AKey);
                    OpString := OpString + AKey
                END
                ELSE IF  (AKey = #8) AND
                        (Length(OpString) > 0) THEN BEGIN
                    Delete(OpString, Length(OpString), 1);
                    ClrEol;
                END;
```

```
END; { WHILE }
Val(OpString, OpCode, ErrorCode);
IF ErrorCode = 0 THEN { valid command number }
    CASE OpCode OF
        1 : BEGIN
            REPEAT
              GotoXY(1,SECOND_PROMPT_LINE);
              WRITE('>');
              ClrEol;
              READLN(OpString);
              Val(OpString, X, ErrorCode);
            UNTIL ErrorCode = 0;
              Push(X);
            END;
        2 : ClearStack;
        3 : ClearX;
        4 : CHS;
        5 : RollUp;
        6 : RollDown;
        7 : Swap;
        8 : X := Pop;
        9 : Square;
       10 : SquareRoot;
       11 : Power;
       12 : Sine;
       13 : Cosine;
       14 : Tangent;
       15 : ArcTangent;
       16 : Loge;
       17 : Exponential;
       18 : AbsVal;
       19 : BEGIN
            REPEAT
              GotoXY(1, SECOND_PROMPT_LINE);
              WRITE('Memory Index > ');
              ClrEol;
              READLN(OpString);
              Val(OpString, I, ErrorCode)
            UNTIL ErrorCode = 0;
              Store(I)
            END;
       20 : BEGIN
            REPEAT
```

```
                                GotoXY(1, SECOND_PROMPT_LINE);
                                WRITE('Memory Index > ');
                                ClrEol;
                                READLN(OpString);
                                Val(OpString, I, ErrorCode);
                              UNTIL ErrorCode = 0;
                              Recall(I)
                           END;
                    21 : Push(GetLastX);
               END
             ELSE
                 OpCode := 1;
          END;
          { erase second prompt line }
          GotoXY(1, SECOND_PROMPT_LINE);
          ClrEol;
      UNTIL OpCode = 0;
      ClrScr;
END;

PROCEDURE ViewBusiCalc.UseIt;

BEGIN
    { initialize calculator and memory }
    Init;
    ClrScr;
    { display memory labels }
    GotoXY(15,1);
    WRITE('Stack');
    GotoXY(50,1);
    WRITE('Memory');
    { display register names }
    GotoXY(1, FIRST_REG_LINE);
    WRITELN('   T');
    WRITELN('   Z');
    WRITELN('   Y');
    WRITELN('   X');
    WRITELN;
    WRITELN('LastX');
    { display memory register numbers }
    FOR I := 0 TO LAST_MEM DO BEGIN
        GotoXY(MEMORY_COLUMN, FIRST_REG_LINE+I);
        WRITE(I:1);
    END;
```

```
{ display operators and commands }
GotoXY(1,OP_LINE);
WRITE('Operators: + - / *');
GotoXY(1,COM_LINE1);
WRITELN(
'Commands: 0. Exit, 1. Enter, 2. ClearStack, 3. ClearX, 4. CHS');
WRITELN(
'          5. Roll up, 6. Roll down, 7. Swap, 8. Pop, 9. Reset');
WRITELN(
' Store >> 10. PV , 11. FV, 12. I, 13. N');
WRITELN(
' Recall>> 14. PV , 15. FV, 16. I, 17. N');
WRITELN(
' Calc. >> 18. PV , 19. FV, 20. I, 21. N, 22. Store, 23. Recall');
{ main loop }
REPEAT
    OpString := '';{ reset command string }
    { display stack registers }
    I := 0;
    FOR RegIndex := TReg DOWNTO Xreg DO BEGIN
      GotoXY(FIRST_REG_COLUMN, FIRST_REG_LINE + I);
      INC(I);
      WRITE(GetReg(RegIndex));
    END;
    { display LastX }
    GotoXY(FIRST_REG_COLUMN, FIRST_REG_LINE + 5);
    WRITE(GetLastX);
    { display memory contents }
    FOR I := 0 TO LAST_MEM DO BEGIN
    GotoXY(MEMORY_COLUMN+2,FIRST_REG_LINE + I);
      WRITE(GetMemory(I));
    END;
    { display error message }
    GotoXY(1, MESSAGE_LINE);
    WRITE('Error Message> ', SayError);
    ClrEol;
    { prompt for operator or command }
    GotoXY(1,FIRST_PROMPT_LINE);
    WRITE('> ');
    ClrEol;
    AKey := ReadKey; WRITE(AKey);
    IF AKey IN ['+','-','*','/'] THEN
        { process operator }
```

```
CASE AKey OF
    '+' : Add;
    '-' : Subtract;
    '*' : Multiply;
    '/' : Divide;
END
ELSE BEGIN { process command number }
    OpString := AKey;
    WHILE AKey <> #13 DO BEGIN
        AKey := ReadKey;
        IF NOT (AKey IN [#13, #8]) THEN BEGIN
            WRITE(AKey);
            OpString := OpString + AKey
        END
        ELSE IF (AKey = #8) AND
                (Length(OpString) > 0) THEN BEGIN
            Delete(OpString, Length(OpString), 1);
            ClrEol;
        END;
    END; { WHILE }
    Val(OpString, OpCode, ErrorCode);
    IF ErrorCode = 0 THEN { valid command number }
        CASE OpCode OF
            1 : BEGIN
                    REPEAT
                        GotoXY(1,SECOND_PROMPT_LINE);
                        WRITE('> ');
                        ClrEol;
                        READLN(OpString);
                        Val(OpString, X, ErrorCode);
                    UNTIL ErrorCode = 0;
                    Push(X);
                END;
            2 : ClearStack;
            3 : ClearX;
            4 : CHS;
            5 : RollUp;
            6 : RollDown;
            7 : Swap;
            8 : X := Pop;
            9 : ResetBusiMem;
           10 : StorePV;
           11 : StoreFV;
```

```
                        12 : StoreI;
                        13 : StoreN;
                        14 : RecallPV;
                        15 : RecallFV;
                        16 : RecallI;
                        17 : RecallN;
                        18 : CalcPV;
                        19 : CalcFV;
                        20 : CalcI;
                        21 : CalcN;
                        22 : BEGIN
                                REPEAT
                                  GotoXY(1, SECOND_PROMPT_LINE);
                                  WRITE('Memory Index > ');
                                  ClrEol;
                                  READLN(OpString);
                                  Val(OpString, I, ErrorCode)
                                UNTIL ErrorCode = 0;
                                Store(I)
                              END;
                        23 : BEGIN
                                REPEAT
                                  GotoXY(1, SECOND_PROMPT_LINE);
                                  WRITE('Memory Index > ');
                                  ClrEol;
                                  READLN(OpString);
                                  Val(OpString, I, ErrorCode);
                                UNTIL ErrorCode = 0;
                                Recall(I)
                              END;
                    END
                  ELSE
                        OpCode := 1;
                END;

            { erase second prompt line }
            GotoXY(1, SECOND_PROMPT_LINE);
            ClrEol;
        UNTIL OpCode = 0;
        ClrScr;
    END;


    END.
```

Listing 13.3 contains a test program for the ViewMemCalc class. Notice how short the program is! Its only function is to send a UseIt message to an instance of the class ViewMemCalc.

LISTING 13.3. Test program TSCALC.PAS for the ViewMemCalc objects.

```
Program Test_Calculator_Objects;

{
Program implements a scientific calculator
}

Uses Crt, ViewCalc;

VAR RPN : ViewMemCalc;

BEGIN
    RPN.UseIt;
END.
```

The following is a sample screen image produced by the test program:

```
              Stack                              Memory
    T 3.00000000000000E+0000         0 3.00000000000000E+0000
    Z 3.00000000000000E+0000         1 1.00000000000000E+0000
    Y 3.00000000000000E+0000         2 1.00000000000000E+0000
    X 1.10000000000000E+0001         3 0.00000000000000E+0000
                                     4 0.00000000000000E+0000
LastX 1.00000000000000E+0001         5 0.00000000000000E+0000
                                     6 0.00000000000000E+0000
                                     7 0.00000000000000E+0000
                                     8 0.00000000000000E+0000
                                     9 0.00000000000000E+0000


Error Message>

Operators: + - / *
Commands: 0. Exit, 1. Enter, 2. ClearStack, 3. ClearX, 4. CHS
          5. Roll up, 6. Roll down, 7. Swap, 8. Pop, 9. Square
          10. Square root, 11. Power, 12. Sin, 13. Cos, 14. Tan
```

```
                    15. ArcTan, 16. Ln, 17. Exp, 18. Abs, 19. Store
                    20. Recall, 21. LastX


        > 1


        > 11
```

Listing 13.4 contains a test program for the ViewBusiMemCalc class. Like the test program in Listing 13.3, this one is short.

LISTING 13.4. Test program TSCALC2.PAS for the ViewBusiMemCalc objects.

```pascal
Program Test_Calculator_Objects;

{
Program implements a financial calculator
}

Uses Crt, ViewCalc;

VAR RPN : ViewBusiCalc;

BEGIN
    RPN.UseIt;
END.
```

The following is a sample screen image produced by this program:

```
              Stack                                Memory
    T  4.50000000000000E+0001         0 1.00000000000000E+0000
    Z  4.50000000000000E+0001         1 3.00000000000000E+0000
    Y  5.50000000000000E+0001         2 1.00000000000000E+0000
    X  3.14159292035401E+0000         3 3.14159292035401E+0000
                                      4 0.00000000000000E+0000
 LastX 1.13000000000000E+0002         5 0.00000000000000E+0000
                                      6 0.00000000000000E+0000
                                      7 0.00000000000000E+0000
                                      8 0.00000000000000E+0000
                                      9 0.00000000000000E+0000


    Error Message>
```

```
Operators: + - / *
Commands:  0. Exit, 1. Enter, 2. ClearStack, 3. ClearX, 4. CHS
           5. Roll up, 6. Roll down, 7. Swap, 8. Pop, 9. Reset
Store >> 10. PV , 11. FV, 12. I, 13. N
Recall>> 14. PV , 15. FV, 16. I, 17. N
Calc. >> 18. PV , 19. FV, 20. I, 21. N, 22. Store, 23. Recall


> 22

Memory Index > 3
```

14 | Polymorphic Arrays

In Chapter 8 I presented a hierarchy of array-based objects. The base class was an array of strings and its subclasses modeled array-based stacks and lists. In this chapter I will take the class that represents an array of strings and use it to demonstrate polymorphic behavior exhibited by a subclass of virtual arrays.

Arrays can be classified into a number of categories according to their storage schemes. First, there are static arrays, whose space is allocated when an application is launched, their size known by the compiler. Second, you have dynamic arrays, whose space is allocated at runtime on the heap. Next, there are the virtual arrays, whose space typically resides on a disk or in extended or expanded memory. Usually, part of the virtual array (especially if it is disk-based) is allocated in traditional RAM or on the heap to speed up access. Thus, the basic differences between disk-based virtual arrays and nonvirtual arrays are:

1. The initialization of virtual arrays involves disk I/O activity. The records storing the virtual array may be initialized to zeros or null values.
2. The access of virtual arrays involves disk I/O. Buffers may be used to store segments of the virtual arrays in memory, with disk I/O performed to swap data segments between buffer and disk.
3. Files storing virtual arrays must be closed if the virtual arrays are to be retrieved in future sessions. This requirement becomes optional, but still recommended, if the virtual arrays are treated as volatile data.

The major difference between virtual and nonvirtual arrays is in their access routines. How does that translate into object-oriented coding in Turbo Pascal? Consider the declaration of the array-of-strings class StrArray:

```
StrArray = OBJECT
    MaxArraySize,
    VSize { current size } : WORD;
    VData : OneStringPtr;
    SortFlag : BOOLEAN;
    CONSTRUCTOR Init (NumElem : WORD { input });
    DESTRUCTOR Done;
    FUNCTION Store ( Data   : LSTRING;   { input  }
                     Index  : WORD       { input })
                          : BOOLEAN; VIRTUAL;
    FUNCTION Recall (VAR    Data    : LSTRING;   { output  }
                     Index  : WORD        { input   })
                          : BOOLEAN; VIRTUAL;
    FUNCTION GetArSize : WORD;
    PROCEDURE Sort;
    FUNCTION Search (SearchData : LSTRING { input }) : WORD;
    PROCEDURE Reverse;
END;
```

This declaration is identical to that of StrArray in Chapter 8, except that the Store and Recall methods are virtual. Listing 14.1 on page 282 shows the library unit implementing the class. If you look at the code for methods Sort, Search, and Reverse, you find that they send messages Store and Recall to access the elements of the array. In Chapter 8, the access of the array elements was made directly using VData^[Index]. While the new arrangement is slightly less efficient, it opens the door for the subclasses of StrArray to exhibit polymorphic behavior simply by redefining the constructor, the destructor, and the virtual methods Store and Recall. This is demonstrated by the declaration of the VirtStrArray:

```
VirtStrArray = OBJECT (StrArray)
    FileVar : TFILE;
    CONSTRUCTOR Init ( NumElem   : WORD;    { input  }
                       DataFile  : LSTRING { input });
    FUNCTION Store ( Data   : LSTRING;   { input  }
                     Index  : WORD       { input })
                          : BOOLEAN; VIRTUAL;
    FUNCTION Recall (VAR    Data    : LSTRING;   { output  }
                     Index  : WORD        { input   })
                          : BOOLEAN; VIRTUAL;
    DESTRUCTOR Done;
END;
```

The virtual array requires a file-typed field to perform disk I/O. The constructor Init requires that the array's size and the name of the data file be specified. The methods Store and Recall perform straightforward random access disk I/O to access the sought element. This is the simplest scheme and the least efficient. The Ith element of the virtual array is stored in record $I - 1$.

You can enhance the speed by reading a group of elements into a dynamic buffer. As implemented, the virtual array does not employ the inherited field VData to create and access a data buffer.

As a refinement of this subclass, I defined another subclass that implements a better virtual storage scheme. The new subclass employs the inherited VData pointer to create a dynamically allocated buffer. Consequently, the virtual data file is logically divided into segments, numbered 0 and up. The index I of a virtual array is mapped into the segment (I DIV Buffer_Size). Once a segment is loaded into memory, the index I is mapped onto the dynamic-array index (I MOD Buffer_Size + 1).

I elected to store one segment in memory at any given time. Therefore, swapping segments is a frequent operation in most cases. Rather than simply writing out the segment in RAM before reading in the new one, I decided to employ "dirty bit" flags. Each array element stored in RAM has an associated dirty-bit flag, which is initially set to FALSE. Once information is written to that element, its dirty flag is set to TRUE. When the time comes to write the resident segment back to disk, only those elements that have their dirty-bit flags set to TRUE are actually written. This mechanism is a real time-saver when only a small portion of the memory-resident segment is updated.

The new virtual array class is declared as follows:

```
SuperVStrArray = OBJECT (VirtStrArray)
    DirtyBit : OneBitPtr;
    SegIndex,
    ElemInRAM : WORD;
    CONSTRUCTOR Init ( NumElem,              { input }
                       MemElem   : WORD;   { input }
                       DataFile  : LSTRING { input });
    FUNCTION Store ( Data    : LSTRING;   { input }
                     Index   : WORD       { input })
                             : BOOLEAN; VIRTUAL;
    FUNCTION Recall (VAR  Data   : LSTRING;   { output }
                         Index   : WORD       { input })
                             : BOOLEAN; VIRTUAL;
    DESTRUCTOR Done;
END;
```

DirtyBit is a pointer to a dynamic array of Booleans. SegIndex keeps track of the segment of virtual data currently in memory. The ElemInRAM field stores the number of virtual-array elements residing in memory. The constructor in this class differs from that of the parent class by having an additional parameter MemElem. This parameter is used to assign a value to the ElemInRAM field. The same information is used in allocating and deallocating the dynamic arrays.

The fact that the methods Store and Recall are polymorphic enables objects of the two virtual array subclasses to receive Sort, Search, and Reverse messages and act using virtual storage mechanisms.

LISTING 14.1. Source code for the PolyMorf library unit.

```
UNIT PolyMorf;


{================================================================


              Copyright (c) 1989, 1990  Namir Clement Shammas

         LIBRARY NAME: PolyMorf

         VERSION 1.0 FOR TURBO PASCAL                    DATE 6/21/1989

         PURPOSE: Exports polymorphic arrays-based objects.


 ================================================================}


{******************************************************************}
{************************} INTERFACE {****************************}
{******************************************************************}


CONST STRING_SIZE = 80;

TYPE

LSTRING = STRING[STRING_SIZE];
OneString = ARRAY [1..1] OF LSTRING;
OneStringPtr = ^OneString;

TFILE = FILE OF LSTRING;
```

```
                    StrArray = OBJECT
                        MaxArraySize,
                        VSize { current size } : WORD;
                        VData : OneStringPtr;
                        SortFlag : BOOLEAN;
                        CONSTRUCTOR Init (NumElem : WORD { input });
                        DESTRUCTOR Done;
                        FUNCTION Store ( Data    : LSTRING;   { input }
                                         Index : WORD        { input })
                                              : BOOLEAN; VIRTUAL;
                        FUNCTION Recall (VAR Data    : LSTRING;   { output }
                                             Index : WORD        { input })
                                              : BOOLEAN; VIRTUAL;
                        FUNCTION GetArSize : WORD;
                        PROCEDURE Sort;
                        FUNCTION Search (SearchData : LSTRING { input }) : WORD;
                        PROCEDURE Reverse;
                    END;

                    VirtStrArray = OBJECT (StrArray)
                        FileVar : TFILE;
                        CONSTRUCTOR Init ( NumElem   : WORD;    { input }
                                           DataFile  : LSTRING { input });
                        FUNCTION Store ( Data  : LSTRING;   { input }
                                         Index : WORD        { input })
                                              : BOOLEAN; VIRTUAL;
                        FUNCTION Recall (VAR Data    : LSTRING;   { output }
                                             Index : WORD        { input })
                                              : BOOLEAN; VIRTUAL;
                        DESTRUCTOR Done;
                    END;

                    OneBit = ARRAY [1..1] OF BOOLEAN;
                    OneBitPtr = ^OneBit;

                    SuperVStrArray = OBJECT (VirtStrArray)
                        DirtyBit : OneBitPtr;
                        SegIndex,
                        ElemInRAM : WORD;
                        CONSTRUCTOR Init ( NumElem,                { input }
                                           MemElem   : WORD;    { input }
                                           DataFile  : LSTRING { input });
                        FUNCTION Store ( Data    : LSTRING;   { input }
                                         Index   : WORD        { input })
                                              : BOOLEAN; VIRTUAL;
```

```
        FUNCTION Recall (VAR Data   : LSTRING;   { output  }
                             Index  : WORD       { input   })
                                    : BOOLEAN; VIRTUAL;
        DESTRUCTOR Done;
END;


{*****************************************************************}
{**********************} IMPLEMENTATION {************************}
{*****************************************************************}


Uses Crt;


{$R-}


VAR DummyBool : BOOLEAN;


CONSTRUCTOR StrArray.Init (NumElem : WORD { input });
BEGIN
    GetMem (VData, NumElem * STRING_SIZE);
    MaxArraySize := NumElem;
    VSize := 0;
    SortFlag := FALSE;
    { assign null strings to dynamic array }
    WHILE NumElem > 0 DO BEGIN
        DummyBool := Store ('', NumElem);
        DEC (NumElem)
    END;
END;


DESTRUCTOR StrArray.Done;
BEGIN
    FreeMem (VData, MaxArraySize * STRING_SIZE);
    VData := NIL;
    MaxArraySize := 0;
    VSize := 0;
END;


PROCEDURE StrArray.Sort;

VAR Offset, I, J : WORD;
    StrI, StrJ : LSTRING;
```

```
                BEGIN
                    IF VSize < 2 THEN EXIT;
                    Offset := VSize;
                    WHILE Offset > 1 DO BEGIN
                        Offset := Offset div 2;
                        REPEAT
                            SortFlag := TRUE;
                            FOR J := 1 TO VSize - Offset DO BEGIN
                                I := J + Offset;
                                DummyBool := Recall (StrJ, J);
                                DummyBool := Recall (StrI, I);
                                IF StrI < StrJ THEN BEGIN
                                    DummyBool := Store (StrI, J);
                                    DummyBool := Store (StrJ, I);
                                    SortFlag := FALSE
                                END; { IF }
                            END; { FOR }
                        UNTIL SortFlag;
                    END; { WHILE }
                END;

                FUNCTION StrArray.Search (SearchData : LSTRING { input }) : WORD;

                VAR Low, High, Median : WORD;
                    NotFound : BOOLEAN;
                    StrMedian : LSTRING;

                BEGIN
                    IF NOT SortFlag THEN { need to be sorted }
                        Sort;
                    Low := 1;
                    High := VSize;
                    REPEAT
                        Median := (Low + High) div 2;
                        DummyBool := Recall (StrMedian, Median);
                        IF SearchData < StrMedian THEN
                            High := Median - 1
                        ELSE
                            Low := Median + 1;
                    UNTIL (SearchData = StrMedian) OR (Low > High);
                    IF SearchData = StrMedian THEN
                        Search := Median
                    ELSE
                        Search := 0;
                END;
```

```
PROCEDURE StrArray.Reverse;

VAR I, J : BYTE;
    StrI, StrJ : LSTRING;

BEGIN
    FOR I := 1 TO VSize div 2 DO BEGIN
        J := VSize + 1 - I;
        DummyBool := Recall(StrI, I);
        DummyBool := Recall(StrJ, J);
        DummyBool := Store(StrI, J);
        DummyBool := Store(StrJ, I);
    END;
END;


FUNCTION StrArray.Store(    Data    : LSTRING;   { input }
                            Index   : WORD       { input })
                                    : BOOLEAN;

BEGIN
    IF Index <= MaxArraySize THEN BEGIN
        IF Index > VSize THEN
            VSize := Index;
        VData^[Index] := Data;
        SortFlag := FALSE;
        Store := TRUE
    END
    ELSE
        Store := FALSE
END;


FUNCTION StrArray.Recall(VAR Data    : LSTRING;   { output }
                             Index   : WORD       { input })
                                     : BOOLEAN;

BEGIN
    IF Index <= VSize THEN BEGIN
        Data := VData^[Index];
        Recall := TRUE
    END
    ELSE
        Recall := FALSE
END;
```

```
FUNCTION StrArray.GetArSize : WORD;
BEGIN
    GetArSize := VSize;
END;

CONSTRUCTOR VirtStrArray.Init(
                    NumElem   : WORD;    { input }
                    DataFile  : LSTRING { input });

VAR OK : BOOLEAN;

BEGIN
    REPEAT
        Assign(FileVar, DataFile);
        {$I-} Rewrite(FileVar); {$I+}
        OK := IOResult = 0;
        IF NOT OK THEN BEGIN
            WRITELN;
            WRITELN('Cannot open file ', DataFile);
            WRITELN;
            WRITELN('Enter filename -> ');
            READLN(DataFile); WRITELN;
        END;
    UNTIL OK;
    MaxArraySize := NumElem;
    VSize := 0;
    SortFlag := FALSE;
    { assign null strings to dynamic array }
    Seek(FileVar, 0);
    DataFile := '';
    WHILE NumElem > 0 DO BEGIN
        WRITE(FileVar, DataFile);
        DEC(NumElem)
    END;
END;

FUNCTION VirtStrArray.Store( Data    : LSTRING;  { input }
                            Index   : WORD       { input })
                                    : BOOLEAN;
BEGIN
    IF Index <= MaxArraySize THEN BEGIN
        IF Index > VSize THEN
            VSize := Index;
```

```pascal
            Seek(FileVar, Index-1);
            WRITE(FileVar, Data);
            SortFlag := FALSE;
            Store := TRUE
        END
        ELSE
            Store := FALSE
END;


FUNCTION VirtStrArray.Recall(VAR  Data    : LSTRING;    { output }
                                  Index   : WORD        { input })
                                          : BOOLEAN;
BEGIN
    IF Index <= VSize THEN BEGIN
        Seek(FileVar, Index - 1);
        READ(FileVar, Data);
        Recall := TRUE
    END
    ELSE
        Recall := FALSE
END;


DESTRUCTOR VirtStrArray.Done;
BEGIN
    VData := NIL;
    MaxArraySize := 0;
    VSize := 0;
    Close(FileVar);
END;


CONSTRUCTOR SuperVStrArray.Init(
                    NumElem,              { input }
                    MemElem   : WORD;     { input }
                    DataFile  : LSTRING { input });


VAR OK : BOOLEAN;
    I : WORD;


BEGIN
    REPEAT
        Assign(FileVar, DataFile);
        {$I-} Rewrite(FileVar); {$I+}
```

```
                        OK := IOResult = 0;
                        IF NOT OK THEN BEGIN
                            WRITELN;
                            WRITELN('Cannot open file ', DataFile);
                            WRITELN;
                            WRITELN('Enter filename -> ');
                            READLN(DataFile); WRITELN;
                        END;
                    UNTIL OK;
                    MaxArraySize := NumElem;
                    VSize := 0;
                    ElemInRAM := MemElem;
                    SortFlag := FALSE;
                    GetMem(VData, MemElem * SizeOf(LSTRING));
                    GetMem(DirtyBit, MemElem * SizeOf(BOOLEAN));
                    FOR I := 1 TO MemElem DO BEGIN
                        VData^[I] := '';
                        DirtyBit^[I] := FALSE
                    END;
                    SegIndex := 0;
                    { assign null strings to dynamic array }
                    Seek(FileVar, 0);
                    DataFile := '';
                    WHILE NumElem > 0 DO BEGIN
                        WRITE(FileVar, DataFile);
                        DEC(NumElem)
                    END;
                END;


FUNCTION SuperVStrArray.Store(   Data    : LSTRING;    { input  }
                                 Index   : WORD        { input })
                                         : BOOLEAN;

VAR I, J, K : WORD;


BEGIN
    IF Index <= MaxArraySize THEN BEGIN
        IF Index > VSize THEN
            VSize := Index;
        { is Index in segment loaded in RAM ? }
        J := Index DIV ElemInRAM;
        IF J = SegIndex THEN BEGIN
```

```
                I := Index MOD ElemInRAM + 1;
                VData^[I] := Data;
                DirtyBit^[I] := TRUE; { set dirty bit }
            END
        ELSE BEGIN
            { write any element in segment with dirty bit on }
            K := SegIndex * ElemInRAM - 1;
            FOR I := 1 TO ElemInRAM DO BEGIN
                IF DirtyBit^[I] THEN BEGIN
                    Seek(FileVar, K + I);
                    WRITE(FileVar, VData^[I]);
                END;
            END;
            SegIndex := J;
            I := 1;
            Seek(FileVar, SegIndex * ElemInRAM);
            WHILE (NOT Eof(FileVar)) AND
                  (I <= ElemInRAM) DO BEGIN
                READ(FileVar, VData^[I]);
                DirtyBit^[I] := FALSE;
                INC(I);
            END;
            I := Index MOD ElemInRAM + 1;
            VData^[I] := Data;
            DirtyBit^[I] := TRUE; { set dirty bit }
        END;
        SortFlag := FALSE;
        Store := TRUE
    END
    ELSE
        Store := FALSE
END;


FUNCTION SuperVStrArray.Recall(
                    VAR Data    : LSTRING;    { output }
                        Index   : WORD        { input  })
                                : BOOLEAN;
VAR I, J, K : WORD;

BEGIN
    IF Index <= VSize THEN BEGIN
        { is Index in segment loaded in RAM ? }
        J := Index DIV ElemInRAM;
        IF J = SegIndex THEN BEGIN
```

```
                                    I := Index MOD ElemInRAM + 1;
                                    Data := VData^[I];
                        END
                        ELSE BEGIN
                            { write any element in segment with dirty bit on }
                            K := SegIndex * ElemInRAM - 1;
                            FOR I := 1 TO ElemInRAM DO BEGIN
                                IF DirtyBit^[I] THEN BEGIN
                                    Seek(FileVar, K + I);
                                    WRITE(FileVar, VData^[I]);
                                END;
                            END;

                            SegIndex := J;
                            I := 1;
                            Seek(FileVar, SegIndex * ElemInRAM);
                            WHILE (NOT Eof(FileVar)) AND
                                  (I <= ElemInRAM) DO BEGIN
                                READ(FileVar, VData^[I]);
                                DirtyBit^[I] := FALSE;
                                INC(I);
                            END;
                            I := Index MOD ElemInRAM + 1;
                            Data := VData^[I];
                        END;
                    Recall := TRUE
                END
            ELSE
                Recall := FALSE
END;


DESTRUCTOR SuperVStrArray.Done;

BEGIN
    FreeMem(VData, ElemInRAM * SizeOf(LSTRING));
    FreeMem(DirtyBit, ElemInRAM * SizeOf(BOOLEAN));
    MaxArraySize := 0;
    ElemInRAM := 0;
    VSize := 0;
    Close(FileVar);
END;


END.
```

Listing 14.2 contains a test program that creates an object of class VirtStrArray and sends it messages. The program prompts you to enter five strings, which are then sorted and displayed. The program employs a loop to allow you to conduct a series of string searches. The input strings are stored in the file VM.DAT. The following message creates the virtual data file and allocates its space:

AnArray.Init(TEST_SIZE, TARGET_FILE)

The stings you type are stored in the virtual array by sending the message AnArray.Store(S, I). Once the array has received its input, it is sorted by sending the Sort message to the object AnArray. The message AnArray.Recall(S, I) is used to recall the elements of the ordered array. The Search message is sent to the object to query the index of a matching string.

LISTING 14.2. Program TSPMORF.PAS to test the polymorphism of virtual-array objects.

```
Program Test_Polymorphic_Array_Objects;

{
    Program tests polymorphic virtual array.

}

Uses Crt, PolyMorf;

CONST TEST_SIZE = 5;
      TARGET_FILE = 'VM.DAT';

VAR AnArray : VirtStrArray;
    I : WORD;
    S : LSTRING;
    Akey : CHAR;

BEGIN
    ClrScr;
    { test the AnArray object }
    AnArray.Init(TEST_SIZE, TARGET_FILE);
    FOR I := 1 TO TEST_SIZE DO BEGIN
        WRITE('Enter string # ',I,' ? ');
        READLN(S);
```

```
                    IF NOT AnArray.Store(S, I) THEN
                        WRITELN('Out of bound index');
                END;
                AnArray.Sort; { sort the array }
                REPEAT
                    ClrScr;
                    WRITELN('Sorted array is:'); WRITELN;
                    FOR I := 1 TO TEST_SIZE DO BEGIN
                        IF WhereY > 22 THEN BEGIN
                            WRITELN;
                            WRITE('Press any key to continue ...');
                            AKey := ReadKey;
                            ClrScr;
                        END;
                        IF AnArray.Recall(S, I) THEN
                            WRITELN(I:2,' ',S);
                    END;
                    WRITELN;
                    WRITE('Search for string (press [Enter] to exit) -> ');
                    READLN(S);
                    IF S <> '' THEN BEGIN
                        I := AnArray.Search(S);
                        IF I > 0 THEN
                            WRITELN('Matches element ', I)
                        ELSE
                            WRITELN('Has no match');
                        WRITELN;
                        WRITE('Press space bar to continue ...');
                        AKey := ReadKey;
                    END;
                    WRITELN;
                UNTIL S = '';
                AnArray.Done; { deallocate dynamic memory }

                WRITELN;
                WRITE('Press any key to end the program ...');
                AKey := ReadKey;
            END.
```

A sample session with program TSPMORF.PAS is shown here:

```
Enter array string # 1 -> Paris
Enter array string # 2 -> London
Enter array string # 3 -> Berlin
```

```
Enter array string #  4 -> Rome
Enter array string #  5 -> Madrid

Sorted array is:

1  Berlin
2  London
3  Madrid
4  Paris
5  Rome

Search for string (press [Enter] to exit )-> London
Matches element 2


Press space bar to continue ...
```

Listing 14.3 is a test program that creates an object of class SuperVStrArray and sends it messages. The program is a modified version of the last one, with the following differences:

1. The size of the virtual array has been increased from 5 to 100 elements.
2. Ten elements of the virtual array may be resident at any given time.
3. The program generates its own strings. A loop is employed to create 100 three-character strings that have a descending order. The Sort message is sent to reverse the order of the elements in the virtual array.

LISTING 14.3. A second program, TSPMORF2.PAS, to test the polymorphism of virtual-array objects.

```
Program Test_Polymorphic_Array_Objects_2;

{
   Program tests polymorphic virtual array.

}

Uses Crt, PolyMorf;

CONST TEST_SIZE = 100;
      TARGET_FILE = 'VM.DAT';

VAR AnArray : SuperVStrArray;
```

```
            I : WORD;
            S : LSTRING;
            Akey, C : CHAR;

        BEGIN
            ClrScr;
            { test the AnArray object }
            AnArray.Init(TEST_SIZE, TEST_SIZE DIV 10, TARGET_FILE);
            FOR I := 1 TO TEST_SIZE DO BEGIN
                C := CHR(127 - I);
                S := C + C + C;
                IF NOT AnArray.Store(S, I) THEN
                    WRITELN('Out of bound index');
            END;
            WRITELN('Sorting ... please wait');
            AnArray.Sort; { sort the array }
            REPEAT
                ClrScr;
                WRITELN('Sorted array is:'); WRITELN;
                FOR I := 1 TO TEST_SIZE DO BEGIN
                    IF WhereY > 22 THEN BEGIN
                        WRITELN;
                        WRITE('Press any key to continue ...');
                        AKey := ReadKey;
                        ClrScr;
                    END;
                    IF AnArray.Recall(S, I) THEN
                        WRITELN(I:2,' ',S);
                END;
                WRITELN;
                WRITE('Search for string (press [Enter] to exit) -> ');
                READLN(S);
                IF S <> '' THEN BEGIN
                    I := AnArray.Search(S);
                    IF I > 0 THEN
                        WRITELN('Matches element ', I)
                    ELSE
                        WRITELN('Has no match');
                    WRITELN;
                    WRITE('Press space bar to continue ...');
                    AKey := ReadKey;
                END;
                WRITELN;
            UNTIL S = '';
```

```
        AnArray.Done; { deallocate dynamic memory }

        WRITELN;
        WRITE('Press any key to end the program ...');
        AKey := ReadKey;
    END.
```

Other Polymorphic Arrays

The classes of dynamic and virtual arrays are but a few examples of array objects.
You can build on the code presented in this chapter to include sparse arrays, virtual-
sparse arrays, EMS-based arrays, and others. Each category requires new constructor, destructor, and virtual Store and Recall methods. All the other methods
implemented in class StrArray are conveniently inherited by all subclasses. This is
the power of OOP and polymorphism!

Index

Area under polynomial, 204
Array, 151
    dynamic array, 151
    lists as arrays, 153
    stacks as arrays, 154
    static array, 151
    virtual, 279
Array objects, 151
Array of objects, 46

Buffers 106, 279, 281

Calculator, 249
    basic, 249
    financial, 252
    memory registers, 251
    scientific, 251
    stack registers, 249
Class, 3
    compound classes and objects, 48, 87
    parent class, 5
    Screen, 90, 92
    subclass, 5
    superclass, 5
Class types
    BusiCalc, 253, 255
    ByteFile, 106, 108
    Calculator, 251, 254
    CalculusPoly, 205, 207

CompressedTextFile, 105, 108
Cursor, 87, 91
EnhancedPrecisionLR, 221, 224
GenFileObj, 103, 107
LinearizedRegression, 222, 224
LinearRegression, 220, 223
MemCalc, 252, 255
MixedCircuit, 241, 242
NumAnalPoly, 206, 207
ParallelCircuit, 241, 242
Polynomial, 204, 207
ProgramFile, 107, 109
RealMatrix, 171, 177
RealVector, 170, 177
Screen, 90, 92
ScreenObj, 77, 79
ScrnObj, 60, 64
ScrnWindow, 61, 64
SeriesCircuit, 240, 242
SimpleCircuit, 240, 242
SpreadSheet, 174, 178
StatMatrix, 175, 178
StrArray, 152, 156, 280, 283
StrList, 154, 157
StrStack, 155, 157
SuperVStrArray, 281, 283
TAlphabet, 15, 16, 36
TCharSet, 8, 1, 36
TDigits, 14, 16, 38

Class types (Continued)
   TextFile, 104, 108
   TiledWindow, 62, 64
   TItem, 129, 132, 149
   TString, 128, 132, 148
   TTitle, 131, 133, 149
   TToken, 130, 132, 149
   TUpperCase, 14, 16, 36
   TWord, 129, 132
   Video, 89, 91
   VideoObj, 78, 79
   VideoText, 88, 91
   VirtStrArray, 280, 283
Coefficient of polynomial, 203
Compound classes and objects, 48, 87
   Screen, 90, 92
Compression, 105
Constructor, 31
Cursor, 87

Data hiding, 41
Decompression, 105
Destructor, 31
Displayable text, 88
Dynamic array, 151
Dynamic binding, 32
Dynamic matrices, 169
Dynamic object, 53
Dynamic vectors, 169

Electrical circuits, 237
   mixed series and paralle resistors, 239
   parallel resistors, 238
   series resistors, 237
   simple DC circuit, 237
Executable programs, 106
Exporting classes, 35

File(s)
   ASCII, 101
   attributes, 101, 103
   binary, 101, 105

   buffers, 106
   executable, 106
   generic, 102
   hierarchy of file classes, 102
   text file, 104

HasA relationship, 48
Heading, 131
HyperTalk, 129

Inheritance, 5
   multiple inheritance, 5
   single inheritance, 5
INHERITED, 21
Intercept, 217, 218
IsA relationship, 6
Item, 129

Linear regression, 175, 217
   enhanced precision, 221
   extended precision, 218
Linearized regression, 219, 222
   procedural parameters and, 222
   transformation functions, 222
Lists as arrays, 153
Loci of polynomial, 203

Mandatory initialization of objects,
      26
Math (polynomial), 204
Matrices, 169, 171
   dynamic matrices, 169
   static matrices, 169
   statistical matrices, 175
   column indices, 175
Message, 4, 5
Message ownership, 5
Method, 5
Method hiding, 42
Mixed series and parallel resistors,
      239
Multiple inheritance, 5

OBJECT, 7
Objects, 2, 3
    array of objects, 46
    assignment of, 45
    basics, 1
    dynamic object, 53
    functionality, 2
    mandatory initialization, 26
    state, 2
Order of polynomial, 203
Override, 5, 14

Parallel resistors, 238
Parent class, 5
Polymorphism, 32, 279
Polynomial, 203
    area under polynomial, 204
    coefficient of polynomial,
        203
    loci of polynomial, 203
    math (polynomial), 204
    order of polynomial, 203

Reverse Polish Notation, 249
RPN, 249

Screen, 59
Self, 11
Series resistors, 237
Simple DC circuit, 237
Single inheritance, 5
Slope, 217, 218
Spreadsheet class, 173
Stacks as arrays, 154

Static array, 151
Static matrices, 169
Static vectors, 169
Statistical matrices, 175
    column indices, 175
Statistical summations, 218
Strings, 127
    heading, 131
    intrinsics, 127, 128
    item, 129
    title, 130
    token, 129, 130
    token delimiter, 130
    words, 128
Subclass, 5
Superclass, 5

Text compression, 105
Text decompression, 105
Title, 130
Token, 129, 130
Token delimiter, 130

Vectors, 169
    dynamic vectors, 169
    static vectors, 169
Video buffer, 75
Video screen, 75
VIRTUAL, 31

Window, 61
    tiled window, 62
    untiled window, 61
Words, 128

IF YOU HATE TYPING READ THIS!

Many programmers dislike typing source code that is already available in electronic form. They find it a complete waste of time to key in listings and spend even more time hunting for typos.

This offer provides you instant access to the code in this book. It enables you to begin using the book's programs and libraries.

Send your order to:

Namir C. Shammas
3928 Margate Drive
Richmond, VA 23235

Please make check payable to Namir C. Shammas.

Please send _____ copies of the Turbo Pascal source code listings disk. Enclosed is a check or money order for $12.50. (Includes shipping and handling. Add $4.00 for shipping if outside the United States or Canada. Sorry, no purchase orders or credit cards.)

Disk format available:

5.25" DSDD _____

3.50" DSDD _____

Please type or print the following information:

Name _____

Company (for business addresses) _____

Address _____

City _____ State _____ Zip Code _____